CATHERINE THE GREAT

CATHERINE THE GREAT

A SHORT HISTORY

ISABEL DE MADARIAGA

YALE UNIVERSITY PRESS
NEW HAVEN AND LONDON
1990

First published in paperback 1993

Reprinted 1994

Set in Linotron Bembo by Excel Typesetters Company, Hong Kong
Printed and bound in Great Britain by Biddles Ltd, Guildford and King's Lynn

Library of Congress Cataloging-in-Publication Data

De Madariaga, Isabel, 1919–
Catherine the Great: a short history/Isabel De Madariaga.
p. cm.
Includes bibliographical references and index.
ISBN 0–300–04845–9 (hbk.)
ISBN 0–300–05427–0 (pbk.)
1. Catherine II, Empress of Russia, 1729–1796. 2. Soviet Union – History – Catherine II, 1762–1796. I. Title.
DK171.D44 1990
947′.063′092 – dc20 90–43666
CIP

CONTENTS

List of Illustrations

The illustrations listed below are between pages 16 and 17:

The illustrations listed below are between pages 152 and 153:

Preface

The reign of Catherine the Great, which lasted from 28 June 1762, the date on which she overthrew her husband, the legitimate Emperor Peter III, until her death in November 1796, is the subject of a great deal of controversy.

In her own time, Catherine was viewed with admiration by many of the leading thinkers of the age, such as Voltaire or Melchior von Grimm, though others, such as Denis Diderot, had reservations about her and about her country. They could point to the discrepancy between her proclaimed objectives and her actual achievements, her search for glory by means of war and her ruthless extinction of a great east European state – Poland – and they accused her of vanity and vainglory.

Nevertheless, eighteenth-century rulers and thinkers recognized her as one of their own kind. Only much later, in the age of the emancipation of the serfs and the aspiration towards constitutional or even democratic government, was her performance disparaged and even her proclaimed aim of ruling in the interests of her people derided as mere hypocrisy.

So much was this the case that serious study of her reign was interrupted for many years. The publication of her papers, which had continued systematically in pre-revolutionary Russia, ceased in 1917, and, though various aspects of her reign were written about in a number of scholarly articles in the Soviet Union, little effort was made until the 1960s to draw this work together. In the interval, a number of popular biographies which paid more attention to the Empress's lovers than to her policies were published in western Europe, though not in the USSR, where the biographical approach to history was frowned upon. It was thus in Britain and the USA, more than in the USSR, that fresh attention was devoted to the Empress, both as woman and as ruler, beginning in the 1960s.

There is always a timelag between the work of scholars and the general histories which draw upon it and put it into circulation for the general public. Hence this book is put before the reader in order to bring the more recent work on Catherine II to a wider audience in schools, colleges and universities than can be reached by specialized publications. My own attention was drawn to the need for such a work when I was invited, some years ago, to lecture to the members of the Sixth Form and the European Society at St Paul's School for boys. I therefore dedicate it to them, though the members of my original audience have long since taken wing.

I wish to express here my gratitude to Dr Janet M. Hartley, who read through the whole of my first draft and pointed out its many weaknesses. Those which remain are my own responsibility. I must also thank Professor A.G. Cross for allowing me to see the unpublished diary of Princess Dashkova's travels in Scotland.

The portraits which illustrate the book (other than that of Catherine II) are reproduced from *Russkiye portrety 18-19-kh stoletiy* by Grand Duke Nicholas Mikhailovich by courtesy of the School of Slavonic and East European Studies in the University of London. The portrait of Catherine II is reproduced from *Britain, Russia and the Armed Neutrality*, Yale University Press, 1962, by Isabel de Madariaga. The illustrations representing Russian life are taken from *A Picturesque Representation of the Manners, Customs and Amusements of the Russians, in One Hundred Coloured Plates* by John Augustus Atkinson and James Walker (London, 1803–4), 3 vols, by courtesy of the British Library.

I am grateful to the Fondation de Ligne at the Domaine de Beloeil for permission to reproduce on the jacket the portrait of Catherine II in their possession.

Note: All dates in this book are given in the Julian calendar in use in Russia in the eighteenth century, which was eleven days behind the Gregorian calendar in use in Europe at the time and now. The only exception, the date of the Polish constitution of 1791, is indicated as being NS (New Style).

I have taken the opportunity in the paperback edition to correct a few mistakes pointed out to me by kind friends.

CHAPTER 1

Catherine Seizes Power in the Russian Empire

Catherine II, who reigned over Russia from 1762 to 1796, had no claim whatsoever to the Russian throne. She was born in 1729 as Princess Sophia of Anhalt Zerbst, the daughter of a minor German prince in Prussian service. She was sent to Russia, at the age of fourteen, in 1744, to marry her fifteen-year-old second cousin, Peter of Holstein Gottorp, grandson of Peter I, who had been named heir to the Russian throne.

Before his death in 1725, Peter the Great had decreed that the Emperor was entitled to name his successor. As a result the succession to the throne in the following forty years was decided by a series of *coups d'état* in which the various claimants relied on the support of the Guards Regiments. Peter I was followed by his widow, Catherine I (1725–7), then by his grandson, Peter II (1727–30); the extinction of the direct Romanov male line now brought Peter I's niece Anna Ivanovna to the throne (1730–40), followed in turn by his great-great-nephew, the baby Emperor Ivan VI (1740–1). Finally, Peter's daughter Elizabeth seized the throne (1741–61) and one of her first steps was to appoint an heir, her nephew Peter, Duke of Holstein Gottorp, the son of her dead sister Anna Petrovna (see Genealogical Table, p. 226).

The marriage of Peter and Catherine (the name Sophia was given when she converted to the Orthodox religion) was not a happy one. The new Grand Duchess spent much of her time developing her intellectual interests, an activity to which her husband was totally indifferent. For a long time she was childless, which undermined her position. But finally, following her first, officially encouraged, love affair, a son, Paul, was born, in 1754. To this day no one knows for certain whether he was the son of the Grand Duke Peter or of Catherine's lover, Sergey Saltykov.

When, soon after Paul's birth, Saltykov was sent abroad on a mission Catherine fell in love again, this time with a young Pole, Stanislas Poniatowski, who was in the suite of the British Ambassador, Sir Charles Hanbury Williams. Sir Charles helped the two lovers, and he was instrumental in procuring financial assistance from England to enable Catherine to pay her debts. But the outbreak of the Seven Years War in 1756 soon rendered the British Ambassador's position in Russia impossible. Prussia, in alliance with Great Britain, was at war with Russia and with France, in alliance with Austria. Russia, though not at war with Britain, was fully engaged in the campaign against Britain's ally, Prussia. Hanbury Williams was recalled in autumn 1757; Poniatowski also had to return to Poland. But he was then sent back to St Petersburg as Polish envoy, though he too was recalled in summer 1758, after Catherine had given birth to a daughter by him, who lived only for some fifteen months.

The failure of the Russian military leadership in 1758 to exploit to the full Russia's military victories over the Prussians led to a crisis at the Russian court, which was deeply divided into a pro-Prussian party led by Catherine's husband, the Grand Duke Peter; a pro-French party, led by the Vice-Chancellor, Count M.L. Vorontsov, and, standing somewhat above them, the pro-British Chancellor, Count A. Bestuzhev Ryumin, who had become the friend and ally of Catherine and had for many years received a pension from England. The pro-French party were successful in impeaching the Chancellor, accusing him of failure to prosecute the war, and they very nearly succeeded in implicating Catherine, by then on very bad terms with her husband. But the Grand Duchess manoeuvred skilfully and succeeded in saving her position. The one person who was really opposed to the war against Prussia, the Grand Duke Peter himself, who harboured a most extravagant admiration for Frederick II of Prussia, got off scot-free.

In December 1761, the Empress Elizabeth died, and Peter now became the Emperor Peter III. Though not stupid, he was totally lacking in common sense, and he quickly set about alienating all the powerful parties at court. He withdrew from the war against Prussia and signed a peace treaty in April 1762, abandoning all Russian conquests, including East Prussia, then occupied by the Russian army. He alienated the Orthodox hierarchy by setting in motion again the taking over of Church lands by the state (a policy inaugurated under Elizabeth). He threatened to repudiate his wife Catherine, to disinherit his son Paul, and to marry his current mistress, Elizabeth Vorontsova, a niece of the Vice-Chancellor M.L.

Vorontsov. And he embarked on a military campaign against Denmark in the interests of his German principality of Holstein Gottorp. Most of his policies were so unpopular at court, so lacking in judgment, that several groups started plotting to dethrone him; some, like Nikita Panin, the governor of the seven-year-old Paul, wanted to proclaim him emperor, with a regency council on which they would of course play a prominent part. Others preferred to proclaim Catherine empress in her own right.

In the meantime Catherine had embarked on a third and more lasting relationship with a young Russian Guards officer, Grigory Orlov, by whom she bore a son in secret, in April 1762, known as A. Bobrinskoy. Thanks to her lover, and his four brothers who occupied strategic positions in the armed forces, the plotters acting on Catherine's behalf were successful, and on 28 June 1762, she was proclaimed empress in her own right in St Petersburg. The extent to which families in powerful positions at court were divided between the rights of Peter III and the claims of Catherine is illustrated by the fact that Catherine's closest woman friend at the time, who took an active part in the plot to put her on the throne, was Princess Catherine Dashkova, the sister of Peter III's mistress Elizabeth.

Peter, who was absent from the capital when Catherine was proclaimed empress, was soon after arrested. He abdicated, and was taken to an estate near St Petersburg, where a few days later he died. It was officially stated that he had died of an attack of haemorrhoids, but it is known that he died at the hands of Aleksey Orlov, one of Grigory's brothers, and of several other officers charged with watching over him. According to Aleksey Orlov, he was killed in the course of a drunken brawl, but there is no doubt that it was in the interests of the Orlov brothers to make him disappear, and that Catherine's position on the throne as empress in her own right was thus made secure. According to the available evidence she was not informed of the plot to murder her husband; on the other hand she must have realized that if he remained alive he would be a constant threat to her hold on the throne, and that her supporters were unlikely to let him live.

What sort of person was Catherine at this stage in her life? We know a good deal about her because she wrote several versions of her memoirs, and conducted an extensive correspondence, much of which has been published. Her memoirs were written at various times throughout her life and, though not written for publication, they were no doubt intended to explain and to justify her actions to her family and to posterity. More genuinely spontaneous are the many marginal notes in books she read, or her jottings in notebooks which have survived. She greatly admired the work of the great French *philosophes*, such as Voltaire, d'Alembert and Montesquieu, and the *Great Encyclopaedia*, edited by Denis Diderot. Her great hero was King Henry IV of France, who had thought Paris well worth a Mass. Many of her extracts reflect her careful reading. They also show an open, generous mind, a strong sense of justice, a strong moral sense, founded on humanitarian rather than religious considerations, and tolerant of sexual irregularities, though not of the seduction of one of her maids of honour by the English Envoy, George Macartney.

Paraphrasing d'Alembert, Catherine noted in 1762: 'One should do good and avoid doing evil as much as one reasonably can, out of love of humanity.' 'It is in the interests of the state,' she also noted, 'the laws of which must always remain sacred to monarchs, because they last for ever while subjects and rulers disappear, that men should be judged according to the law.' And she added that princes might occasionally deviate from the law in the interests of mercy, but never in order to make it more cruel. On another occasion she jotted down: 'Liberty, the soul of everything, without you all is dead. I want the law to be obeyed, but I want no slaves. I want the general aim of making people happy, but no caprice, no fantasies, no tyranny which might undermine it.' 'I want to establish that courtiers should learn that the best way to flatter me is to tell me the truth. Even a courtier will adopt this practice when he sees that you like him and that it is the road to favour.' Throughout her reign Catherine showed herself humane and not at all vindictive. In a striking breach with the practice in previous violent changes of ruler (1730, 1741) Catherine prosecuted and exiled none of the high-ranking officials who had previously served Peter III. A very few were dismissed; some were moved to posts outside the capital. Most of them soon returned to high office.

Thirty-three years old when she became empress, Catherine was at this time a small, slender woman, handsome, with blue eyes and dark hair, and great charm of manner. All the reports from foreign envoys concur in describing her gaiety and the ease and lack of pomp and ceremony at her court. Her lover, Grigory Orlov, was given an official position as general in command of the artillery, but did not otherwise interfere in government. Whether she ever thought of marrying him we cannot know, but at the first rumour, in 1763, that a marriage might be contemplated, there was so much opposition that any such idea was promptly and permanently abandoned.

Catherine was of course quite inexperienced in government, and had to rely on those around her. But she was well educated in the literature of the enlightenment, she had read Tacitus and Suetonius on the intrigues surrounding the Roman emperors and the role of the Roman Praetorian Guards, and she was acquainted with German political thought and German administrative practice as it had developed in the small courts of the Holy Roman Empire and in Austria. She had had to convert to the Orthodox religion on her marriage, but religion sat lightly on her. She fulfilled all her religious duties punctiliously and maintained good social relations with the Church hierarchy, but she disapproved of any sort of fanaticism and of forcible conversions. She held that the state should regulate the Church and hence had very little sympathy with Roman Catholicism, which was in her view a religion which aimed at political control, as for instance in Poland, France or Spain.

Though Catherine attempted in public to put a brave face on the difficulties of her situation as empress without any legal right to the throne, several of the foreign envoys remarked on the evident strain she laboured under at the time. To what extent did she feel herself secure on the throne? There were a number of plots, some merely a matter of incautious and drunken talk against a possible marriage with Grigory Orlov. Far more serious however were two conspiracies which were designed to remove Catherine and replace her not by her son Paul, but by a different candidate, Ivan VI, the baby Emperor who had reigned briefly in 1740–1, until he was dethroned by Peter's daughter Elizabeth. In Elizabeth's reign he had become an 'unperson'. All references to his reign were deleted from laws and documents, as though he had never been. The ex-Emperor Ivan VI was kept in prison all his life, mostly in the great fortress of Schlüsselburg on Lake Ladoga, and deprived of any education. As a result he was backward if not mentally defective. Instructions had been issued under Elizabeth that in the event of an attempt to release him he was to be killed by his guards, instructions which were repeated and endorsed under Catherine by her chief minister at the time, Nikita Panin.

Catherine was therefore very alarmed when she heard in 1763 of a plot among a group of Guards officers, who had been among her supporters, to place Ivan VI on the throne. The plot in reality amounted only to talk among men dissatisfied with their rewards for helping Catherine to seize power. But the extent of Catherine's fear is reflected in the penalties finally awarded: loss of rank, and exile to hard labour in Siberia for the two ringleaders, and lesser penalties for the remainder.

Far more serious was a genuine attempt to release Ivan VI and proclaim him emperor organized in 1764 by a disgruntled young Ukrainian, V. Mirovich, whose ancestors had lost their estates under Peter the Great. At the head of a detachment of troops, who did not in fact know what they were doing, he attempted to break in to the inner court in Schlüsselburg where the ex-Emperor Ivan was held. Hearing the commotion, the two officers who were guarding Ivan followed their orders and killed him, whereupon Mirovich gave himself up, since his rising had lost its main object. The death of Ivan could not be hushed up, and Mirovich was tried, sentenced to death and executed – the first execution to take place for many years, since the death penalty had been abolished by Elizabeth in 1754. The whole episode, coming on top of the murder of Peter III, was extremely damaging to Catherine, particularly as the two guards who actually killed Ivan were quietly allowed to disappear – they had of course only been obeying orders.

Russia was not easy to govern. Its sheer size, extending from the Polish frontier to the Pacific Ocean, rendered communications slow and difficult, though the Russians were able to use the river systems which crossed Siberia from south to north, flowing into the Arctic Ocean, to speed up their transport. These rivers extending from, the Ob, to the Yenisei, to the Lena and to the Kolyma, with their many tributaries and portages, formed the staging posts for Russian expansion into Siberia. By the time of Peter I, Russians had already advanced into Kamchatka. In 1742 Alaska was explored, and a few settlements founded in search of furs. Russia then began to move southwards down the west coast of America, founding Fort Ross in 1812, just to the north of San Francisco, then still part of the Kingdom of New Mexico in the Spanish Empire.

European Russia benefited considerably from such navigable rivers as the Narva, the Dvina and the Volkhov, which flowed into the Baltic Sea; the northern Dvina, which flowed into the White Sea; the Don and the Dnieper, flowing into the Black Sea, and the Volga and the Yaik, into the Caspian. Naturally enough Russian rulers had always tried to secure control of the mouths of these rivers, in order to safeguard their communications and particularly their import and export trade with the west or through the Caspian to the east. The city of Archangel on the White Sea had been founded at the end of the sixteenth century as the port for trade with England and the Dutch. Access to the Baltic Sea was only finally secured by Peter the Great, when he defeated Sweden in the Great Northern War (1700–21). It was here, on the Gulf of Finland, that Peter built his new capital, St Petersburg, and his new naval base, Kronstadt. Even so, it was only with the annexation of the Baltic provinces of Livonia (modern Latvia) and Estonia in 1712 that Russia had access to ice-free ports in the Baltic, namely Riga and Reval (modern Tallin). In the south, Russia was still cut off from the Black Sea by the Crimean Tartars, though she was by now the dominant naval power on the Caspian from the port of Astrakhan.

This vast territory had but a small population, totalling some fifteen and a half million in 1725, and a very low population density even in the most densely settled areas of the country. Most of the heartland of old Muscovy, around Moscow, had a population density of about 11–15 per square kilometre; in the north-east, around St Petersburg, the density fell to 1–5 per square kilometre, and large areas of the south and south-west did not reach one person per square kilometre. The whole of Siberia had a population of about 400,000.

The population was relatively homogeneous, mostly composed of Slavs. The major group was the Great Russians, settled around Moscow, extending north, east, west and into Siberia; there were White Russians, or Belorussians as they are called today, in the region bordering on the Lithuanian frontier (Lithuania formed part of the kingdom of Poland–Lithuania), around Smolensk. There were Ukrainians in Little Russia and in the lands on the left bank of the Dnieper known as Slobodska Ukraine, which had been settled by Ukrainians moving there in the seventeenth century. (The population was also largely Ukrainian on the right bank of the Dnieper river, which was at that time under Polish sovereignty.)

There was also a substratum of non-Slavonic peoples in Russia. There were Finns in what was known as Russian Finland, around Vyborg, and many still lived in north-east Russia. There were Tartars around Kazan' and on the Volga, as well as Chuvash, Mordvin and Kalmuck tribes, some still nomadic; further east, in western Siberia there were the Bashkirs. In far-off Siberia there were the Buryats and the primitive Samoyeds and Yakuts.

The two Baltic provinces and that part of the Ukraine called Little Russia were known as regions 'living under their own laws'. According to the conditions laid down by treaty when the Baltic provinces were first annexed by Russia in 1712, Livonia and Estonia were allowed to maintain their own form of administration, social structure, religion and language. There was a German, mainly noble, landowning class, which provided the personnel for the noble law courts and participated in the *Landtag* or Diet. The burghers in the cities participated in town government and in the city law courts. All the peasants, who were mainly Latvian and Estonian, were serfs. The language was German and the religion Lutheran.

The Little Russians too had preserved many features of their way of life before their annexation by Muscovy in 1654 when, under the leadership of the Hetman Bogdan Khmel'nitsky, the Ukrainian Cossacks, who were mainly Orthodox, revolted against their Polish Catholic overlords and placed themselves under the suzerainty of Orthodox Moscow. Neither the Baltic provinces nor Little Russia were subjected to the Russian laws; the inhabitants did not pay Russian taxes (for instance, the poll-tax) nor were they conscripted into the Russian armed forces.

Finally, there were the Cossacks. In addition to an army of some 186,000 men, Russia disposed of a number of irregular cavalry formations, the so-called Cossack Hosts. The Cossacks lived on the margin of settled society, in the Ukraine or Little Russia, or in an island on the Dnieper, 'below the rapids', which was the headquarters of the Zaporozhian Host, extending widely on both banks of the river; or on the Don, where the town of Cherkassk was the centre; or on the Volga, and on the Yaik, a river bordering on Kazakhstan and where the Host had its capital in Yaitskiy Gorodok. As irregular forces some of them had at one time served the Polish–Lithuanian Commonwealth, to which the Cossack Hosts of Right-Bank Ukraine still owed a nominal allegiance. As a social group the Cossacks had gradually come together over the centuries as refugees from Catholic Poland or Moslem Turkey, or fugitive peasants and serfs from Orthodox Russia. They lived by fighting, either as irregulars who hired themselves out and received money and ammunition from Poland or Russia, or by brigandage, and also by cattle-rearing or, more recently, by agriculture, or by fishing as on the Yaik. They elected their own leaders (*hetman*, or *ataman*) and officers, known collectively as the *starshina*. The Zaporozhian Host and the Don Cossacks had for years defended the advancing southern frontier of Russia against slave-raids by the Crimean Tartars or attacks by the Ottoman Turks. Always an unstable element in

Russian society, as the eighteenth century advanced efforts had been made by the Russian government to regularize their administration and the form of their military service. The Cossacks of the Don had so far proved to be the most adaptable, but even their leaders intrigued occasionally with the Turks in the hope of securing more independence for themselves.

The Russia over which Catherine II began to rule in 1762 had been superficially 'Europeanized' in the reign of the dynamic and forceful Peter the Great (1682–1725), who had attempted to modernize Russia's administration and her armed forces. The first twenty years of Peter's reign were taken up by war, and his reforms were largely improvised and piecemeal, but in the second half of his reign he set about endowing Russia systematically with new social and administrative institutions.

The Russian form of government is often described as an autocracy; this is a confusing notion, for it is merely a grander way, because it more closely echoes the Greek word for sole ruler, namely *avtokrator*, of saying that it was an absolute monarchy like most European states at the time. Peter I took over the definition used by King Charles XI of Sweden to express his conception of the nature of Russian government: 'His Majesty is a sovereign monarch who is responsible to no one for his actions, but has the power to rule his state and his lands as a Christian lord according to his will and good understanding.' Nevertheless, the Russian government gave the impression of being more powerful, more authoritarian, than other European governments at the time, because there seemed to be no limits on the tsar's will, no obstacles of a legal or social nature to his power. In other European states, even where there were no effective representative institutions, no diets or parliaments, there were traditions, acquired rights, often described as 'fundamental laws', which rulers in practice respected, whatever their theoretical powers.

The Russian tsar (emperor after 1721) was the sole source of law. All Muscovite institutions were swept away by Peter I, who introduced a new structure modelled to a great extent on Swedish administration. At the top of the pyramid there was a senate. This in no way resembled the model of the Roman Senate, but was a small council of very senior appointed officials, charged with the co-ordination of policy at home and abroad. The Senate had its own secretariat divided into departments, at the head of which was the Procurator-General. His role was an important one, for he was the intermediary between the Emperor and the Senate; he set the agenda and decided on the business. He was moreover the head of a network of procurators throughout the land whose task it was to see that decisions taken by governors or local courts were in accordance with the law of the land.

Beneath the Senate there was a number of functional 'colleges', such as the College of War, the College of the Navy and the College of Commerce. These colleges were the equivalent of a modern ministry or department of state, but Peter had adopted the principle of collective decision-making from his Swedish model, so that the colleges were placed under a president (usually a Russian), a vice-president (often a foreign expert) and a number of members of the collegiate 'boards'. Peter also gave a permanent status to the security service, which had existed at times in the seventeenth century. This body, which had various names throughout the eighteenth century, is most conveniently called the Secret Chancery. Its main function was to investigate any manifestation of opposition to the tsar, ranging from criticism of his (or her) policies to the assertion that Peter I was a changeling, or Antichrist, or that rule by women who 'had more hair than wit' was unnatural. It did not have its own staff throughout the country, but local agencies would arrest and despatch to its headquarters in the capital anyone accused of treason, or even of making disrespectful remarks about the tsar when drunk. An accusation could be launched by anyone calling out the words, 'Word and business of the lord.' Whereupon accuser, and accused, and many only distantly involved, would be arrested and only rarely released. The Secret Chancery used torture and had a terrible reputation for cruelty, and though it was much smaller it was a worthy ancestor of the GPU, NKVD or KGB of modern times (see pp. 137–8).

The country as a whole was divided into some thirteen vast provinces, or *guberniya* in Russian, under a governor, which in turn were divided into sub-provinces and districts. Peter had attempted to set up an elaborate network of administrative offices and courts, but after his death most of this apparatus was dismantled, since it cost too much to maintain and there was not enough educated manpower to staff it. As a result the Russian countryside was very 'under-administered', and often very disorderly. Bands of brigands wandered at will, and had to be put down by the army, since there was no police force, and noble landowners could wage a veritable war on each other using their peasants as troops.

The most obvious and the most effective of Peter's reforms was his remodelling of the armed forces. He built upon the work of his predecessors in creating a standing army mainly composed of infantry; he completely phased out the old cavalry levy of Muscovite days, and replaced it with regiments of dragoons, which soon ceased to be composed exclusively of nobles; and he modernized the artillery. He also created two Guards Regiments to act as training corps for noble officers. Nobles joined the Guards in the ranks, but on promotion an officer in the Guards ranked above an officer in the army. The Guards were a privileged and elite corps from the beginning. The nobles, who had already been bound to serve the tsars intermittently in previous reigns, were now called on to provide continuous, uninterrupted, salaried service, as officers or officials. The peasants and the common people were conscripted to serve in the ranks. As in the civil administration, Peter employed many foreign experts in the armed forces, but the topmost posts remained in Russian hands. Peter is also remembered in Russia as the founder of the Russian navy. First in the northern port of Archangel, then in his newly built capital on the Finnish gulf, St Petersburg, he set about establishing Russia as a maritime power, both in the military and in the commercial sense. Though after his death rulers in other countries expected that his successors would not be able to maintain the military and naval eminence Russia had reached, yet from now on what Russia would do had to be taken into account by those who made foreign policy in eastern and in western Europe.

Thus, whereas in the seventeenth century Muscovite Russia had played a relatively small part in European diplomacy and had only sent occasional missions to the capitals of other countries, from Peter I's reign onwards foreign countries maintained ambassadors and envoys at the Russian court and Russia also had her own diplomatic representation abroad. For obvious geopolitical reasons, Russia's role in international affairs was more important in eastern Europe. The basic orientation of her foreign policy was laid down in the treaty of alliance with Austria in 1726, while friendly relations were maintained with Britain and Denmark. Russia was anxious to defend her Baltic acquisitions against possible Swedish attack, egged on by France, just as she feared the Ottoman Turks, who were also subsidized by France. Relations with England were conditioned by commercial considerations. The trade in naval stores (pitch, hemp, iron, timber, masts, sailcloth) was very valuable to both sides and was eventually regulated by a treaty in 1734 which gave very favourable terms to England.

In 1733 Russia, acting in alliance with Austria, intervened actively to force the election of her own candidate, Augustus III of Saxony, to the throne of Poland, and to keep out a French candidate, but her objectives were limited and she was excluded from the settlement of the peace in the west. Again, in 1735, Russia went to war with Turkey, but in spite of Russian victories she was forced to abandon her conquests, in the peace of Belgrade of 1739, because of the defeat suffered by her ally Austria. The Russian army created by Peter had now showed itself to be more effective against the Turks than the Habsburg armed forces.

Russia took no part in the War of the Austrian Succession (1740–8), but the victories of Frederick II of Prussia led her to consolidate her alliance with Austria, in order to strengthen her position in the event of attack on her Baltic possessions. As a result of the union between the Empress Elizabeth of Russia and the Empress Maria Theresia of Austria in 1746, Russia became one of the leading powers in the so-called diplomatic revolution of 1756, the change-over from the traditional hostility between France and Austria to an alliance between the two countries, supported by Russia, with the aim of defeating and partitioning Prussia. In the so-called Seven Years War which broke out when Frederick II made a pre-emptive strike by invading Saxony in August 1756, Russian armies showed themselves able to stand up to the Prussian forces. Russian victories such as Gross Jägersdorf (1757) and Kunersdorf (1759), the occupation of East Prussia, the brief raid on Berlin in 1760, all served to increase Russian self-confidence. Russia had now become a fully integrated member of the European states system.

CHAPTER 2

Russian Society in 1762

In his efforts to modernize Russia Peter had also endeavoured to give a more western appearance to his country in external ways. Officers and men were made to wear uniforms of western cut, and nobles and townsmen were compelled to shave their beards, and don the wigs and the brocades of the court of Louis XIV, while their wives too were expected to wear the elaborate headdresses, the skirts and embroidered petticoats of western fashion. Women of the upper class were brought out of the seclusion which had been their destiny in Muscovite days, and Peter obliged the great nobles to build modern stone palaces in his new capital and to give balls and receptions, though these were not quite as refined as those of Versailles in view of the Tsar's practice of forcing both male and female guests to drink to excess.

Precedence, that is to say the order in which people are placed in society, the armed forces or the bureaucracy, had been organized in a most clumsy and complicated way in pre-Petrine days. The system known as *mestnichestvo*, or 'placing', laid down that no man should be placed in public service under a man who had been junior in rank to the first man's father. Disputes over this complicated system of precedence had had a bad effect on military efficiency since the best soldier could not be appointed to command an army over the head of a man whose father had been senior to his own father. With the introduction of foreign officers and infantry regiments in the mid-seventeenth century the system became increasingly pernicious and it was finally abolished in 1682. However, no society, and certainly no armed forces, can exist without some command structure reflected in an established order of precedence, and in 1721 Peter issued the so-called Table of Ranks which laid down the order of ranks in the military, naval, civil and court hierarchies in Russia. He abandoned traditional Russian names for ranks and functions – which had already largely ceased to be used – and introduced new titles borrowed mainly from German practice. There were fourteen ranks. The first included field marshal, admiral of the fleet and chancellor; the fourteenth and lowest included ensign, ship's commissar and court butler.

A unique feature of the Russian system moreover was that any man, whatever his social origin, who rose to the lowest rank of commissioned officer in the armed forces (the fourteenth) automatically became a hereditary noble, with all the privileges this entailed. In the civilian service a man in the fourteenth rank became a personal noble, and acquired hereditary nobility when he rose to the eighth rank. Hereditary nobility was much prized because it enabled the man who had achieved it to buy an estate with serfs attached to it. Personal nobles and non-nobles were not allowed to buy these estates, though in Peter's reign many non-nobles who had earlier been granted estates in payment for service were allowed to keep them.

Such tables of precedence were of course in use in other countries too but priority in England or France, for instance, was usually given to social rank. Thus a man's rank at court depended on his title (prince, duke, earl) rather than on his rank in service (captain, colonel, general). Indeed in most cases courtiers did not have a service rank, since service was not compulsory for the nobility, whereas in Russia the title of prince (which was hereditary and which not even the tsar could grant), count or baron did not take precedence over service rank. Rank in service had precedence over rank in society, and the Table of Ranks served to grant hereditary nobility to those who rose high enough in government service. This enabled a number of veterans grown grey in fairly junior positions to rise to hereditary nobility, but it did not lead to a massive influx of promoted nobles into the top posts since, in spite of what is often written about him, Peter I was not anti-noble. He merely wished to be free to use manpower, including noble manpower, in the most efficient way.

In his short reign Peter III had introduced one very substantial change in the relationship between the nobility and the state. In a manifesto published on 18 February 1762 the nobles were specifically freed from compulsory service to the state. They were expected to continue to serve, at least for a number of years, in a military, sometimes a civil capacity; and they were not allowed to leave service in time of war. But the element of compulsion, which the nobility had come to regard as humiliating, had now been removed, and in time of peace nobles were free to return to their estates and to occupy themselves with agricultural improvements or cultural activities, or simply to be idle. Nobles did in fact continue to serve, because few of them could live without the extra income service provided. But the Manifesto of February 1762 changed their attitude to the state. They began to regard it less as an oppressive and overarching tyranny, and more as a series of institutions which they could influence, criticize and even remodel, if it did not fulfil their needs.

Slightly over half the peasants in Russia were serfs belonging to landowners, who were usually nobles. Serfdom had been legally codified in Russia in the middle of the seventeenth century, when it had already almost entirely disappeared in western Europe. There were still pockets of industrial serfs in Scotland in the eighteenth century, and serfdom survived in a few of the areas of France bordering on Germany. Otherwise serfdom flourished mainly in eastern Europe, in Prussia beyond the Elbe, in the Habsburg lands and Hungary, and in Poland.

There has been considerable controversy among historians about the origins, nature and development of Russian serfdom. Broadly speaking there have been two schools of thought. There were those who believed that serfdom arose as a result of economic factors, namely the indebtedness of the peasant to the landowner, who was as a result able to extend to him the process of debt slavery which already existed in Russia. Debt slavery consisted in the personal and voluntary enslavement of oneself (and/or one's family) for a limited period, for one life or for ever. It was frequently resorted to by people driven to despair by destitution. A second school of thought considered that serfdom was the consequence of deliberate action by the state, as the result of a decree allegedly issued towards the end of the sixteenth century which prohibited peasants from leaving the land they were cultivating at the time, and authorized landowners to recover them if they ran away.

This is a necessarily simplified account of a very complex question. The consensus today seems to incline to the view that sixteenth-century serfdom, that is forbidding the peasant to move from the village where he was then working and to leave the master he was working for, was introduced around 1580 by state action. The Muscovite army was at this time composed of a cavalry levy of military servitors (the future nobility), who were granted estates in service tenure to enable them to perform the service required of them. This included procuring expensive chain mail and iron weapons, maintaining their families and answering the tsar's call with horses, men-at-arms, servants, food and fodder. Land without labour was useless.

Gradually the military servitors came to regard the land granted to them in service tenure, to enable them to perform their military duties, as property which they could exploit economically. The pressure of the service class led the state to grant the demand that the peasant should be fastened to the land. At first peasants who had successfully fled for five, ten, later fifteen years could not be recovered by their owners. But gradually the landowners succeeded in putting through decrees enabling them to recover their serfs however long ago they had fled. Finally the total enserfment not only of the peasant but also of his family was enshrined in the Code of 1649, a code of law which was drafted by an Assembly of the Land, a representative body composed of deputies from the Church, the nobility and the towns, which met in 1648. When Peter I ceased to grant land in service tenure, and replaced it by salaries in 1714, land which had been granted in this way in the past was treated as though it were private hereditary property. The culmination of this trend came with Peter III's Manifesto of February 1762, freeing the nobles from compulsory service. The relationship between state, noble and serf was now unbalanced; the state could no longer (in theory) compel the noble; the noble could still compel the serf.

By the end of the reign of Peter I the position of the privately owned serf had become almost identical with that of a slave in the New World except that there was no colour bar separating master and servant. But in Russia the serf was liable to conscription in the armed forces and paid taxes to the state; he could be bought and sold, with or without his family, with or without land. According to the Code of 1649 the serf had no right to complain against his master, unless he were denouncing him for treason. In the eighteenth century there were a number of outrageous cases of the sadistic treatment and of the murder of large numbers of serfs by psychopathic landowners and noblewomen. It proved very difficult to prosecute the guilty owing to the way in which nobles closed up to protect members of their own order. On the other hand most masters were ordinary human beings and did not ill-treat their serfs by the standards of their time.

Not all peasants were serfs of individual landowners. The Church had vast estates cultivated by ecclesiastical serfs; these peasants could

1 *Catherine II.*

2 *Prince Grigory Potemkin, Catherine's favourite and president of the College of War.*

3 *Prince A.A. Vyazemsky, Catherine's long-serving Procurator-General (above left).*

4 *Colonel I.I. Mikhel'sen, conqueror of Pugachev, was descended from an English family which had served in Sweden and then in Russia (above right).*

5 *A.V. Khrapovitsky, Catherine's secretary.*

6 *Count I.G. Chernyshev, vice-president of the College of the Navy, and his family.*

7 *Count A.G. Bobrinskoy, Catherine's son by Grigory Orlov.*

8 *A* cocagne: *free food and wine on a public festival.*

9 *An orthodox wedding ceremony.*

10 *A popular amusement: the original scenic railway.*

not be sold or given away, but they could be taken off the land to act as servants to members of the ecclesiastical hierarchy. Other peasants lived in and were attached to villages on land which belonged to the state. These state peasants could be granted with land as rewards to high officials or could be conscripted to work in industry, building projects, transport or the armed forces. Peter I attached state peasants to mines and foundries, and allowed non-noble entrepreneurs and industrialists to buy villages with settled peasants to be attached in perpetuity to industrial enterprises and manufactories as industrial labour (these serfs did not become the private property of the owner of the enterprise but had to be sold with it); or state peasants could be 'assigned' to enterprises for part of the year to perform auxiliary duties such as burning charcoal, transport, even growing food. The former became known as 'possessional' peasants, because they were attached to the enterprise itself. The latter were known as 'assigned' peasants. There were also 'court' peasants, who belonged to the emperor and the imperial family, and some groups whose status was not clearly determined, who were the descendants of soldier–peasants who had been settled along the southern frontiers in the seventeenth century to defend them against Tartar slave-raids. These soldier–peasants or 'one-homestead men' persistently maintained that they were nobles (they were certainly free), and indeed some of them owned serfs.

Both for economic reasons and for reasons of social prestige, the nobility pressed throughout the first half of the eighteenth century to be granted a complete monopoly of the ownership of serfs. They were finally successful, and by 1754 non-nobles had to sell their serfs, and in 1762 non-noble industrialists and manufacturers were also forbidden to buy serf villages for their enterprises, though they could keep those they already owned.

An important feature of Russian peasant life was the commune. There has also been much controversy about its origins, its nature and its functions. The commune was an institution of self-government in the village. The male population elected a number of 'elders' and officials, who organized the work, administered justice at the village level, decided which young man was to be conscripted into the armed forces, issued passports, allowed peasants to work in towns away from the village, collected and allocated communal taxes and the money dues owed to the landowner, provided land for new households, arranged marriages and cared for widows and orphans.

The commune also performed two very important functions: it

allocated the amount of state tax to be paid and it saw to it that the peasant household had enough land to be able to pay the tax. Peter I had introduced a new form of basic tax in Russia in 1721, which replaced the previous tax on hearths and homesteads. This was the so-called poll-tax, which was primarily allotted to the upkeep of the army. It was a tax levied on all males whatever their age, though in fact the taxes to be paid by the very young and the old were distributed among the households in the commune. In order to introduce the tax, a census of the male population was carried out, but it was so inaccurate that it had to be followed by a 'revision'. As a result the name 'revision' has been used ever since to describe the census, which was carried out every ten or fifteen years. The tax payable by a village, which amounted to seventy kopeks per person per annum (about twenty pence at that time) was calculated according to the number of males registered in the census, including babies, old men and those who had died between two censuses. (It is difficult to give an exact value in terms of purchasing power to seventy kopeks; in 1720, one chetvert (5.75 bushels) of flour cost one ruble fifty kopeks. In the 1790s in the Ukraine one could buy fifty apples for one kopek, but this was an exceptionally fertile area.) In order to spread the burden fairly, the commune decided how much each household should pay, according to the number of young, fit men, the size of the holding, the presence or absence of small children and so on. Periodically, the commune arranged for the redistribution of the land, meadows and woods between families according to changes in their circumstances. In this way the level of taxation was to some extent adjusted to the means to pay, and the means to pay were adjusted to the tax liability.

It has been argued by Russian historians that the commune was an institution antedating serfdom, spontaneously developed by the peasantry over the centuries, which later adapted itself to the functions of administration, justice, public order, taxation and economic exploitation required by the landowners and the state; and on the other hand that it was an organization introduced and maintained by the landowners with the backing of the state, in order to enable them to control the peasants, extract government taxes and their own dues from them, and police the countryside. The former explanation seems more probable, since the peasant commune has existed not only in Russia but in other countries. But the commune acquired more importance in Russia because some sort of self-administration was necessary in view of the vast empty spaces where people might go for days without seeing a soul, villages were cut off from each other and landowners were very often non-resident. Moreover the commune was an equally important feature of the life of the state peasants.

Landowners exploited their estates in two ways: either by exacting money dues (*obrok*) or labour dues (*barshchina*) or by demanding both together. In theory landowners were free to fix the amount of money to be paid per annum, or the number of days to be worked per week. In practice, however, in most cases they were bound by the customs of the village and by the need to leave the peasants enough of what they produced to clothe and keep themselves, or enough time to work their own plots. In the mid-eighteenth century, on average, the money dues amounted to about two rubles per year per male serf, while, where labour dues were the custom, peasants worked three days a week for the landowner, three days a week for themselves and rested on Sundays. There was however nothing to stop the landowners from demanding more. Where serfs were engaged in crafts, such as metalworking, spinning and weaving or transport, or where they were allowed to leave the village to work in the neighbouring towns they would be expected to pay their owners higher money dues. The Princes Kurakin for instance sent some of their serfs every winter to work as cabdrivers in St Petersburg. On large estates serfs provided practically all the skills needed to maintain it, such as carpenters, blacksmiths, grooms and farriers. Women were also expected to contribute woven goods and the serfs provided supplies of food, vegetables and firewood to landowners living in nearby towns.

The state peasants paid the poll-tax of seventy kopeks per annum, but they paid an additional tax or money due, calculated to even up the financial burden weighing on them with the burden on the private serf, who had to pay dues to his landowner as well as the poll-tax to the state. The additional tax paid by the state peasants was one ruble per annum.

Between the tiny class of nobles, numbering some 50,000 males in 1752 (as against some 500,000 in France in the 1780s), and the vast mass of peasants there was a small class of people, variously estimated at between 3 and 8 per cent of the total population, who lived in towns (total numbers are very difficult to assess accurately). There were very few towns in the western sense of the word. Only Moscow and St Petersburg had more than 100,000 inhabitants; a few cities ranged between 20,000 and 30,000, a few more up to 10,000, but many settlements which counted as towns in law had only 500 to 1,000 inhabitants. Of the total number of town-dwellers, only about 250,000 (171,000 according to one authority) were actually registered as tax-paying members of the urban 'estate' and entitled to enjoy certain rights as well as obliged to perform certain duties. The remaining urban population, which by 1762 outnumbered the registered town-dwellers, included officials and clerks, members of the armed forces, some resident nobles and a floating population of the kind necessary in towns everywhere in those days to enable it to function at all: water-carriers, street-cleaners, porters, linkmen, watchmen, pastrycooks, cabdrivers, grooms, cattle-drovers, servants of all kinds. There was also a constant coming and going of peasants from the countryside bringing stores of food, fodder, firewood and so on to market or to landowners from their estates.

As envisaged by Peter the Great, the town was not a unit. It was composed of a number of different legally defined sectors of the population, each of which came under its own separate authority. Thus government officials resident in towns were under the authority of the employing body; officers and soldiers came under the College of War; serfs who got into trouble were dealt with by their owners, and only serfs on leave to work in towns or state peasants with permits from their local elders came under the overall jurisdiction of the local governor. Nobles, clerics and foreigners also came under central government authority. All the transitory, 'unregistered' town-dwellers were dealt with by the governor.

The registered townsmen comprised all those engaged in trade, manufacture and crafts. The merchant class, usually known in modern English and American works as the 'merchantry', the nearest one can get to the Russian *kupechestvo* (which included industrialists and entrepreneurs), had been divided by Peter into two groups or 'guilds'. These guilds incidentally in no way resembled guilds in the west since they were not concerned with the organization of particular crafts, the admission of apprentices, the production of goods or the control of quality and quantity. They were merely convenient social divisions based on how much capital a merchant owned, enabling the government to know who could pay taxes and who was reliable enough to be allowed to act as a government agent. The first guild comprised bankers, wholesalers, doctors and apothecaries, ships' captains, gold and silversmiths and icon-painters; the second included all other craftsmen, retail traders and so on. Many of the poorer merchants did not engage in trade at all but were craftsmen or market-gardeners. The two guilds were replaced by three in 1742.

The administration of the urban estate was based on the assembly of all the registered townsmen who elected a number of officials to a town council or *magistrat* which was both an administrative and a judicial body. Registered townspeople paid the poll-tax like the peasants, but at the rate of eighty kopeks, and like the state peasants they paid an additional sum of forty kopeks per annum as dues to the state. As in the case of the peasants the tax was assessed on all the males registered in the last census as belonging to the urban estate in a given town, and the town assembly undertook the task of allocating the amount actually paid by a given household in accordance with its capacity to pay. Merchants could not leave the town without the permission of the town council unless they had paid all their taxes; and permanent departure from one town to another was frowned on because it might deprive the town of a solid citizen able to take more than his fair share of the tax burden. Bound to his place of residence, like the serf and the state peasant, the registered merchant was also burdened with an enormous range of duties which he had to undertake for the state at his own expense. He collected taxes and excise on the salt and alcohol monopoly, arranged transport for military supplies, billeted troops, collected the special taxes for the building of barracks, acted as a sworn witness or as an arbitrator and so on. Sometimes up to one-half of the merchants in a given town were occupied in these unpaid administrative tasks to the detriment of their business.

The local town councils, or *magistraty*, throughout Russia came under the jurisdiction of the Main Council (Glavnyy Magistrat) in St Petersburg, which ranked as a college. In theory, the local town council judged all matters affecting the members of the guilds and the registered inhabitants of the town, but the local governors did not hesitate to override the decisions of the town councils and to exercise arbitrary power over the merchant class. Urban society was thus composed of layers throughout Russia, and the town as a whole had no legal existence or coherence; there were no institutions dealing with the whole of its population. The members of the merchant guilds had more interests in common with their opposite numbers in other towns than with the other residents of their own town.

The Russian Church had viewed Peter's innovations with dismay. Russia had been converted to Christianity in the ninth century, from the Roman Empire of the east, namely Byzantium. But if the liturgy and ritual were Byzantine Greek, the language of the Church was Slavonic, the common ancestor of modern Russian, Ukrainian, Bulgarian, Serbian and other languages which to this day are mostly written in the Cyrillic alphabet, based on Greek letters. But whereas the spoken language of Russia evolved, the language of the Church, and hence of intellectual life, remained Old Church Slavonic, rather as Latin was the common language of the Church and of intellectuals in the west. As a result Russia was cut off from Latin culture and even from Greek unless works were translated from Greek into Old Church Slavonic by monks, usually for their own use. The Russian Orthodox Church was convinced of its superiority to all other Orthodox communions, because it was the only Church not under the overlordship of the Moslem Ottoman Empire since the fall of Constantinople in 1453. It was equally convinced of its superiority over western Latin Christianity, ever since the final breach between the two communions in 1448, and was determined to protect the Russian faithful against contamination by the questing western secular spirit, even at the cost of intellectual stagnation, which was viewed as a small price to pay in order to safeguard one's eternal salvation.

Even more determined to turn their backs on the west and all its works were the so-called Old Believers. They were schismatics who had broken away from the Orthodox Church in the seventeenth century in protest at the revision of the liturgical books which had been undertaken on the authority of the Patriarch Nikon. The Old Believers held that they were true Orthodox, faithful to the uncorrected liturgy, and in the seventeenth century they suffered a great deal of persecution. They fled to the north-eastern forests, to Siberia, to the Volga, they joined the Cossacks. They were heavily taxed under Peter the Great, and one of their methods of evading persecution was to shut themselves up in one their wooden churches and set fire to themselves. By the eighteenth century various sects existed of which the most important were the priested, that is to say those who accepted the services of a priest ordained in the Orthodox Church; and the priestless, who regarded all Orthodox priests as corrupted and therefore had to do without the ministrations of the clergy.

As a result of its outlook on this life and the next, the Church was deeply hostile to the innovations of Peter the Great. True believers refused to shave off their God-given beards, and rejected the drunken parodies of Church ritual which Peter indulged in. Similarly, Peter's efforts to introduce secular education in Russia met with the massive indifference of the bulk of the population, though he was successful in founding a number of institutions for training the technicians he needed to man the army, the newly created navy, the administration (experts in fortification, artillery, shipbuilding and navigation, clerks and bureaucrats), and in building up some basic mining, metallurgical, textile and armaments industries.

In the years after Peter's death in 1725, the great machine he had created stumbled along much more slowly, and with no clear direction. But Russia gradually absorbed the new orientation he had forced on society. Bowing under the despotism of the tsarist political system, the nobles nevertheless grew to enjoy western culture, which became even more accessible with the foundation of Moscow University in 1755. They benefited from increasing commercial contacts through Peter's new capital on the Gulf of Finland, St Petersburg, and from intellectual exchanges with the west through the Academy of Sciences, founded in 1726. Many Russians now visited the west on their own initiative, to study or to enjoy western culture. The Russian government continued to send numbers of nobles abroad to western universities. But the millions of peasants remained untouched by, if not actively hostile to, many of the features of Peter's new regime and bound by a social structure which perpetuated the arbitrary despotism of one legally defined group over another.

CHAPTER 3

Catherine's First Years

When Catherine II seized the throne in June 1762 Russia was just emerging from the long and costly Seven Years War. Her financial situation was disastrous, the revenue uncollected, the armed forces unpaid, the administration in disorder, the Church hierarchy dismayed at the threatened secularization of their lands and the Church peasants in uproar in the hope of being removed from the Church and the monasteries and transferred to the category of state peasants. Inexperienced though she was, Catherine had every intention of being a working ruler and she dealt quickly and efficiently with most of the problems which faced her. She was able to evade an attempt by her leading minister, Nikita Panin, to limit her power by establishing a council composed of people appointed by her, but whom she could not dismiss, who would have to countersign her decrees. Panin, and the few leading officials who shared his views, were moved not only by personal ambition, but by fear of the influence which favourites might acquire in the reign of a woman. They looked back to the situation which had existed under Catherine I, the Empress Anna and the Empress Elizabeth, when power had been concentrated in the hands of men, not institutions. But Catherine saw through Panin's plan, while some of those she consulted pointed out the dangers of allowing too much power to people whom she could not remove from their positions once she had appointed them. As one of her friends put it, 'an imperial council brings the subject too close to the sovereign and the subject may begin to harbour hopes of sharing power with the sovereign'. By December 1762 the plan had failed.

The more intractable problems which faced her, such as those of the armed forces and the Church, Catherine transferred to specially appointed commissions of officials and experts, always taking care to add some of her own supporters to these commissions to neutralize possibly hostile officials. Revenue-collecting was dealt with by transferring the collection of the poll-tax from soldiers to newly appointed civilian officials. The administration was given a quick overhaul; the number of officials, tiny in relation to the size of the country, was increased in 1764, their salaries were doubled to prevent bribery and the number of prosecutions for bribery reached unprecedented heights – including the prosecution of one of the highest officials in the land, the Procurator-General A. Glebov. Pensions were introduced for long-serving officials in the hope that they would no longer be tempted to feather their nests for their old age at the expense of the public. A new Procurator-General, Prince A.A. Vyazemsky, was appointed in 1764. He was to become Catherine's right-hand man in the internal administration of Russia, a loyal, competent and faithful servant until he retired in 1792. He was at the head of the network of procurators attached to all government institutions, and Catherine considerably increased their number. She urged the Procurator-General to enforce the duty of the procurators to challenge the decisions even of higher-ranking officers if they seemed to go beyond the law.

In addition Catherine introduced an important change into the role of the governors of the provinces. They were now formally entrusted with the welfare of the province they ruled, with the duty of seeking to improve economic, social and judicial conditions, and given direct access to the Empress herself, to whom they were encouraged to submit proposals for reform.

Catherine's interest in the political literature of the period was soon manifested to the general public. In common with all her predecessors in the eighteenth century, she was fully aware of the chaotic state of Russian law. The last codification had taken place in 1649. The Code was drafted by the Assembly of the Land (see p. 16), but it had to be approved by the tsar before it could be enforced. Since the Code of 1649 had been issued thousands of new laws had been promulgated, often without any clear reference to previous laws on the same subject. The result was that neither the courts nor the Russian subjects knew what the law in force actually was. This led to constant lawsuits, lengthy appeals and endless chicanery. Moreover, laws were drafted in a very slovenly manner so that their actual meaning was often in dispute.

Law had been neglected in Russia. There was no tradition of legal training, as was the practice throughout Europe, where faculties of law formed part of medieval universities. Not until the foundation of

Moscow University in 1755 did the teaching of jurisprudence begin, at first in Latin or in German, based on Roman law or on the natural law theories current in Europe at the time. The teaching of Russian positive law only began in 1767. None of the high government officials who surrounded Catherine had been trained in law, and Catherine herself, of course, knew only what she had picked up from her reading.

In order to find a way out of this chaos, Catherine embarked on an original experiment. She determined to summon a large assembly composed of deputies from the nobility, the towns, the free peasants, the Cossacks and the non-Russian tribes (Tartars, Kalmucks, Kazakhs, Bashkirs, Mordvins, Chuvash, Cheremiss, Votyaks and even the distant Yakuts), the government departments and the Church to draft a new code of laws. Not surprisingly in view of Catherine's essentially secular turn of mind, the clergy were not represented as a social estate, but the Holy Synod, which had been set up by Peter I to govern the Church, was invited to send a deputy as a government department. Previous rulers had in the past set up bureaucratic 'commissions' which had produced draft partial codes, and had invited representatives of the nobility and the towns to the capital to discuss portions of the drafts. But these gatherings had been small and private, and had in any case led to nothing.

Catherine however attempted something new: to call together an elected representative body somewhat resembling the old Muscovite Assemblies of the Land, such as the one which had drafted the Code of 1649. But she did not want her elected body to pretend to any political role in the government of the country (as the seventeenth-century Assembly of the Land had enjoyed), so the gathering was not called Assembly of the Land, but Legislative Commission, to underline the continuity with the previous commissions in the eighteenth century, and the break with the seventeenth-century precedent. Catherine may also have been influenced by the arguments of the French *philosophe* Diderot in the *Great Encyclopaedia*, in the entry 'représentants', in which he stresses the need for the sovereign to hear the voice of the people through its representatives.

The election of deputies to a Legislative Commission was proclaimed in December 1766, and at once enlivened political life throughout the country. All nobles were entitled to vote in districts where they held estates, and women landowners were allowed to vote by proxy, but not to attend the district electoral assemblies of the noble order. The noble district electoral assemblies began by electing a 'marshal of the nobility' who then proceeded to conduct the elections. Similarly in the towns all registered town-dwellers were called together to elect a 'town chief' who then organized the elections. When the members of the merchant guilds attempted in some towns to restrict the right to take part in the elections to merchants alone the Senate quashed the elections and ordered them to be held afresh. The state peasants voted by means of indirect elections in each province. The groups of electors were also invited to compose 'instructions' for their deputies, setting out their hopes and grievances.

The Legislative Commission, composed of some 29 deputies of government institutions, 142 deputies of the nobility, 209 deputies of the towns, and some 200 deputies of the state peasants and other social groups (including 54 deputies from the non-Russian tribes), met in Moscow at the end of July 1767. They were immediately presented with a lengthy 'Instruction' written by Catherine herself, to guide them in their debates. It was certainly unusual at the time for a ruling monarch to expound his or her views on how a government should be organized, and we have no evidence to indicate the reasons which moved Catherine to embark on this novel enterprise. Frederick II of Prussia had, it is true, published his own political maxims, and this may have inspired her to emulate him. Be that as it may, she now expounded in 20 chapters and 526 articles her vision of how Russia was and should be governed. The Instruction is not however original. Catherine drew very largely on *The Spirit of The Laws* (1748) by the French *philosophe* Montesquieu in her analysis of the nature of government and society. Montesquieu was the author of one of the most influential works published in the eighteenth century, and was one of the first to analyse the social structure of societies and the political rights of men in their relationship to the corresponding form of state. Catherine drew also on the recently published work of an Italian jurist, Cesare Beccaria, entitled *On Crimes and Punishments* (1763), which was one of the most cogent attacks on the cruelty of the penal system as it then existed in all countries. Another source was the *Institutions Politiques* of Baron Bielfeld, which summed up the principles of German cameralism and which Catherine arranged to have translated into Russian in 1768–75. But if the Instruction is not original in content, it is original in the arrangement of the material, which Catherine copied out at length several times and showed to many of her advisers. As a result of their criticisms she omitted some of the most radical sections, particularly her criticisms of serfdom, from the final draft.

Catherine's Instruction has often been seriously misunderstood.

Some contemporaries believed it to be a code of laws; some later historians have even believed that it was a constitutional blueprint for Russia. It is therefore necessary to spend a little time on this important document. The Instruction is not particularly well organized and reflects the sources which Catherine had recently read and which had impressed her. Sometimes she seems to contradict herself, sometimes she deliberately quotes different points of view (for instance on whether nobles should participate in trade), sometimes she fails to integrate ideas derived from different sources. The Instruction is thus a mixture of statements about what Russia is, what it ought to be, what government and the administration of justice ought to be, and how society in general ought to be organized. A supplement, issued in 1768, dealt with 'the police', that is with all the general questions of public order, public health and administration of urban life. A second supplement dealt with the revenue and expenditures of the state.

The Instruction thus deals with political, judicial, social and economic issues. It starts off by proclaiming that Russia is a European state. This is a kind of manifesto against those who believed that Russia was closer to an Asiatic despotism than to a European monarchy. Catherine then defines the government of Russia: 'The Sovereign is absolute; for there is no other authority but that which centres in his single person, that can act with a vigour proportionate to the extent of such a vast dominion' (art. 9). This is one of the statements in the Instruction which has led subsequent historians to argue that she perverted the meaning of Montesquieu. Thus Montesquieu argued that each form of government was centred around a basic principle: honour in the case of a monarchy; virtue in the case of a republic; and fear in the case of a despotism. Among monarchies, he distinguished a 'moderate' monarchy, in which the power of the ruler was limited by the existence of 'fundamental laws' which bound him and which he could not alter; in a 'moderate' monarchy, laws were safeguarded by the existence of a 'depositary' in which they were held, and the power of the ruler was limited by the existence of social institutions such as the corporate rights of nobles or of cities, or of the Church, which the ruler could not override. Montesquieu also drew the attention of his readers to the existence of 'moderate' monarchies which had 'political liberty' as their main principle. He was clearly referring to England, and he argued that it was the separation of the executive (the king), the judiciary (the courts) and the legislature (parliament) which guaranteed this political liberty. Despotisms were for Montesquieu mainly oriental states such as the Ottoman Turks, or Persia, and also very large states, which were difficult to govern if power was diffused too widely. Among these latter he included Russia.

Catherine had been an avid student of Montesquieu for several years, and admired him greatly. Yet she could not publicly accept his classification of Russia, which was a very large state, as a despotism, as a country in which authority could not be exercised effectively unless it were despotic. Therefore Catherine adapted what her French master had to say about despotism to monarchy, and declared that Russia was an absolute monarchy because such a large state could only be governed in accordance with a system in which the sovereign rules alone but subject to fundamental laws, the limitations of which he voluntarily accepts.

The concept of fundamental laws was much in vogue in the eighteenth century, yet it remained very elusive. It did not mean a written constitution. Fundamental laws were basic traditions which were so deeply rooted in a given society that no monarch, however absolute, not even say Louis XIV, would act in opposition to them without extremely grave cause.

Absolute rulers thus respected a certain number of habits and institutions. These usually included respect for the 'state' or dominant religion in a country, like Roman Catholicism in France or Anglicanism in England; or for the law of succession, which excluded women in Bourbon France, but not in the Habsburg lands; or for the existing rights and privileges of social groups, like the nobles, or of urban corporations like the free cities of the Holy Roman Empire. Catherine wished to argue that Russia was not an Asiatic despotism, ruled by fear, but an absolute monarchy, in Montesquieu's sense of the term, with fundamental laws. In spite of the huge size of the Russian Empire, which required absolute power in the ruler in order to be effectively governed, she argued that it was not a despotism. In other ways, however, the Empress followed Montesquieu closely. She argued in favour of a depositary of the laws, that is to say an institution charged with ensuring that newly promulgated laws should not be contrary to the existing fundamental laws of the state. Liberty was defined as 'the right to do whatsoever the laws allow'. Equality consisted in that 'the citizens should all be subjected to the same laws'.

Contrary to normal Russian practice, Catherine went into great detail on the nature and administration of the law and the organization of justice. Laws, as she defined them, 'comprehended all the fundamental institutions, which ought never to be altered, and the number of such can never be large'. Here she was clearly referring again to fundamental laws, to what we would call today constitutional laws, establishing for instance the state religion, or the order of succession to the throne. Laws were backed up by 'momentary regulations, which depend upon circumstances', that is to say rules for the carrying out of the laws, or what we would call today executive actions. Finally there were 'injunctions' or orders which were issued to deal with a particular emergency. Laws, regulations and injunctions were of course made by the sovereign acting alone, but all laws should be simple and clear, and leave no opening for doubtful interpretations.

The Instruction went into great detail on the analysis of crime, distinguishing between crimes against religion and manners, which should be punished by for instance depriving the offender of the benefits of religion, or by public humiliation; crimes against peace or public security, which would deserve imprisonment, corporal punishment or, in the case of murder, death; and crimes against property, which should be dealt with by fines.

Nowhere is Catherine's acceptance of a rational and legal order better illustrated than in her definition of high treason. To begin with she distinguishes between sacrilege and *lèse-majesté*. The sovereign may rule by divine right, but he is not divine, and it is not therefore sacrilege to commit an offence against him, or even against his effigy. Coining false money, in her view, is not therefore high treason, but 'robbery of the state'. Words, let alone thoughts, do not constitute a crime unless accompanied by deeds. And Catherine adds that satirical writings, in monarchies, should be regarded as misdemeanours, not crimes, and that great care should be taken in restraining such libels, since severe censorship can be 'productive of nothing but ignorance, and must cramp and depress the rising efforts of genius and destroy the very will for writing'.

Clearly justice played a large part in Catherine's thinking for she pays a great deal of attention to the role of the judge, the validity of evidence, the kind of proofs required to reach a verdict. It is here that Catherine echoes both Montesquieu and Beccaria in her denunciation of torture: 'The usage of torture is contrary to all the dictates of nature and reason: even mankind itself cries out against it, and demands loudly the total abolition of it.' She gives the example of a great nation which has rejected it 'without any sensible inconveniencies', and is probably referring to Great Britain.

Though she had no training in jurisprudence, the Empress had a sense of the meaning of legality, of the need to replace arbitrariness by due legal process. In states under 'a moderate government' (that is to say absolute monarchies ruled according to fundamental laws – what Catherine believed Russia should be or was), citizens could not be deprived of life, liberty or property without judicial formalities, though people belonging to different social orders, nobles, townspeople or peasants, might bring their lawsuits or be charged before different courts and suffer different penalties. Judges should have no right to interpret the law. Only the sovereign, who makes the law, can do that. Judges must judge according to the letter of the law, because this is the only way of ensuring that the same crime is judged in the same way in all places at all times. If a strict adherence to the letter of the law leads to injustice, then the sovereign, as lawgiver, will issue the necessary new laws. But the ruler must never himself be a judge.

In dealing with the structure of society, Catherine maintained that there must be 'some to govern and some to obey'. Nobles were the descendants of those who in the past had distinguished themselves more than others, primarily by military service. Yet since any state would be destroyed without justice, so nobility could be acquired by civil as well as by military virtues, by judges and officials, as well as by soldiers. The 'middling sort of people' were also free. They comprised those who inhabited the towns and practised the crafts, trades, arts and sciences, all those who were not noble by birth but had been educated in civil or church schools and all those non-nobles who worked as officials or clerks in government offices.

In the published Instruction there was no chapter dealing specifically with the serfs, but Chapter 11 which deals with slavery was very drastically cut after a first and much longer draft had been shown to several of Catherine's advisers. In the published version Catherine states that a ruler should avoid reducing people to a state of slavery, unless constrained by the utmost necessity, and that the civil laws should guard against the abuse of slaves. Finally, quoting Montesquieu, she states that a large number of slaves should not be freed all at once or by a general law. The unpublished drafts of Chapter 11 have survived, and they show that Catherine had originally included a proposal, also derived from Montesquieu, that serfs should be allowed to accumulate sufficient property to buy their freedom and that servitude should be limited to six years. She also proposed issuing a law to the effect that once a serf had been freed he should never be enserfed again.

The supplement on the police is more closely modelled on German cameralist thought, that is to say the science of government which had been worked out in the small German courts throughout the seventeenth and eighteenth centuries, which held that the state was the prime mover in the organization of government and society, and that it could achieve its aims by the minute regulation of all forms of activity. (See pp. 69–70.) According to Catherine's Instruction the functions of the police should include ensuring the decent performance of religious services, supervising the purity of morals (avoidance of luxury, curtailment of drunkenness, regulation of public baths, of public spectacles and so on), hygiene (cleanliness of water, quality of food and drink, control of disease), weights and measures, care of cattle and pasturage, building regulations, fire prevention and fighting, prevention of disorder and brigandage, control of the hiring, firing and paying of servants, caring for the poor and sick, by forcing the fit to work, and feeding the infirm. The police should not be entitled to inflict severe punishments, but only to deal out summary justice and fines for what were in effect breaches of regulations rather than crimes against the laws.

The final supplement deals with what Catherine called 'the administration of finances'. The Empress appears to have been influenced in the preparation of this part of her Instruction by some of the ideas of Adam Smith, which may have reached her through the Russian lawyer, S.I. Desnitsky, who had been a pupil of his in Glasgow and who submitted memoranda to her. She analyses the objects for which revenue is necessary, for example public order, public utility, the magnificence of the throne and defence. She then turns to the sources of revenue, namely taxes; and to the sources of wealth, namely population, agriculture, exploitation of natural resources and trade, and ends on the hopeful statement that 'the sum total of the expences might not, if possible, exceed the revenue'.

After the formal opening of the Legislative Commission at the end of July 1767 the Empress's Instruction was read aloud to the deputies. One may imagine the impact which such a document must have had on fairly low-ranking, very moderately educated, sometimes illiterate army officers, tradesmen whose horizon was limited by their own province, peasants and primitive tribesmen from Siberia. The deputies had all brought written statements of the grievances of their electors, on the lines of the *cahiers de doléances* which deputies to the States General in France were instructed to produce in 1789. They were often very eloquent accounts of the injustices and the exploitation suffered by members of all classes, but they were usually drawn up in a language which did not reflect the bracing ideas of the enlightenment. Now under the impact of the Empress's Instruction, it became possible to discuss a whole range of political concepts using the terminology which the Empress had launched, sheltering behind her own statements. The Instruction brought before the deputies ideas on law, justice and humane and civic behaviour such as had never been publicly proclaimed in Russia. The debates in the various sessions were often enlivened by deputies quoting this or that paragraph of Catherine's Instruction in support of controversial ideas.

Yet the Legislative Commission did not produce a code. Its sessions were unwieldy, its work badly organized; moreover the time needed for all the preparatory work had been grossly underestimated. A number of drafts of portions of a code were prepared but nothing had received final approval in the Commission when war broke out between Russia and Turkey in October 1768. Catherine prorogued the full assembly, for many of the noble deputies were called upon to serve in the army, and she and her government needed to concentrate their energies on waging war. A number of sub-commissions continued in being until the early 1770s, when they too petered out. Nevertheless, the debates in the full assembly, the discussions in the sub-commissions, the draft codes of the rights of nobles, townspeople, Cossacks and peasants and the material included in the lists of grievances provided the Empress (and subsequent historians) with a vast amount of information about the needs, wishes and opinions of local people upon which she was able to draw in later legislation. The draft codes also enable one to follow differing trends of opinion in Russian society on serfdom, the rights of peasants and nobles, the status of Cossacks, and on many other social and political issues.

No complete new code of laws was ever promulgated in Catherine's reign. But she issued a number of partial codes, such as the Statute of Local Administration of 1775, the Code of Commercial Navigation and the Salt Code (dealing with the state monopoly of salt) of 1781, the Police Ordinance of 1782, the Charters to the Nobility and the Towns of 1785, the Statute on National Education of 1786, which went a long way towards modernizing and filling the gaps in existing Russian law. Some of these laws will be dealt with in more detail later. Some of them refer back quite specifically to parts of Catherine's Instruction. As she wrote to Voltaire on 1 October

1777 when she sent him a copy of the Statute of Local Administration of 1775:

> the building of our laws is rising little by little: the Instruction for the Code is the foundation. I sent it to you ten years ago. You will see that these new regulations do not fall below its principles, but rather follow from them; they will soon be followed by regulations on finance, commerce, police, on which we have been working for two years. After that it will be a simple and easy task to draft a Code.

The fact that no complete code was produced led both contemporaries and subsequent historians to assume that Catherine had other quite different reasons for calling together the deputies from the different estates. She was assumed to be vain (which was true), and many thought that the principal purpose both of the Instruction and of the Legislative Commission was to throw dust in the eyes of her 'enlightened' correspondents in the west, and to dazzle them with the spectacle of the political progress of backward Russia. She was believed to have summoned the Commissioned in order to strengthen her claim to be a legitimate ruler, and was regarded as a systematic hypocrite, only too well aware of the difference between theory and reality, and making no genuine efforts to improve the lot of her people. For many subsequent historians this interpretation was confirmed by one salient fact: the absence of deputies from the serf peasantry in the Commission.

Again, there were those who believed that the idea of consulting the people about the drafting of the laws as well as many of the principles put forward in the Instruction indicated that Catherine had passed through a 'liberal' phase at the beginning of her reign, and that she subsequently became more authoritarian, and after the French Revolution even reactionary. These interpretations need to be considered if a convincing synthesis of her beliefs and her policies is to be made.

The idea that the principal purpose of such an expensive and time-consuming operation (remember that the Empress wrote out the many drafts of her Instruction with her own hand) was only to throw dust in the eyes of western intellectuals suggests that these same intellectuals had a somewhat inflated opinion of themselves. It was possible for Catherine to win their golden opinions by corresponding with them, as she did with Voltaire, and Falconet, buying his library and leaving it in his possession, as she did with Diderot, inviting d'Alembert and Beccaria to come to Russia (who both refused), appointing Melchior von Grimm, the editor of the *Correspondance littéraire et politique*, the gossipy, well-informed, private newsletter of current literature, poetry, drama and politics as her personal agent in Paris. There was no need for her to embark on an enterprise of such major dimensions as the Legislative Commission.

The problem of the representation of the serfs raises the whole question of the nature of political representation in the eighteenth century in those countries in which representative institutions existed such as for instance Great Britain, the Netherlands, Poland, Sweden. Traditionally, three social orders or 'estates' were represented in parliamentary institutions. These were the nobility, the Church (in France it was the First Estate) and the so-called Third Estate in France, which corresponded to the Commons in England. One must bear in mind that the American and the French Revolutions are a great divide, separating the Old Regime type of parliaments, in which social groups with interests based on property were represented, from the modern institutions, in which the opinions of individuals are represented as of right, by means of the principle of universal suffrage.

Under the Old Regime parliamentary bodies often lacked systematically worked-out regulations for calling them together and electing their members. If they were composed of more than one chamber, the members of the upper or noble chamber might be elected by all the nobles, or by noble heads of families only, or all nobles might be summoned to attend in person. Towns would be represented by heads of guilds or corporations; or the corporations – not the inhabitants – might elect deputies to represent them. It was taken for granted that only people with some standing in society should be called upon to advise the ruler in a parliament and to participate in the making of laws. The reverse of 'no taxation without representation' was 'no representation without taxation'. Only those who paid taxes should share in decisions about taxes. No one could have any such weight unless he were free, that is to say his opinions did not depend on the need to conciliate an employer or an owner, and he need not fear for his livelihood and that of his family. Standing therefore tended to be identified with status (noble or urban) and ownership of property. Thus in Sweden, the only country in which there was a 'Fourth Estate' of peasants, only those peasants who lived on state land elected deputies, but not those who lived on noble land, whose opinion might be conditioned by their dependence on the landowner, though they were personally free. Similarly in eighteenth-century England, no servant had a vote.

Moreover, it was commonly believed that deputies 'represented', that is to say spoke for, the interests of social groups, and did not express their own individual opinions. Thus the deputies of the Dutch towns represented the countryside around them, just as the estate of the peasants was abandoned in Denmark on the grounds that the peasants were represented by the nobles. There is a remnant of this belief in modern Britain, where an elected Member of Parliament represents not only his electors, but all the people in his constituency, whether they voted for him or not; and where he is supposed to use his independent judgment in the interests of the people he represents, though this latter aspect of his function has declined as a result of the increasingly rigid party discipline.

Thus the assembly called together by Catherine in 1767 has to be seen in the context of eighteenth-century ideas of representation and compared with similar institutions in other countries. In England at this time only a small percentage of the population actually voted in general elections, and in many constituencies elections were uncontested. In the counties, the vote was limited to landowners down to the forty-shilling freeholder, that is to say a man who owned land with an income of forty shillings a year. Peasants had no vote. In the boroughs the franchise was very varied, often limited to the members of the borough corporation, themselves subject to the pressure of a local political magnate. Over 40 per cent of the borough members of Parliament were returned by fewer than 100 electors. There was thus nothing democratic about this system, and there seems to be no reason to expect that the system adopted by Catherine in 1766 should conform to modern notions of democratic representation, rather than to Russian historical tradition and contemporary practice elsewhere.

Representation in the Legislative Commission was in fact extremely broad. The state peasants, who were legally free in the sense that their landlord was the state, were invited to send deputies chosen by indirect elections in constituencies as large as a sub-province. All householders in a town were invited to choose deputies, also by indirect election, while all nobles living in a particular district (there were several districts in a sub-province) were invited to choose a deputy. There was no choice between candidates standing for different opinions or policies. It was a process of selection of a suitable person to speak in the Legislative Commission about the needs of a given community and to give advice to the Empress on the nature of Russia's problems and how to solve them. The final decision was hers. And in order to make the post of deputy more acceptable, all those chosen to serve were given a salary to cover their expenses according to their rank, and a medal to distinguish them.

Finally, it is obvious that there was nothing 'liberal' in the political sense in which the word is used today about the Legislative Commission. It was never intended to discuss the Russian form of government or to limit the absolute power of the ruler of Russia, and Catherine had made perfectly clear in her Instruction that she considered absolutism to be the only form of government suitable to Russia. There never was a 'liberal' phase, let alone a constitutional one, in Catherine's reign. But there are of course degrees of absolutism, and the impression of liberalism can be given simply when an absolute government is somewhat less arbitrary than its predecessors and interferes less in the daily life of the people. Catherine was much less arbitrary than Peter I.

CHAPTER 4

The First Turkish War

On Peter III's accession in 1762 Russia had still been engaged in fighting against Prussia in the so-called Seven Years War (1756–63), as the ally of Austria and France. He had forced Russia to change sides at once, withdrawing his troops from military co-operation with the Austrians, and making peace with Prussia in April 1762. On her accession Catherine inherited this situation, which rendered Russia very unpopular with her ex-allies. As a result she was left out of the negotiations leading to the peace treaties of Hubertusburg and Paris which put an end to the Seven Years War in 1763. Russia was left dangerously isolated and Catherine was forced to re-examine the general principles of Russian foreign policy and her system of alliances.

The objectives of Russian foreign policy were implicit in her geopolitical situation, but were also influenced by traditional friendships and enmities. Since the sixteenth century Russia had been striving to extend her borders on three fronts: in the north-west, she had sought an outlet to the Baltic Sea in order to free her foreign trade from the stranglehold exercised on it first by the Livonian knights, then by the Prussians, the Poles and the Swedes. Peter I had finally been successful in this area with the annexation of Livonia and Estonia in 1721. In the west Russia was also striving to reassert her authority over Belorussian and Ukrainian lands which had once formed part of the medieval principality of Kievan Rus' and which had subsequently accepted the overlordship of the grand dukes of Lithuania, who were in turn joined in a dynastic union with the kings of Poland; or which had come under the direct overlordship of Poland herself. To the south Russia had had for centuries to defend herself against the Tartars of the Crimea, the descendants of the Mongol overlords, who raided Russian lands regularly, seizing thousands of prisoners every year for the slave-markets of Constantinople.

Little by little, as Russia grew stronger, defence had changed into attack. Russia hoped to acquire a foothold on the Black Sea, even though this did nôt imply access to the Mediterranean, the gates of which were locked up by the Turks at the Dardanelles. Peter the Great had three times tried and failed to establish a permanent base in the Sea of Azov at least (also a sea closed by the Turks). Not until 1739 was this achieved, but it was still not enough to render the territory secure. The military lines, or settlements, of farmer–soldiers which had marked the steadily advancing southern Russian frontier were further strengthened by the Cossack Hosts, such as the Don Cossacks, the Ukrainian or Little Russian Cossacks, and the Zaporozhian Cossacks.

Control of an outlet to the Baltic, of the western lands now Polish and of the south was desirable also for commercial purposes. It implied also the control of a number of waterways important for internal and external trade. Peter I's conquest of Livonia had secured for him the great port of Riga at the mouth of the River Dvina, down which produce from the north-western forests of Russia and Poland, such as timber, masts, pitch, hemp, tar, as well as flax and hides, was floated. Such goods could now be exported directly, particularly to the maritime powers of western Europe, England, France and the United Provinces of the Netherlands. Estonia too provided a useful naval base at Reval. St Petersburg was to develop into a major port, but it was icebound for part of the year. The western lands controlled the headwaters of the River Dnieper and its many tributaries, central also to the commercial development of the area, which – though it was not navigable because of the rapids – ultimately required control of the whole course of the river and of its estuary on the Black Sea. Similarly control of the mouths of the Rivers Bug and Dniester, at present in Turkish hands, would enable Russia to dictate the terms of the export of goods from what was then southern Poland and Turkish Moldavia. These ambitions remained unfulfilled at Catherine II's accession.

When he withdrew from the Seven Years War in 1762, Peter III had signed not only a treaty of peace but a separate treaty of alliance with Prussia with a view to his impending war against Denmark. Catherine did not ratify this treaty. The long war had left Russia exhausted. In an undated note, probably belonging to the mid-1760s, Catherine wrote, 'The only advantage Russia has drawn from the peace treaty is peace. The finances were exhausted to the point that every year there was a deficit of 7 million rubles. . . . The army had not been paid for eight months'. A policy of peace and recuperation was clearly indicated.

The man Catherine appointed in October 1763 to carry out her foreign policy, Nikita Panin, was the *Oberhofmeister* or Grand Master of the Court or governor of the Grand Duke Paul. He had previously been Russian ambassador first in Denmark, then in Sweden, and knew the politics of the Baltic well. He did not give up his post with the young Grand Duke, which provided him with a secure base at court and living quarters in the Palace, but became officially the 'senior member' of the College of Foreign Affairs as well.

In the early 1760s Prussia was the only major state prepared to offer Russia its friendship. France was traditionally hostile, in spite of the brief rapprochement between the two powers during the Seven Years War. Austria had been totally alienated by the Russian change of sides in the war. England maintained friendly relations with Russia in spite of the recent hostilities, because of the close trade relations in iron and naval stores between the two countries, regulated by the commercial treaty of 1734 – a trade which had not been interrupted during the war though the two countries had fought on opposite sides.

But England was not prepared to agree to the most important condition Catherine put forward in discussions of a treaty of alliance between the two countries. The Empress wanted to secure British assistance in the event of a war against her most dangerous enemy, namely the Turk, just as Britain demanded assistance in the event of war with her most dangerous enemy, namely France. But Britain utterly refused to agree to the Russian condition, largely in order not to jeopardize British trade with the Ottoman Empire, the so-called Levant trade, by siding with Turkey's enemy. Catherine reduced her demands to subsidies for action in Poland and Sweden, but Britain again refused on the ground that Parliament would not agree to pay subsidies in time of peace.

In these circumstances Catherine was finally induced by Frederick II's pressure to sign a treaty of alliance with Prussia in 1764 by which the two powers undertook to come to each other's assistance with subsidies in the event of attack by one power, with armed force in the event of attack by two powers. This treaty laid down the broad framework of Catherine's foreign policy for the next sixteen years. As developed by Nikita Panin, it was an essentially defensive policy, and he hoped to extend it into a 'northern system' which Britain, Sweden, Poland and Denmark would be invited to join, thus counterbalancing the Family Compact of France and Spain, allied to Austria, the so-called Catholic bloc. One of the terms of the Russo-Prussian treaty of 1764 was that the two powers, Russia and Prussia, should co-operate in settling problems, as they arose, in Poland and Sweden, to their joint advantage. These countries were both at this time limited monarchies, that is to say the king was not fully sovereign, his power being limited by some form of representative institution such as a diet or parliament.

It was most important for the fulfilment of Panin's policy that the pro-Russian party should win power in Sweden and keep it. Since the introduction of limited monarchy in Sweden in 1720, the government had been in the hands either of the Caps, or pro-Russian party, or of the Hats, or pro-French party. Both parties however were strongly opposed to any effort by the King of Sweden, Adolf Frederick, and even more of his queen, Louisa Ulrica, the sister of Frederick II of Prussia, to restore royal absolutism. Russian policy too was aimed at preventing the restoration of absolutism, because it was widely believed that an absolute king would be more likely to attempt to use military force to recover the lands Sweden had lost to Russia in the treaties of 1721 and 1743. The pro-French Hats were in power in 1763, and the Russian Ambassador worked hard together with the British Envoy in order to break the Franco-Swedish alliance and bring Sweden into Panin's 'northern system', for it was Britain's policy to counter France wherever she could. By means of massive bribery, the two envoys helped the Cap party to secure an overwhelming victory in the elections to the Diet of January 1765. For the time being Russia and her friends, Britain and Denmark, ensured that there would be no restoration of absolutism in Sweden.

The government of the Commonwealth of Poland–Lithuania in late-eighteenth-century Europe was quite unlike that of any other country. To begin with the country was composed of two parts, the kingdom of Poland and the Grand Duchy of Lithuania, which meant that though there were some common institutions such as the Diet (or Sejm), there were a number of duplicated posts, for example the commanders of the military forces (such as they were) in Poland and in Lithuania respectively. Often described as a crowned aristocratic republic, the Commonwealth had a king who was not hereditary but elected. The Diet too was elected by the Polish and Lithuanian nobles, a very large class of people, numbering perhaps some 10 per cent of the population (a much larger electorate than existed at the time in England). The Diet elected a Permanent Council, which sat between sessions of the Diet, and a number of the highest officials. The king appointed some of these highest officials too, but he could not remove them.

Unique to the Polish–Lithuanian Commonwealth was the so-called *liberum veto*. The *liberum veto* entitled any single deputy to the Diet to veto a decision, even when it was approved by a majority. Thus all decisions reached by the Diet had to be unanimous in order to be implemented. If any single deputy opposed a decision, it was declared invalid and moreover all the decisions taken in the session of the current Diet were also wiped out. It was unfortunately always possible to find one deputy who either for reasons of principle, more often because he was bribed, opposed one of the decisions taken. As a result the Polish government staggered on from crisis to crisis, while the country was ruled in fact by a small number of extremely wealthy aristocratic magnates whose estates (with serfs) were bigger than several English counties, and who maintained large retinues of poor noble hangers-on. There existed one method however by which the *liberum veto* could be circumvented. This was the 'confederation'. A group of nobles would get together to proclaim a confederation in order to achieve certain aims. A Diet would be summoned, known as a Confederated Diet, and it could take enforceable decisions by majority vote. When it had achieved its purpose it would dissolve itself, and Poland would revert to its normal constitutional anarchy.

A system of this kind was perfectly devised to enable powerful neighbours to meddle in internal Polish affairs, starting with the election of a king. Austria, France (traditionally Poland's ally), Prussia and Russia were all interested in the election of a king who would be subservient to them in foreign policy or war. Indeed, ever since 1716, Peter the Great had been the guarantor of the constitution of Poland–Lithuania, which meant in practice that the Poles could not change their constitution without Russian consent. Thus when the King of Poland, who was also the Elector Augustus III of Saxony, died in October 1763, the various rulers began to manoeuvre to place their candidates on the throne.

Austria (then allied to France) supported another member of the Saxon ruling house, but Catherine considered that the new King of Poland would be less independent, less able to oppose Russian policies, if he did not have a base in the Holy Roman Empire, outside Poland, where his authority would be greater than in the Polish–Lithuanian Commonwealth. She therefore preferred the election of a native Polish candidate to the throne. She had moreover already decided on the man, namely her former lover, Stanislas Poniatowski, who belonged to one of the greatest Polish families and could therefore count on a good deal of support. As early as 2 August 1762, not long after her accession, she had written to her former lover, 'I am sending Count Keyserling off immediately as ambassador to Poland to make you king.'

Frederick II of Prussia, who had also been left somewhat isolated and disgruntled at the end of the Seven Years War (he felt that Britain had let him down), was happy to co-operate with Catherine and keep out an Austrian candidate. Thus the two powers, acting together, by a combination of bribery and force (Russian troops had entered Poland at the request of the Poniatowski faction), ensured the election of Stanislas Augustus as King of Poland on 26 August 1764.

This was a first triumph for Catherine but she now overplayed her hand. Not content with having placed her nominee on the throne, a man attached to her by personal as well as by political ties, she attempted to build up a political party for herself in Poland by manipulating its constitution. She made use of the presence in Catholic Poland of large religious minorities, the Protestants, both Calvinist and Lutheran, and, more important for her purposes, members of the Russian Orthodox communion, of whom there were a great many in eastern Lithuania (modern Belorussia) and south-eastern Poland (modern Ukraine) and who came under the jurisdiction in religious matters of the Orthodox Church in Russia. The members of the religious minorities had little by little been deprived of all political rights in Poland in the seventeenth and eighteenth centuries, notably the right to elect deputies to the Diets and to occupy high administrative, military or judicial posts. Catherine now embarked on a campaign to abolish religious discrimination in Poland, counting on the support of Frederick II to advance the cause of the Protestants. All this was carried out in the name of the enlightenment which, as an intellectual movement, was deeply engaged in the attack on organized religion and particularly on the Catholic Church, and in the promotion of the secularization of the state.

A number of different political groupings existed in Poland on which Catherine could play. There were those who favoured constitutional reform designed to introduce strong government, but were indifferent in matters of religion; there were those who opposed any political reform and clung to the full range of privileges for Catholics, and there were those who wanted constitutional reform but no concessions to religious minorities. Catherine manoeuvred between these groups, demanding extensive political rights for the religious minorities of a kind which a country which was officially Catholic could not possibly grant. She even persuaded the government of George III of England to support her demand that the Protestants and the Orthodox in Poland should enjoy rights denied to both non-conformists and Catholics in Great Britain.

The result of Catherine's constant pressure, backed by the presence of Russian troops, was an explosion. A 'confederation' was formed at Bar, a town in the far south of Polish Ukraine, in 1768, led by conservative Polish magnates, and Poland was soon in the throes of civil and foreign war. Russian troops flooded the country, and a frontier incident on the border between Polish Ukraine and Turkey gave the Turks the pretext they needed to declare war on Russia. They were not only alarmed at what seemed to be an enormous extension of Russian military might in a country which they had come to regard as a buffer state, but were also egged on by France, the traditional ally of Poland and Turkey, and equally alarmed at Russian aggressiveness.

Since no other power was involved, Frederick II, who had tried to avoid war by restraining Catherine's demands in favour of the religious dissidents, limited himself to the grudging payment of annual subsidies (he was notoriously stingy). Catherine fought the war alone, with two armies, one operating in Poland and advancing towards the Dniester, and one advancing down the Dnieper towards the Crimean peninsula.

The most striking event however, and one which awoke the western powers to the full extent of Russia's military power, was the appearance of the Russian Baltic fleet in the Mediterranean. This could not have been achieved without the co-operation of Great Britain. In the knowledge that France was supporting the Turkish war effort, and giving verbal encouragement to the Confederates of Bar in Poland, Britain offered facilities to the Russian navy not only in her ports (Hull, Portsmouth) but in her naval bases in the Mediterranean (Gibraltar and Menorca). There were many British officers and ships' captains in the Russian fleet, and one, Samuel Greig, rose to be one of the most important Russian admirals, responsible for Russian maritime development. Squadron after squadron left the Baltic in 1769 and 1770, sailed through the Channel

(Britain warned the French not to interfere) and arrived in Leghorn, in the Grand Duchy of Tuscany, one of the bases used by Russia. The main fleet was placed under the overall command of Aleksey Orlov, the brother of Catherine's lover Grigory (who had no experience as a naval officer), and sailed towards Greece, where an attempt was made to persuade the Greeks to rise against their Turkish overlords in the name of freedom and the Orthodox Christian religion. The attack on the mainland of Greece was not very successful but some of the islanders threw off Turkish rule and accepted that of Russia. The Russian fleet systematically pursued the Turkish fleet in the Aegean Sea and eventually succeeded in destroying most of it at the battle of Chesme on 25 June 1770, in which British officers took a prominent part. The battle did not perhaps have an immediate effect on the course of the war, but it ranks with Peter the Great's victory over the Swedes at Poltava in 1709 as one of the decisive battles in Russian history, proving that the fleet created by Peter I in the Baltic Sea was powerful enough to support Russian aims in the Mediterranean.

On land too Russia was victorious in 1770. Russian forces under General P.A. Rumyantsev (according to court gossip he was really the son of Peter the Great) advanced into Moldavia and defeated a large Turkish army at Larga in July, following this up with another great victory over an even larger Turkish army on 21 July at Kagul. The principalities of Moldavia and Wallachia were new occupied by the Russian army. However, the extent of Russia's victories began to alarm not only her enemies but also her friends, and events elsewhere slowed down the pace of her advance.

In the first place, Russia lost control of Sweden. In the Diet of 1769 the Hats defeated the Caps. This made no immediate difference, but Crown Prince Gustavus departed on a visit to Paris, and was there when his father, King Adolf Frederick, died in 1771. This gave the new King of Sweden an excellent opportunity to reach an understanding with France. The French had now decided that nothing could be done to oppose Russia in Sweden unless the power of the King were strengthened. Gustavus seemed to share their views, and the French government decided to support his efforts to overthrow the existing constitution and strengthen the role of the Crown. Frederick II too was reluctant to endorse the peace terms which Russia was now proposing to the Turks, notably the independence of the Crimean peninsula (which Russian troops were about to occupy) and of the Danubian principalities of Moldavia and Wallachia, as well as the cession to Russia of the ports of Kerch and Yenikale, which controlled the passage from the Sea of Azov into the Black Sea, and even an island in the Aegean, unless he received some compensation which would in his view restore the balance of power. He brought pressure to bear on his ally Catherine by means of two meetings which he held with the Emperor Joseph II in 1769 and 1770, designed to show her, by flirting with the Emperor, that he was not necessarily to be counted on to support all her aims. He had already long before decided on the compensation he wanted, namely that part of Polish territory which separated Brandenburg from East Prussia, and also the free city of Danzig, thus depriving Poland of an outlet to the Baltic and enabling him to control Polish trade.

Austria too began to be alarmed at the extent of Russian victories. She particularly objected to any suggestion that the Turks should be deprived of the principalities of Moldavia and Wallachia on the Danube, whether by transferring them to Poland as compensation for what Poland might lose, or by occupation by Russia, or by so-called 'independence'. Her anxiety led her to sign in July 1771 a highly secret treaty with the Turks by which she committed herself to come to their assistance in exchange for Turkish subsidies and territorial concessions.

By the end of 1770, Catherine had realized that she would have to modify her peace terms, and that neither her ally Prussia, nor the increasingly hostile Austria, were going to allow her to make extensive acquisitions (though Russia was doing all the fighting). In conversations in St Petersburg, in December 1770, between Catherine and Frederick II's brother, Prince Henry of Prussia, which were light-hearted yet serious, the idea of compensation for Prussia in Poland was trailed; Russia would then agree to lower her demands for territorial cessions by Turkey, in exchange for some solid territorial gains for her too on her Polish frontier. Later in 1771 Catherine, having discovered the existence of the secret treaty between Austria and Turkey, gave up any idea of removing Moldavia and Wallachia from the Turkish Empire, and hinted instead that Austria too might receive compensation in Poland for Russian gains at the expense of Turkey. Austria was now faced with the stark choice: should she maintain her treaty of July 1771 with the Turks, and fight Russia in order to assist the Turks, with no help from any other European power? Or should she abandon the Turks and join Prussia in seeking compensation in Poland for Russian victories over the Turks? Early in 1772, Austria finally made up her mind to abandon the Turks. Preliminary agreements were reached between Prussia and Russia in January 1772, and between Russia, Prussia and Austria in March, and the final treaty of the first partition of Poland was signed on 25 July 1772. Russia acquired the whole course of the River Dvina and Belorussia; Prussia acquired West Prussia and Ermeland, thus joining up East Prussia to the rest of the Prussian dominions, and cutting Poland off from the sea; but she did not acquire Danzig. Austria was amply compensated in Galicia.

In spite of the occupation of the Crimea, which took place in the summer of 1771, Russia had now many reasons to wish for peace. There had been an extremely serious outbreak of plague – perhaps the last great European epidemic – in Moscow and southern Russia, probably introduced from Constantinople with the movement of Turkish troops into Moldavia and Wallachia. It lasted from August to December 1771, killing about 55,000 people in Moscow and 120,000 throughout the Empire. The setting up of quarantine houses and other medical precautions created an atmosphere of panic in Moscow and led to rioting, in the course of which a mob murdered the Archbishop in October 1771. The strain of the war on Russian manpower and Russian finances was considerable, and a truce was signed in May 1772 between the Russian and Turkish commanders. But the negotiations which ensued were interrupted when the Turks received news of a further weakening of the Russian position.

For the new King of Sweden, Gustavus III, aroused by the parition of Poland to the danger which weak government implied for his country, determined to bring about a restoration of royal absolutism before Russia was free from the war with Turkey and in a position to turn against him. On 8 August 1772, he suspended the existing constitution and arrested the leaders of the estates in the Diet. The possibility that Gustavus's *coup d'état* might lead to war in the Baltic led the Turks to stiffen their peace terms, and the winter of 1772–3 passed in anxious expectation. But owing to the careful diplomatic manoeuvring of the powers concerned to maintain peace in the Baltic, Britain, Denmark and Prussia, war in the north was avoided and Catherine was able to concentrate on a further campaign against the Turks in 1773. It proved disappointing and fresh plans were drawn up for the following year. However, the situation changed again with the death of the Sultan, Mustapha III, in 1774, and the accession of his brother, Selim. General Rumyantsev, the Russian Commander-in-Chief, was now authorized to open direct negotiations with the commander of the Turkish forces should the opportunity arise. Catherine needed peace more than ever in view of the Cossack revolt which had broken out in western Siberia in October 1773 and which might well require troops to be diverted to put it down (see Chapter 5).

This time Catherine was fortunate. A brilliant Russian victory at Kozludzhi on 9 June 1774 was followed by a Turkish request to negotiate. Discussions were carried on between the two military commanders and the peace of Kutschuk Kainardzhi, which put an end to the war, was signed on 10 July 1774. The peace treaty was very advantageous to Russia: Azov, Kerch, Yenikale, Kinburn and the little strip of coast on the Black Sea between the Rivers Dnieper and Bug were ceded outright to Russia. The principality of Crimea was to become independent of the Turks, under its own ruler (though under the spiritual overlordship of the Sultan). A large war indemnity was to be paid by the Turks. Russia was to be allowed to send merchant ships through the Straits into the Mediterranean, and could of course build warships for use within the Black Sea. One clause in this treaty was however to acquire great importance in the nineteenth century, and to lead eventually to the Crimean war of 1854. This was the clause which allowed the Russian Ambassador in Constantinople to 'make representations' in favour of a Christian Orthodox Church the Russians would be allowed to establish, 'and of those who serve it'. The clause did not entitle Russia to intervene on behalf of all Christians, or all Orthodox Christians, in the Ottoman Empire, but only on behalf of one particular Church. It was later interpreted in a much wider sense.

Though Russia had only acquired a toehold on the northern coast of the Black Sea, it was enough to enable her to develop a forward policy. She had gained access from the port of Azov to the Black Sea and, though the estuary of the Dnieper was still dominated by the Turkish fort of Ochakov, opposite the Russian fort of Kinburn, the estuary was large enough to permit the construction of a fleet. Catherine saw at once that, if the Turks violated the commitment to respect the independence of the Crimea, Russia was now in a strong position to bring pressure to bear by sea on the Turkish Empire. The balance of power in the area had been altered in favour of Russia, who, as a result of her victories, had also acquired prestige (and a large number of skilful captains of privateers) among the Greek peoples under Turkish rule. After the ratification of the treaty of Kutschuk Kainardzhi, a formal embassy was despatched to Constantinople in 1775; two frigates were converted into merchant ships and permission was requested to allow them to pass through the Straits into the Mediterranean. Russian consuls were appointed in a number of Greek Mediterranean islands, in accordance with the treaty; they were usually Greeks in Russian uniforms, who according to one French account threw their weight about in an insulting manner. But they were also instruments of Russian policy.

The other European powers were fully aware of the significance of the Russian victory. All of them realized that the independence of the Crimea was unlikely to last, and that the strategic situation in the Black Sea now favoured Russia.

CHAPTER 5

The Crisis of the 1770s

War implies additional stresses and strains for state and society alike. In the case of the serfs these stresses came on top of years of resentment at the injustice of their situation. At the accession of Catherine in 1762 there had been the usual spate of risings on serf estates, very often on estates belonging to the Church. These were the kind of riots which normally marked the accession of a new ruler, since this always aroused the hope that serf estates would be removed from private ownership and become state owned. (It is noteworthy that peasants never demanded *total* freedom from *any* overlord; the greatest degree of freedom they could conceive of was to be 'registered' to the ruler, that is to become state peasants.)

Four events in the 1760s contributed to peasant ferment. The first of these was the Manifesto issued by Peter III in February 1762, which freed the nobility from compulsory service to the state. The serfs were perfectly capable of grasping that the logical consequence of freeing the noble from servitude to the state was freeing the serf from servitude to the noble – since this servitude had only been instituted in order to make the noble's service possible. Naturally enough they expected a law to that effect to be enacted, and when it did not come they assumed that the 'wicked' nobles had intervened to suppress or conceal it. Rumours circulated in the villages about secret manifestos, and occasional riots took place which had to be put down.

The unrest was bound to be fed by the second important event of the 1760s. A major change occurred in the status of the Church peasants in 1764. The idea of removing the Church peasants, and the income Church lands generated, from the Church, and handing the Church estates over to the state, had already arisen in the reign of the Empress Elizabeth, but had not then been carried out. Catherine II postponed action on her accession, since she had promised at the time to protect the interests of the Orthodox Church. But shortage of money, after the expenses of the Seven Years War, as well as her own negative attitude to monasticism, led her to revive the policy of secularization once again, and it was finally put through in the winter of 1764. About one million Church peasants were now freed from ecclesiastical control, and the administration of the estates was handed over to a College of Economy. The peasants were now known as 'economic peasants', and they ceased to perform any labour dues for the Church, such as working on building or maintenance of churches, monasteries, transport or cultivation of the land, and instead paid a money due and the poll-tax of seventy kopeks to the state. The government took the opportunity to streamline the number of male and female monasteries and convents, reducing their numbers from 572 to 161, and laying down the sums each was to receive from the confiscated revenues. The allowances for the maintenance of metropolitans, archbishops and bishops, the metropolitan churches and the bishoprics and the parish churches were also laid down. The balance of the income went into the state's coffers. Not unnaturally the spectacle of the removal of such a large number of peasants from private control was bound to arouse fresh hopes in the serfs.

The general absence of individual rights which characterized Russian society had already led to the passing of a law in 1760, during the reign of Elizabeth, which weighed heavily on all communities. According to this law any townsman, state peasant, Church peasant or serf could be sent to settlement in Siberia, with his wife and small children, simply by the decision of the elders of the community to which he belonged or, in the case of private serfs, of the landowner. In all cases, the government would give a receipt which would be counted against the next recruit levy for the armed forces. On present evidence we do not know how widely this power was used in any community, or by owners of serfs, because the records of convoys being despatched to Siberia do not specify whether those included are convicts sent after trial and conviction by the courts, or 'compulsory emigrants' banished by their communities or their landlords to settlement. But it is known that peasants exiled other peasants from their villages under this law as late as the beginning of the twentieth century. (Settlement in Siberia should not be confused with transportation in English penal legislation, since emigrants or even convicts sentenced to settlement were not condemned to hard labour; they were granted land, issued with tools and given tax exemption for a number of years in order to enable them to establish new agricultural communities. However, the horrors – and the mortality – of the journey by sea to Australia and by land to Siberia were about equal.)

The power of the landowner, already very great, was further increased by a decree of 1765, which authorized serf-owners to send insolent serfs to hard labour in Admiralty establishments, and to ask for them back after a number of years. Again we do not know how often this power was used, but John Howard, the English prison reformer who visited Russia twice, saw serfs sent under this law in the dockyards of Kronstadt in the 1780s.

It was above all among the peasants 'assigned' to work in the metallurgical industries in the Urals that serious unrest broke out in the early 1760s. They numbered about 144,000 male peasants in all and what they particularly resented was the long absence from their villages imposed upon them by the need to travel anything up to 500 versts each way, journeys which could well take two months. In one of the earliest examples of Catherine's positive interest in the peasant problem, she ordered Prince A.A. Vyazemsky to undertake an inquiry into the unrest among the assigned peasants in December 1762, as a result of which in 1764 the peasants were given greater control over the organization of their work, and peasants were no longer 'assigned' to enterprises.

There was not very much large-scale rioting in the 1760s but 1767 saw as many as twenty-seven revolts on private estates, in many of which the landowners were murdered; the revolts had frequently to be put down by soldiers, and the cost of the operation was laid on the serfs. Though most of these revolts were directed at particularly harsh individual landowners, they may well have been sparked off by news of the calling of the Legislative Commission and even of the tenor of its debates (see Chapter 3). Serfs were not invited to elect deputies to the Commission, though they lived cheek by jowl with the communities of state peasants who did elect deputies. Rumours of 'changes in the laws' undoubtedly reached them, but such changes as occurred in the interval were not in their favour.

In May 1767 there was severe rioting on the estates of the family of one of the Empress's secretaries, and the serfs who had submitted petitions to the Empress, contrary to the existing law, were duly punished. Several senior officials were however ordered to 'admonish' other landowners who had been guilty of over-burdening or ill-treating their serfs and provoking them to revolt. While Catherine was travelling down the Volga to Kazan' in spring, 1767, she received some 600 petitions. Historians have frequently repeated that these petitions were submitted by serfs complaining against the ill-treatment of their landowners. But, according to Catherine herself, most of them came from free peasants complaining of shortage of land. Only a few were submitted by serfs complaining against their masters, 'which were returned to them with the instruction not to submit such petitions in future'. However, faced with this rural disorder Catherine restated the existing law regarding complaints by serfs against their masters, pending the issue of a new law by the Legislative Commission.

The presentation of petitions on any subject directly to the ruler in person had been forbidden since the beginning of the century. As many as fifteen decrees had been issued on the subject before Catherine's accession in 1762. Serfs were specifically forbidden to complain against their masters by the Code of 1649, unless they were denouncing them for plotting against the state or the person of the tsar. In a decree issued on 22 August 1767 Catherine now dealt with the two questions of serfs petitioning the Empress in person and serfs complaining against their masters. The new decree allowed serfs to petition the Empress through the proper channels (specified government officials) but this concession was invalidated by the repetition of the article of the Code of 1649 which forbade serfs to submit petitions against their landowners unless they were reporting cases of treason or attempts on the life of the tsar. The penalty for those who 'dared to submit forbidden petitions' was punishment with the knut in accordance with the Code of 1649 and exile to hard labour in the silver mines of Nerchinsk in Siberia.

The decree of 22 August 1767, judging by the way it was drafted, was evidently a temporary expedient, designed to deal with the particular cases which had recently arisen, and to last until a new law was produced by the Legislative Commission. However, no new law was issued, and the decree therefore acquired permanent status. There has unfortunately been no study of the extent to which and the manner in which it was actually applied, but it was bound to exacerbate the feeling of injustice under which the serfs smarted.

Catherine herself disapproved of serfdom, as one can tell from marginal notes and private jottings she made at various times, and from the original draft of Chapter 11, dealing with serfdom, of her Instruction to the Legislative Commission. She saw only too clearly how closely the status of domestic or house serfs approached to slavery. She was also fully aware of the danger that ill-treatment of the serfs by the nobles might drive the former into revolt. An undated note of hers to the Procurator-General, Prince Vyazemsky, makes her views quite clear: the position of the serfs was so critical, she wrote, that only peace and humane institutions could forestall a general movement to throw off 'an unbearable yoke'. 'If we do not agree to reduce this cruelty and moderate a situation intolerable for human beings, then sooner or later they will do it themselves.' Catherine drew back however from the task of regulating the relationship between landowners and serfs by law. The problems implicit in any attempt to intervene between masters and serfs were beyond the power of her government to solve, lacking as it was in experienced officials and agents other than the serf-owners themselves. She sponsored a number of attempts by noble landowners in her intimate circle to introduce new relationships, based on hereditary leases, on Crown estates, most of which failed, among other reasons because the peasants themselves strongly opposed the changes. On the whole, what the serfs desired was to become state peasants; they did not conceive of individual holdings or the break-up of the commune.

Until Catherine's reign, the moral right to own serfs had never been questioned in Russia. The distribution of peasants attached to land had initially been considered not as a reward for service, but as a means of making service possible, by providing for the upkeep and the weapons of the warrior and enabling the magnates to support the tsar with their counsel. That the contract between the tsar and the military servitor had steadily changed its nature throughout the seventeenth century and Peter's reforms, notably when Peter in 1714 introduced salaries for officers, while allowing them to keep their serfs, did not affect the noble's conviction of his right to the land and the labour which he now owned. However, by the mid-eighteenth century, and particularly under the impact of Catherine's Instruction to the Legislative Commission and the thought of the enlightenment, some Russian nobles, notably Prince D.A. Golitsyn (a diplomat who lived for many years in Paris and The Hague), began to question the morality of serfdom. A public debate was launched by Catherine herself in 1765 when she proposed that the Free Economic Society, a body whose formation she had sponsored to further the study of agriculture and crafts, and which survived until the Bolshevik Revolution, should arrange an essay competition. This was at the time a fashionable form of intellectual activity and a way of provoking debate around specific subjects which intellectual academies indulged in. Rousseau's *Discours sur les sciences et les arts* was written for just such a competition sponsored by the Academy of Dijon.

The theme proposed by Catherine was: 'What is most useful for society – that the peasant should own the land or only moveable property, and how far should his rights over the one or the other extend?' The competition attracted many entries, including one by Voltaire, and it is a reflection on the state of Russian public opinion on the subject that only seven out of 160 entries were submitted by Russians. The prize was awarded to an entry by a French writer, Beardé de L'Abbaye. His essay painted the realities of serfdom in harsh colours but advocated only the gradual freeing of the serfs, leaving the land in the hands of the landowners. It was duly published in a Russian translation. The new anti-serf current of thought immediately provoked a counter-current. For the first time the supporters of serfdom found it necessary to defend it by stressing both its moral value (the patriarchal and humane care which the landowner took of his peasants, who, like children, were incapable of standing on their own feet), and its economic justification, namely that land without labour attached to it was useless to the landowner.

However, freedom without land was also held to be useless by many of the peasants. As the serfs of I.D. Yakushkin, one of the participants in the plot against Nicholas I on 14 December 1825, put it, 'We are yours but the land is ours.' The crux of the problem, in the eighteenth century, as later, at the time of the emancipation of the serfs in 1861, was the huge financial investment, the sophisticated financial methods and the administrative skills which would have been necessary to transfer enough land to the peasants to enable them to live, without ruining the landowners, whose income from their land enabled the government to pay relatively low salaries to officers and officials.

The only occasion on which Catherine dared to intervene between landowners and serfs was in 1765, in the provinces of Livonia and Estonia. The amount of work the serfs were supposed to do had been recorded in Swedish times in books, called in Russian *bakkenbukhi*. Catherine had toured the Baltic provinces in 1764, and had been impressed by their Germanic orderliness. But the standard of living of the peasantry was very low, particularly as the practice of allowing peasants to leave the land and earn a living elsewhere, paying a money due to the landowner, did not exist. It was moreover much easier for Catherine to act in the tiny Baltic provinces, with a total population of some 350,000, than in Russia. Thus she was able to make a tacit bargain with the nobles in 1765, guaranteeing the continuation of their traditional institutions in exchange for a fresh regulation of the amount of work the serfs were supposed to do, and the endorsement of the peasants' right to appeal to the lowest law court in cases of ill-treatment or dispute with their landowners. In the Baltic provinces her policy was supported by her Russian officials, always glad to cut down the privileges of these more Europeanized regions of the Empire.

The question of the serfs was also raised in the debates at the Legislative Commission, but in the context of the noble rights to ownership of the land, and of the rights of peasans to trade in towns. Some nobles spoke in favour of allowing serfs to hold land on long leases, or even argued that the peasants should be free. The Commission was very perplexed by a government-sponsored proposal that nobles should be allowed to transform 'serf villages' into 'free villages'. Nobody quite understood what this meant, or what the status of individual peasants in these 'free villages' belonging to landowners would be. The whole proposal seems to have been an attempt by Catherine and her closest advisers to test opinion in the Commission on the issue of improving the lot of the serfs.

It has frequently been stated by historians that the rural unrest of the 1760s arose in great part because of the large number of state peasants whom Catherine distributed as rewards to those who had helped her to seize the throne. Yet the number of settled estates given away during these years was quite small: 18,275 male peasants or souls were distributed in 1762 to those who had helped her to the throne. From 1762 to 1772, about 48,000 male peasants were granted. (Peasants attached to the land and domestic serfs were usually described as 'souls' in Russian official documents.) But no Russian state peasants and none of the peasants who had belonged to the Church estates were given away. Imperial grants of land played no part in preparing the way for the revolt in the south-west which broke out in 1773, as has sometimes been stated.

The outbreak of war in 1768 diverted the Empress from her projects for reform. Russia had neither the manpower nor the bureaucratic skills to cope with waging a war at the same time as undertaking large-scale reform. War too weighed heavily on the common people of Russia, particularly the peasants, whether serf or state peasant. In the first place, the conscription of men was immediately stepped up. The peacetime average call-up in Catherine's reign was usually one man in 500, but she had been able to refrain from calling up any recruits in the years 1762–7. The first levy of her reign, one man in 300, took place in 1767. On the outbreak of war three levies were ordered, and some 50,000 men were conscripted between October and December 1768. In all a total of 323,360 men were conscripted in five years. This was an enormous drain on manpower and always caused bitterness and anguish in the villages.

War also led to a heavy increase in taxation. The poll-tax of seventy kopeks per head remained the same but the additional money dues paid by all the taxable peasants except the serfs were increased from one ruble to two rubles per annum. The price of spirits to the consumer was raised from 2.34 rubles per pail (equivalent to some 2.70 gallons) to three rubles, and a number of indirect taxes were imposed or increased.

The origin of the widescale revolt which swept across south-eastern Russia in 1773–4 must however be sought elsewhere. It was above all the tense situation in the smallest of the Cossack Hosts, the Cossacks of the Yaik, which sparked off the revolt. Already deeply divided between the elite and the common Cossacks over the allocation of fishing licences, the Yaik Cossacks were aroused to anger in 1771 by an order to supply a number of men for a new corps to be formed under the name of the Moscow Legion, to be used in the war against Turkey. This seemed to threaten the Cossacks with 'becoming regulars', which they regarded as contrary to their traditional form of service. Moreover they feared that, as regular soldiers, they would be forced to shave their beards which, since a large number of the Yaik Cossacks were Old Believers, would offend against their religious beliefs. Appeals to distant St Petersburg led nowhere, and in January 1772 the tension erupted in a mutiny in which the Russian commander (who was in fact a German) was killed. A Russian regular detachment was immediately sent to put down the revolt; it defeated the rebels in June 1772, and after the usual lengthy investigations the ringleaders were sentenced to the usual variety of corporal punishments, exile to hard labour or settlement in Siberia, or service in ordinary units of the army. A large fine was also imposed on the rebel Cossacks. The sentences were carried out publicly in July 1773 in Yaitskiy Gorodok.

Rage and resentment simmered in the Cossack Host on the Yaik, and it needed but a spark to trigger off a second rising. The spark took the form of the appearance among them of a 'pretender', a Don

Cossack deserter named Emelyan Pugachev who claimed to be Peter III, the murdered husband of the Empress Catherine. 'Pretenders' had been a common phenomenon in Russian history since the extinction of the first Russian dynasty, the descendents of Ryurik, in 1598. Their emergence responded to the people's need to hope for something better than the known present. A 'pretender' nearly always claimed to be someone who had a right to rule but had been deprived of his throne by the wicked boyars before he could show himself as the true friend of the common people. Thus 'pretenders' claimed to be Aleksey, the son of Peter the Great, who was supposed to have miraculously survived the sentence of execution passed on him by his father; or the baby Emperor, Ivan VI, dethroned in 1741, who had escaped from the attempt by his gaolers to kill him in 1764; or, of course, Peter III, who had reigned only six months and had escaped from the wiles of that wicked woman, his wife, supported by boyars who had suppressed the ukaz he was believed to have promulgated freeing the peasants from bondage to the nobility. It was indeed very difficult to recruit sufficient widespread support for a revolt against established authority, unless the revolt was carried out in the name of an authority which seemed to be equally legitimate. Hence, when Emelyan Pugachev raised the standard of revolt on the Yaik, he did so in the name of the Emperor Peter III. He was not the first to pretend to be Catherine's dead husband, but this time the Cossacks wanted to believe in him.

When Pugachev launched his rising in September 1773, he put forward a programme designed to appeal to the Cossacks of the Yaik. In his manifestos he promised them, as their tsar, to restore the old, free conditions of service, free access to the fisheries and to pasturage, arms and ammunition and guaranteed salaries. His first followers were in fact Cossacks and also members of the non-Russian tribes, the Tartars and the Kalmucks. There was at first no specific appeal to the Russian peasantry, but Pugachev's following was soon increased by large numbers of Cossacks and smaller numbers of regular soldiers who went over to him, while their officers were shot or hanged, and by 'assigned peasants' (those who were temporarily attached to industrial enterprises) and 'possessional peasants' (those who were permanently attached to these same enterprises). Western Siberia, where the revolt began, did not have a large population of privately owned agricultural serfs. In the province of Orenburg for instance they formed only some 20 per cent of the peasant population. After mopping up a number of small and lightly garrisoned forts on the Yaik river, Pugachev turned on the largest town in western Siberia, the centre from which the Yaik Cossacks were governed, namely Orenburg, but his attempt to take it failed, and he settled down to starve it into surrender.

Meanwhile the government in distant St Petersburg, still concentrating on the principal task of defeating the Turks, sent detachments to deal with what seemed at first to be a minor matter. But the first government troops to reach the area were defeated. This enabled Pugachev to extend the revolt into the province of Ufa and into Bashkiria, a province where the bitter and savage struggle of the semi-nomad Bashkirs against the conquering Russian colonizing forces, as late as 1735–40, was still remembered and where a deep hatred of the mining and metallurgical industries established by their new masters lay only just below the surface. Thus while Pugachev's lieutenants laid siege to a number of important forts and towns the Bashkirs attacked the foundries in the Urals. But government reinforcements were arriving, and in March 1774 the forces of Pugachev outside Orenburg were crushingly defeated, and the six-months siege was lifted. Pugachev himself, and a few close associates, escaped into Bashkiria, collecting new followers among Bashkirs, Russian factory serfs and assigned peasants, and suddenly, in July 1774, he appeared before the city of Kazan' on the Volga, with some 20,000 men. Almost defenceless, the city fell on 12 July 1774 to the rebels, who looted and destroyed a great part of it, killing the men and capturing the women.

The government troops were not far behind, under the command of Colonel Mikhel'sen, one of the many Baltic officers in the Russian army. After strenuous forced marches, he caught up with Pugachev at Kazan' and on that same 12 July, defeated the rebel leader outside the city. Undaunted, Pugachev withdrew, regrouped his forces and returned to give battle, but this time he was completely routed. Only two days earlier, on 10 July 1774, peace between Russia and the Ottoman Empire had been signed, thus freeing the Russian army for action against the rebels. General Peter Panin, brother of the head of the College of Foreign Affairs, was placed in overall charge of the necessary measures, and the future field marshal A.S. Suvorov was ordered to command the detachments detailed to hunt down Pugachev. But neither of them had anything to do with Pugachev's final downfall.

Abandoning all hope of being crowned tsar in Moscow Pugachev now turned southwards down the Sura river, back towards the land which he knew best, but where his true identity was also most likely to be known. Now, his appeals for support were more than ever before specifically directed to the enserfed peasantry, urging them to murder their masters and to follow their 'emperor', who promised them freedom and the 'old religion'. The motley force advanced from town to town, breaking open the liquor stores, seizing money and grain, killing and looting, capturing and raping the noblewomen and murdering the noblemen, and forcing the inhabitants to take the oath of loyalty to their 'tsar'. Hard on their heels came Colonel Mikhel'sen, who caught up with them at last outside Tsaritsyn on the Volga (later Stalingrad, now Volgograd) and defeated the rebel force, which was now no more than a rabble, towards the end of August 1774. Pugachev himself escaped with a few companions, but the great adventure was over at last. Hoping to save their own skins, some of those still with him determined to betray Pugachev to the forces of order. They seized him, as they were fleeing in the wastes around Lake Elton, and handed him over to the commandant of the tsarist forces in Yaitskiy Gorodok, where the revolt had begun.

But it was not yet completely over. Pugachev's most inflammatory manifesto, which he had issued on 31 July 1774, had been carried from village to village along the Sura and the Volga, in an area densely settled with small estates worked by their proprietors, who were thus in close contact with their serfs. Urged to revolt against their masters, the serfs rose and killed their landowners, or captured them in order to deliver them to the 'Emperor Peter III' himself. Disturbances rumbled on well into the autumn, while in Bashkiria the leaders of the rebels, always concerned with their own tribal aims, continued the struggle into November.

This was the last, and the most politically mature, of all the great Cossack and peasant revolts which punctuated the history of Muscovy and Russia. The rural unrest of the 1760s had taken the form of isolated revolts against individual landowners, on specific estates. It had not coalesced into wide-ranging movements, except on Church estates where, according to Catherine herself, 150,000 peasants were in open revolt when she came to the throne, and among the 'assigned' peasants in the Urals where disturbances had taken place in many mines and foundries in 1762–3. But Pugachev was not content with massacring landowners and officials, he attempted to construct an alternative government for Russia, centred around the rival tsar, Peter III, who had risen in order to recover his throne from his immoral wife. Thus, from the beginning of the revolt, Pugachev issued manifestos proclaiming his policy towards Cossacks, members of the various non-Russian tribes, industrial serfs, peasants assigned to work as auxiliaries in industrial enterprises, state peasants and serfs, and a category which embraced to some extent all of the above, namely the Old Believers. His policy was not always very coherent, since it was not easy to reconcile some of the conflicting interests, for instance those of the non-Russians, who wanted to destroy the foundries, and those of the industrial workers, who wanted to take them over.

The ultimate political aim of Pugachev and his immediate followers, insofar as they succeeded in formulating it clearly, was the repudiation of the Russian state as founded by Peter the Great. There were to be no regular armed forces, no conscription, no taxation, the land was to belong to those who worked it, there were to be no nobles, no government officials, no foreign officers or uniforms, no European clothes, no shaven chins. Government and society were to be organized as one great Cossack community, in which all would enjoy Cossack freedoms and the right to elect their officers and in which the Cossacks would be the privileged class. It was an essentially backward-looking political movement, rooted in the old pre-Petrine tradition of the relationship between tsar and people, and in the Old Belief. But, simple though the political outline of this Arcadia might be, the conduct of military operations on a wide scale forced the general staff of the revolt to set up their own government and administration in the territories which at any given moment they occupied. Thus Pugachev set up his own College of War, borrowing the name from the institution set up by Peter I in St Petersburg. His most senior lieutenants took the names of well-known Catherinian ministers; Zarubin Chika called himself Field Marshal Count Ivan Chernyshev after the President of the College of War in St Petersburg, Count Z. Chernyshev, while Ovchinikov called himself Count Panin after the man in charge of foreign affairs. The College of War was charged with keeping records of income and expenditure, of supplies of food and fodder, and of the distribution of weapons and military supplies. It carried on an extensive correspondence with the authorities set up to govern in the territories 'liberated' from central government rule, authorities which were usually modelled on the traditional Russian pattern of peasant communal self-government or on elective Cossack institutions. It dealt with the organization of conscription and taxation (for the mirror government borrowed many practices from tsarist administration) and with prisoners of war, and recreated for its own purposes the administrative structures it had overthrown.

Many remarkable leaders emerged briefly from a variety of backgrounds to lead the rebel forces, and the records of their administration are all the more striking in that many of them, including Pugachev himself, were illiterate. Some of Pugachev's followers had been deputies to the Legislative Commission, which suggests that there was a real link between what was discussed there and the popular movement. Unfortunately we do not know whether the deputies were aroused to indignation by the refusal of the nobles to contemplate any easing of the burden of the serfs; or whether they were influenced by the rhetoric of the enlightenment in Catherine's Instruction and in some of the speeches by the deputies. In any event the peasant leaders did not prove capable of welding their followers together into an efficient military force, let alone a credible administration. The peasants had no military experience, and were usually armed only with pikes or pitchforks. Only the Cossacks were mounted and properly armed, and on the whole they despised the peasants, as warriors have usually felt only contempt for toilers on the land. The whole array was undermined by lack of discipline fostered by drink, cupidity and the desire for revenge on the people who had once been their masters. Pugachev's credibility as tsar was undermined too when he 'married' the daughter of a fellow Cossack, and set up her court, complete with ladies in waiting, regardless of the fact that he already had a wife and two children of his own as Pugachev, and was, as Emperor Peter III, 'married' to Catherine II. Captured officers were executed by the dozen, and when Pugachev's convoy of barges was seized by Mikhel'sen at Tsaritsyn in August 1774, numbers of captured noblewomen and girls destined for his harem were freed. A modern historian has estimated that as many as 4 or 5 per cent of the Russian noble class were killed, usually in a very brutal way. 'Of the 1,572 noble victims [as distinct from officials] including women and children, 42% were hanged, 40% were bludgeoned or tortured to death, 9% were shot, 5% stabbed, 4% beheaded, and 1% drowned.'

The barbarity of the rebels was countered by the ruthless savagery of the forces of order. As territory occupied by Pugachev's forces was liberated, thousands of peasants and Cossacks, many priests, minor officials and townsmen, and even occasionally officers who had sided – usually involuntarily – with the rebels were arrested and confined in makeshift gaols in Orenburg, Kazan' and other cities. Anyone found guilty of murder was harshly punished with the knut and/or hard labour in Siberia; some were executed. Count Peter Panin, in particular, issued a proclamation threatening the most savage mutilations as a punishment for those who refused to denounce murderers and their accomplices, well-knowing however that he had no power to carry out his threats. Nevertheless, according to his own computation, 324 rebels were executed, 399 suffered the knut and the loss of an ear, and about 7,000 more suffered some form of corporal punishment, such as 'whipping under the gallows'. Yet the sheer numbers involved had all along forced the more far-seeing military commanders to be more moderate. Thus most of the 10,000 prisoners taken after the freeing of Kazan' in July 1774 were released after taking a new oath of loyalty, without any punishment, and with fifteen kopeks for the journey home.

Some of Pugachev's principal lieutenants had been captured and executed in the course of the fight. But the remaining ringleaders, including Pugachev himself, were taken to Moscow, interrogated (though not tortured) and subjected to a formal trial at the end of December 1774. Five of them were sentenced to the barbarous forms of execution common at the time throughout Europe and the remaining eighteen to various forms of mutilation, corporal punishment, exile to settlement, or hard labour. The sentences were carried out before a hushed crowd early in January 1775. On the secret orders of Catherine herself, Pugachev, and the others sentences to be quartered, were beheaded first, in order to reduce the degree of physical pain inflicted. At the time the executioner was blamed for having slipped up, and it is only in the twentieth century that Catherine's personal intervention behind the scenes has been established. The need for her to act in a completely clandestine fashion is an interesting reflection on the nature of absolute power.

Catherine was anxious that all traces of the revolt should be swept away as soon as possible, and she wished to celebrate the great victory over the Ottoman Empire without allowing it to be overshadowed by the horrors of the Pugachevshchina, the name given in Russian to the Pugachev revolt. Thus most of the prisoners still held in Moscow were released without punishment and on 17 March 1775 a manifesto was issued proclaiming a general amnesty for all those involved in any degree in the revolt; pending cases were reviewed and punishments were reduced, though some army officers were still punished under military law. As far as the government was concerned, however, though steps had still to be taken to compensate nobles who had lost all their property, and women whose husbands had been killed, as well as to restore industry, the whole tragic episode was to be forgotten.

No other eighteenth- or nineteenth-century popular revolt attained such dimensions anywhere in Europe. It is usually described as a peasant war in Soviet historiography, though peasants did not form the majority of those who took part. Numbers vary widely. According to a Soviet historian, some three million people were involved in the revolt, of whom 40 per cent were peasants. However this figure seems to apply to the total population of the area over which the revolt spread in the course of a year. According to an American historian, some 200,000 took part, while an incomplete list of some 4,000 prisoners shows that 27 per cent were Cossacks, 22 per cent belonged to non-Russian tribes and 29 per cent were peasants, including state peasants, industrial serfs and private serfs. Casualties were high, particularly among the rebel forces; the total losses are estimated at some 22,000, of which up to 18,000 may well have been incurred by the rebels. Similarly material losses were considerable. Much of the city of Kazan' was burnt down; many other towns suffered serious damage, and the destruction and looting of the foundries and metallurgical enterprises was estimated to have cost over five million rubles, while many private estates were destroyed.

Did the revolt present a serious danger to the Russian state? One must remember that it took place at a time when Russia's resources were gravely strained by the continuing war with Turkey, and soon after a serious epidemic of the plague had ravaged Moscow and the south of Russia. Yet, in spite of the pressures upon the central government, at no time did the Pugachevshchina really threaten the stability of the regime. Pugachev's motley forces never tried to penetrate to the heart of the country (though many in Moscow feared that he might), to the real centre of serfdom. He kept to the outlying region of the south-west and only succeeded in launching a mass movement among the enserfed peasantry in the Volga area, in the very last months of the revolt, from July 1774 to his capture in September. He was able to seize a number of ill-defended towns by sheer weight of numbers, but where towns – and even factories – defended themselves with skill and courage, he failed, and his hold on the towns he passed through was short-lived. His ill-armed and undisciplined peasant troops could not stand up against regular soldiers, even when these were heavily outnumbered. Cossacks and soldiers might desert to him in small outposts, but the army in general remained loyal to the government. Pugachev was also hampered by political disunity, for his Bashkir allies deserted him after his defeat at Kazan' and withdrew to continue the struggle in their own territory.

Taking the revolt as a whole, one must conclude that it was not primarily a peasant war, but a Cossack revolt, initiated by a specific Host, the Yaik Cossacks, the furthest from the central government and the most primitive and backward-looking. Its aims were to secure the Cossacks' traditional freedoms and to 'turn everyone into a Cossack'. The Cossacks did not think of launching a widespread peasant rising, they thought in terms of their own aims and at first waged the war in their own territory, Orenburg, and that of their allies the Bashkirs. When final defeat stared them in the face, they returned to their base on the Yaik. It is more than probable that had it not been for the coincidence of the arrival of a wildly imaginative and undoubtedly charismatic leader among them, discontent among the Yaik Cossacks would have continued to rumble, without reaching flashpoint.

The government certainly realized that the Cossacks had been the mainspring of the movement, and it took steps to curb both the innocent and the guilty. The town of Yaitsky Gorodok and the Yaik river were renamed Uralsk and Ural, and placed under a government-appointed officer. The Don Cossacks, who had been loyal to the government (perhaps because they knew perfectly well that Pugachev was not Peter III), lost some of their autonomy, but in exchange their higher-ranking officers were accepted as the equals of the Russian nobility. The Zaporozhian Host, which had not been involved in the revolt at all, and which had fought bravely against the Turks, suffered more than any other. Since the Turks had ceded to Russia the lands between the Host and the Black Sea, the Cossacks were no longer necessary for its defence, and were indeed an obstacle to its settlement and economic development. Under the ruthless hand of the new chief of the armed forces, G.A. Potemkin, the Zaporozhian Host was broken up in 1775. Its *hetman* and senior officers were interned in the Solovetsky monastery prison on the White Sea, and the rank and file continued to live locally, but not as registered Cossacks.

CHAPTER 6

The Reform of Local Administration and of the Legal System

Catherine celebrated the end of the war with the Ottoman Turks and the repression of the Pugachev Revolt with a manifesto dated 17 March 1775 in which she deliberately set out to stress the return of happier times. Not only did she proclaim an amnesty for those guilty of participating in the Pugachev Revolt (see Chapter 5) but some thirty-two taxes were repealed, including the special taxes imposed to finance the war, and a number of pre-existing taxes. Catherine's concern with hygiene was reflected in the specific repeal of the tax on bathhouses introduced by Peter I. An amnesty for all crimes committed within the previous ten years was proclaimed, and all crimes undetected for ten years were to be consigned to oblivion. The armed forces too were rewarded by granting to nobles serving in the ranks the right to be punished in accordance with their status as nobles, and to non-noble private soldiers the right not to be subjected to corporal punishment without trial. An amnesty was also proclaimed for deserters and for runaway state peasants who returned within a year, but not for serfs. (Catherine had included serfs in her original draft, but when she submitted it to her Council for State, it met with objections so strong that she was persuaded to remove this provision.)

If the manifesto served to tidy up the past, it also pointed the way to the future. Ever since the convocation of the Legislative Commission Catherine had been considering ways and means of improving local administration, in the interests of the government, and to meet the complaints put forward by the deputies. They had complained of the huge distances they had to travel in order to conduct lawsuits, the disorder, brigandage and lack of policing in the countryside, and the absence of any educational facilities particularly in the smaller towns. From the government's point of view, the way in which local administration had collapsed before the hordes of

Pugachev rendered the need to strengthen its presence in the provinces even more glaring.

There is evidence that, in the years between the outbreak of war in 1768 and the signature of the peace in 1774, Catherine had continued to study with a number of advisers how to approach the problem of local administration in view of the shortage of qualified manpower and the need to keep expenses within bounds. She drew on a number of plans which had been submitted to her and also studied the legal systems of the Russian Baltic provinces, which were based on the German model. The solution Catherine found for her problem took the form of a system of local government relying on the co-operation of the free estates of the Empire, namely the nobles, the townspeople and the free or state peasants. They were to be drawn in to occupy a number of elective posts, many of which would be given temporary rank in the Table of Ranks, and a salary, thus rendering service in the provinces more attractive to the noble, and less of a burden to the townsman or the peasant. Such a policy implied a restructuring of the social organization of Russia, defining the personal and property rights of the various classes and laying down the terms of their service. It was a long-term policy, which was bound to take some time to work out and implement, but a pilot project was tried out first in 1772 in the two provinces taken from Poland in the first partition, Mogilev and Polotsk, which became Belorussia.

Catherine worked hard at her new plan. She wrote out many drafts in her own hand (some chapters went through as many as eleven different drafts), and spent much time closeted with her principal advisers. These included the Procurator-General, Prince A.A. Vyazemsky, and a Baltic noble, Count Jacob Sievers, who knew England well and may have been instrumental in drawing her attention to the *Commentaries on the Laws of England* by Sir William Blackstone, which had replaced Montesquieu's *Spirit of the Laws* as her bedside book and which undoubtedly influenced her thinking on law and administration. (Sievers was also instrumental in introducing the paintings of Hogarth to Russia.) The new Statute for the Administration of the Provinces of the Russian Empire, a book of some 215 pages, was promulgated on 2 November 1775. Its basic principles were the decentralization and multiplication of administrative offices and courts of law; the separation of functions, namely setting up separate institutions to deal with administration, finance and justice; the establishment of separate bodies to deal with matters concerning the nobles, the merchantry and townspeople, and the state peasants; and the recruitment of elected representatives of these social estates to participate in the functioning of the new institutions.

In practice this meant first of all that the existing twenty-five provinces were to be divided into over forty provinces of between 300,000 and 400,000 inhabitants, each of which was in turn to be sub-divided into districts of between 20,000 and 30,000 people. (The old sub-province was done away with.) In principle, no administrative office should now be more than a day's journey away from a village, town or settlement. Administration was in the hands of a governor, assisted by a board, and a deputy governor in charge of finance, including collecting the poll-tax, indirect taxes and the dues from the state peasants. Subordinate offices were set up in the capital of each district. One or more provinces were placed under the supreme authority of a very high-ranking *namestnik* or lord lieutenant.

Under the overall supervision of the governor, a network of law courts was established: at the centre, in the provincial capital, there were the central civil and criminal courts, from the decisions of which an appeal could be lodged with the Senate in St Petersburg. The system of courts then branched out, with an upper, a district and a lower land court for the nobles; an upper and a district court, or *magistrat*, for the townspeople, and a higher and a lower summary court for the state peasants. To all these courts the members of the corresponding estate had the right to elect 'assessors'. Their function was not, however, that of a jury, which decided whether the accused was guilty or innocent, but that of advisers to the judge.

A further court was set up, which was in all probability modelled to some extent on the English concept of an equity court. This was the Court of Conscience. There was only one equity court in England, which was one of the chambers of the Chancery Court. But Catherine set up the courts of conscience in each province, because, as she put it, 'England is a small country, and there is no great inconvenience in bringing lawsuits in London, but to drag affairs from the ends of the earth to the capital is inconvenient, and it is better for current affairs to be judged by local courts'. Catherine's Courts of Conscience dealt with cases concerning all classes, and assessors from the corresponding class were elected as required. They were to deal with cases of witchcraft, sexual offences, lunacy and minors but they were also the courts in which cases involving more than one social class could be heard, and they could act as a court of arbitration with the agreement of both parties to a dispute. In addition it was to this court that those who had been arrested and held for more than three days without a specific charge being brought against them could appeal to be freed on bail (except in cases of murder, treason, brigandage and so on). This was a very new departure in Russian penal practice and it is probable that it was based on the concept of the English *habeas corpus* about which Catherine had made some personal notes from the *Great Encyclopaedia*.

At the lowest level, police functions in the towns were placed in the charge of a town provost (*gorodnichi*) with a small corps of armed men, and in the countryside of a land commissar (*zemskiy ispravnik*), who seems to have been intended to function somewhat like an English justice of the peace. He was responsible to the Lower Land Courts, on which two assessors elected by the local nobility and two assessors elected by state peasants also sat. But neither the town provost nor the land commissar could themselves sentence offenders or impose any punishments; they had to bring them before the lowest-level courts of law, the Lower Land Court in the countryside, and the district *magistrat* in the towns.

The Statute also contained provisions designed to care for the welfare of the people as a whole, in accordance with the political philosophy commonly accepted at the time in Europe, which goes by the German name of *Polizeiwissenschaft*, or the science of policing the state, and which Catherine had already drawn on in the supplement on the police of her Instruction (see Chapter 3). The term police state has an unpleasant sound to modern ears, conveying as it does the idea of a police force above the law and dominating society. But in the eighteenth century, an *état policé* was the usual description of a well-ordered state, and the science by which the ordering of the resources of the state, and their use for the common good, was to be achieved was known on the continent of Europe by the German name quoted above, or by the name of 'cameralism', a reference to the 'chamber' of the ruler, where all decisions about the management of the political economy of the state were taken. The science of cameralism was known by its German name, because it had been most highly developed and most often applied in the small German courts of the Holy Roman Empire. However, one of the most influential exponents of this science was Nicolas de la Mare, who had been the assistant to the Lieutenant of the Police, La Reynie, appointed by Louis XIV to introduce public order into Paris. Peter I had already adopted some of the ideas of the cameralists, in particular their concern with public health, and good order in the cities. Catherine was familiar with both French and German writings in this field, and, moreover, by the second half of the eighteenth century there were many examples of the successful application of cameralist ideas in Central Europe by which she might be influenced.

The bodies charged with welfare functions were the boards of social welfare, established under the governor's board of administration in each provincial capital. They were composed of the governor, and two assessors from the higher noble land court, the town court or *magistrat*, and the state peasant court. The Board was to deal with the setting up of schools at provincial and district level, hospitals, almshouses, workhouses and houses of correction. Finally the Statute sketched out the social institutions which were to be further developed in 1785 (see Chapter 10). These were the noble assembly, convened every three years by an elected 'marshal of the nobility', and which in turn elected all the noble officials in local government. The marshal also chaired a committee charged with the care of noble widows and orphans in the province. Similar institutions were set up for the townspeople under a 'town chief' (*gorodskoy golova*).

Such a vast programme of reform required time, money and manpower to implement it. In ten years the number of provinces had risen from twenty-five to forty-one, and by Catherine's death in 1796 there were fifty. The number of districts had increased from 169 to 493. The cost of local administration went up enormously, since in order to attract people to serve in the provinces and the towns, and to reduce the temptation to accept bribes, most of the posts were salaried. From 1.7 million rubles in 1774, the cost of local administration rose to nearly eleven million rubles in 1796. Similarly the number of people employed permanently, or temporarily in elective posts, rose from just over 12,000 in 1774 to about 27,000 in 1796. Of these over 10,000 were elective posts, to be filled in theory by over 4,000 nobles, 3,800 merchants and townspeople and 2,700 peasants. The nobles and townspeople were allocated positions in the Table of Ranks for the period of their service. The infrastructure of chancery clerks, copyists, guards, porters, servants and so on increased in proportion. Even so, considering the size of the population and of the territory, the number of Russian administrative staff in the provinces was very small in comparison with for instance Prussia or Austria.

The provisions of the Statute, which meant carving up provinces, creating districts, determining which existing towns or indeed villages should be upgraded to become district centres, setting up new courts and offices, were applied slowly and steadily over some twenty years. In the course of those years Catherine developed the remaining elements of her policy, the administration of the cities, and the organization of the social 'estates' which were to be called on to assist in the implementation of her policies.

The next great piece of legislation in her programme was the Police Ordinance of 1782, which on the one hand laid down the regulations for the organization of the policing of towns, and on the other codified the law in relation to a number of civil and criminal offences such as smuggling and selling contaminated goods.

Cities and towns were to be divided into quarters and wards, under the overall administration of the town provost, assisted by a police board. They were responsible for the maintenance of public order, but were also charged with a whole array of functions which in the modern world would be split up between different ministries, such as public hygiene, inspection of public baths, public morals, streetlighting, control of the building line, fire prevention and fire fighting, control of foodstuffs, inspection of weights and measures, control of the labour market, indeed all the many functions which the current *Polizeiwissenschaft* attributed to the police. According to a modern Soviet scholar it is this Ordinance which for the first time in Russia legalized the holding of public assemblies and the formation of associations by laying down the terms on which they were allowed to function.

The police were given power to deal with very minor offences such as being drunk in the street or theft of goods worth less than twenty rubles, and they could only inflict small fines or short periods of detention (not corporal punishment). So-called verbal courts, where procedure was oral and cases had to be cleared up in a day, were charged with more complicated cases. It is important to remember that there was no central police force. Each city and town had its own police under the control of the governor and the board of administration. Though the police had to be informed of the presence of visitors, it was not a security organ, but a local body charged with the maintenance of public order in many social fields.

The question now arises: how well did this new administration work? This is a very difficult question to answer with any precision because of the lack of detailed studies. It was on the whole not too difficult to decide on the new provincial centres, and in most cases on the district towns. In many cases some attention was paid to the potential for economic development but in some areas of Russia settlements legally regarded as towns were so small as to be useless, while largish villages might be found on neighbouring estates belonging to landowners or to the state. Thus landowners were sometimes bought out, and serfs raised at a stroke to the status of state peasants living in towns. State peasant villages were transformed overnight into district centres, sometimes much against the wishes of the local inhabitants who did not want to cease to be peasants and become townsmen.

Some of the problems arose not so much because those charged with implementing the Statute acted in an arbitrary manner but because the Statute itself was drafted in a way which paid little attention to Russian realities. It assumed the existence in all areas of the required number of educated nobles and townspeople capable of filling all the elective and appointed posts described in the Statute, whereas in many cases there were very few resident nobles in a province, or no first-guild merchants in a town. Moreover, many members of the merchantry in the tiny settlements – often numbering no more than 200 people – selected to act as district towns were illiterate. In some cases, Catherine authorized the election of nobles to urban posts and, particularly in Siberia, the employment of sons of priests or members of the merchant estate or even state peasants in posts which should theoretically have been filled by nobles.

The reform of the local administration and the establishment of the new law courts in 1775 threw a heavy new burden on the already overburdened Russian officials. Throughout Catherine's reign the quality of the officials she could draw on, and of their support services, in the form of clerks, copyists and so on, was often very poor. Illiteracy was widespread among the older nobles of low military rank who filled up the lower reaches of the bureaucracy. It was also widespread among the young nobles who reported to the Herald Master's College, the institution which allocated them to jobs in the armed forces or as officials, when they reached the right age, before the Manifesto of 1762 freed them from compulsory service. Of the 435 who presented themselves to be given posts in that same year 1762, 74, or 17 per cent, were unable to read the Manifesto; thirty-two of the illiterates were over twenty, including 7 who were between fifty and sixty. (Incidentally more than half of the 74 owned land but no serfs.) In 1767, of 1,528 signatories to the local instructions presented by noble deputies to the Legislative Commission, 178 left others to sign for them or made their mark. Moreover not only were many nobles illiterate, others drank or were brutal, and if well connected could terrorize a whole district.

Catherine's legislative programme made increasing demands on the inadequate supply of officials, and she wrote despairingly to Potemkin on 19 October 1783 that she did not know where to turn. 'I don't dare take army men . . . I have looked around the court, and beg you to advise me who should be promoted in accordance with seniority to the rank of privy councillor; there is not much choice I know, but sometimes in the Senate one can use a stop-gap [*bouche trou*] with a well-known name, I confess though that I wish there were better people. . . .'

In the first few years after the promulgation of the reform a number of high-ranking officers found it profitable to take up posts as governors in the provinces, but on the whole the high aristocracy preferred service in the armed forces and in the capital, near the court. As a result, the quality of the officials – mostly retired middle-ranking army officers, from captain to major – was mediocre, particularly after war broke out again in 1787 and made heavy demands on manpower. Mainly totally untrained in law, without any sense of legality and lawful procedures, accustomed to the command system and the brutality which predominated in the army, they were ill-fitted to carry out their duties in the manner which the theoreticians of good civil administration laid down in their textbooks. Even at the higher levels, among the better-educated and more public-spirited nobles it was difficult to train officers, who were accustomed to take arbitrary decisions, to respect rules of procedure, not to remove cases from one court to another or to interfere in the jurisdiction of lower courts whenever they felt like it.

Moreover, in the background there lurked always the well-established Russian tradition of favouring one's relatives and taking bribes. From the evidence of memoirs, and of occasional general works, it is clear that it proved difficult to instil the concept of service to the public into those who had long been accustomed to regard government service as a means of enriching themselves or their families. Nevertheless, there were honest judges, competent governors, enterprising nobles, merchants and peasants. Life became easier once problems could be dealt with locally instead of being referred to the distant capital, and many governors attempted to beautify provincial towns with new stone buildings and to introduce a more lively social life into what had previously been cultural deserts.

It is also very difficult, in the present state of research, to be sure how well the law courts functioned. There is no doubt that life was made easier for people in the provinces, who no longer had to travel hundreds of miles to the nearest court of law. The local waiting lists to hear cases seem to have shortened considerably, though there was still great delay with the processing of appeals. At the end of Catherine's reign, in 1796, the Senate was said to have over 11,000 cases undecided; this seems a very large number, but it was roughly one year's intake, which in view of the paperwork required by Russian procedure, and in comparison with figures in other countries, does not seem excessive. But the quality of the justice meted out may not have improved much. There was still in 1775 no bar in Russia at which lawyers were trained. The first professor of Russian law to give lectures in Russian at the one and only university, that of Moscow, was Simon Desnitsky, who had studied in Glasgow under Adam Smith and who was appointed in 1767. He was subsequently responsible, at Catherine's request, for translating Blackstone's *Commentaries on the Laws of England* into Russian in 1778–80. In most criminal cases it was not the state which undertook the prosecution, but the individual who had been injured, who had also to bear the costs (as in England at the time). And there was no trained counsel for the defence. Procedure was entirely written and litigants relied on the services of intermediaries, so-called *stryapchiye*, who prepared documents and undertook to plead for their clients, but whose training was entirely practical. Many Russian nobles had by the second half of the eighteenth century attended courses in jurisprudence in foreign universities, but not nearly enough to staff the new courts.

Very little is known about how the new type of court, the Conscience Court, functioned. Only two studies of its activities have been published so far. Many western historians have assumed that it ceased to exist in the reign of Paul I (1796–1801), and have failed to realize that though some of these courts might have been abolished then, they were restored under Alexander I. The conscience courts, to which two assessors of each social estate were elected to sit when members of that estate were involved, may have proved easier to set up, particularly in undeveloped and rural areas where there were few nobles. They certainly seem to have heard cases which strictly speaking did not belong within their jurisdiction at all, such as criminal cases, even murder. Indeed the most recent historian of the Conscience Court has commented on the large number of criminal cases which came before one of these courts, concerning 'theft, forgery, incest, rape, arson, neglect of an illegitimate child, thirteen cases of murder, three of which referred to a noble torturing his serfs to death'.

The conscience courts also heard cases involving minors and the mentally deranged, and on the whole they took extenuating circumstances into account and sentenced people found guilty to milder penalties than the other courts. Those records which have been studied show that an increasing number of cases were brought before them. In St Petersburg, for instance, the number rose from 32 in 1780 to 244 in 1793; St Petersburg might be thought of as exceptional, but other courts dealt with very much the same number of cases. There are however very few records of the court being used to demand that a person detained in prison should be charged or released within three days in accordance with the provision of the Statute. Three only have been noted so far in the eighteenth century and one in the nineteenth. It is possible that people of low social and intellectual ability simply did not understand the idea of *habeas corpus* in its Russian disguise, or did not know how to use the procedure, and there was no one to advise an accused person in the absence of defence lawyers. Nevertheless, the conscience courts continued to function well into the nineteenth century, being phased out only in the 1840s. Catherine herself, it should be noted, had very great faith in the usefulness of the Conscience Court, as she wrote to Voltaire on 20 September 1777: 'The experience of the last two years has shown us that the Conscience Court set up by my regulations has become the grave of pettifoggery,' or as she later observed to her secretary, 'the Conscience Court is the pulse which shows the moral tone of a province'.

Almost nothing is known of the way the upper and lower peasant courts operated. State peasants, it will be remembered, had the right to elect peasant assessors to these courts, and it appears that in fact they often elected nobles. The courts were intended to hear cases brought by peasants against peasants in the first place, and many or most of such cases were probably settled within the communes by the village elders applying customary law. Cases in which peasants sued members of other social estates, such as nobles or townsmen, may well have been brought before the conscience courts. One of the few cases of which a record has been published showed two serfs accusing their master of sexual harassment.

Catherine's hope when she embarked on her reform of the law courts had been that the number of appeals would be reduced and that most civil and criminal cases could be decided locally. In this she was mistaken. Cases continued to be heard in the wrong courts, that is townsmen appeared before noble courts, or more surprisingly nobles before town courts; state peasants appeared before noble courts, and sometimes even serfs appeared before courts as plaintiffs or defendants. Clearly the whole concept of trial by one's peers, of special courts for different social estates, was too complicated for the general public to assimilate, and the difficulties were compounded in the many cases in which the plaintiff and the defendant belonged to different social estates. In principle cases were supposed to go before the court of the social estate of the defendant, but in practice they were heard by courts corresponding to either plaintiff or defendant, or neither.

Least of all is known about the activities of the land commissars in the country and the town provosts in the towns. Because the land commissar was elected by the nobility, he was likely to be a hereditary noble, though even this is not certain; in areas where there were few resident nobles, he could simply be appointed by the Crown from 'people with rank', which might mean personal nobility only. His rank in the Table of Ranks was 9, which did not confer hereditary nobility. The land commissar was supposed to investigate an offence by a peasant, or a serf if requested by the landowner, where the offence was not one which could be dealt with under the estate code, or by customary law.

A classic example of the arbitrary behaviour Russian officials were only too likely to indulge in occurred to Jeremy Bentham. In 1787, while he was visiting his brother Samuel, who was then working for Prince Potemkin, the Land Commissar of the local district, Cherikov, arrived to arrest Samuel (who was away at the time) for a debt of 200 rubles, allegedly owed to a couple of merchants. Samuel as a colonel in Russian service ranked as a hereditary noble. When Jeremy refused to pay his brother's alleged debt, the Land Commissar placed him under house arrest. Jeremy protested at once to the Governor-General of the province of Mogilev. From Jeremy's further account it seems that though the Land Commissar was overbearing and far exceeded his powers, the Governor-General and the local Governor treated Bentham with consideration. Evidently Potemkin's protection extended over him.

There has been for a long time a tendency to assume that, because certain officials were nobles, they would automatically and always act in the interests of the nobility, and that the town provost, appointed by the Crown in the eighth rank, that is a hereditary noble, would similarly subordinate the city to noble interests. This is to take far too simple a view of the way things actually happen. The land commissar has often been regarded as the tool of the nobles, designed to keep the serfs in order. But it is clear from the various 'instructions' submitted by nobles to the Legislative Commission that the nobles hoped that he would reduce the constant bickering between *nobles* over estate boundaries, and that he would control the violent behaviour of nobles using their peasants to steal crops, timber and hay from their neighbours' fields, woods and meadows. In turn, the very rich Moscow merchants were not likely to allow themselves to be bullied by a mere army major appointed to the post of town provost. And the town provost would not be faced with many issues in which nobles and townspeople were in conflict.

Many of the boards of social welfare set up as a result of the Statute of 1775 took their work seriously. Indeed these boards can be regarded as the first attempt by the government to set up an elementary secular social welfare system, drawing upon the co-operation of society. The boards were each allotted an initial sum of 15,000 rubles upon the interest of which they were supposed to develop their activities. A percentage of the port taxes was also granted to the boards in some port cities like St Petersburg or Riga. But these sums were supplemented by voluntary contributions from the local nobility and merchantry and even from rich peasants. The extremely efficient board of St Petersburg had raised its capital to over 31,000 rubles by 1781 from private and official benefactions. By 1803 it had risen to 561,590 rubles, which included 5,000 rubles from the English colony and 5,000 rubles from the other foreigners living in the city; and the total capital of the boards in forty-one provinces had risen to over five million rubles in assignats and nearly 800,000 rubles in silver, starting from a total of 615,000 rubles. The response of society to the encouragement from above to embark on measures of public welfare was thus much more considerable than nineteenth-century Russian historians have been willing to credit.

The Statute of 1775 also laid down elaborate provisions for the establishment of medical services in the provincial and district towns, the need for which had been made all too tragically clear by the great plague epidemic in Moscow in 1771. Smallpox too had become increasingly virulent and frequent, and Catherine had already in 1768 struck a blow at this devastating disease when she was inoculated with great public pomp by the English expert, Dr Dimsdale. Her example was followed by many among the nobility, and inoculation hospitals were set up in 1768 in St Petersburg, in 1771 in Kazan', in 1772 in Irkutsk, and in many other towns. Inoculation also became a common feature in serf and state peasant villages.

According to the Statute of 1775, each province and district was to have a physician, a surgeon, two surgeon's assistants and two apprentices, as well as an apothecary. New cemeteries were established outside the precincts of cities and downwind from them, so that the air should not be contaminated. The boards of social welfare were also to be responsible for hospitals, which should be built downstream and outside the town, and Catherine specified in great detail the need to keep rooms clean and aired, and to provide for the comforts of the patients with clean sheets, water jugs and bells to summon assistance on their night-tables. A hospital had already been built in Moscow in 1767 named after Paul (which still exists). A second hospital was built in 1775, the Catherine Hospital, which survived until the mid-twentieth century and was visited by Archdeacon William Coxe in 1778. His description shows that Catherine's initial prescriptions has been fully carried out, down to the bell on the night-table. Each patient had a separate bed, and there were nine beds to a ward sixteen feet square. In the 1790s Prince D.M. Golitsyn, who had been ambassador in Vienna for many years and had provided Catherine with much information about Austrian welfare institutions, built the Golitsyn Hospital in Moscow at his own expense.

Catherine also attempted in the Statute to modernize the Russian penal system by establishing prisons in which people were held before being tried and for people waiting to be transported to exile or hard labour; she also set up houses of correction to which people could be sent for minor crimes, and workhouses for the poor, where they could work off their keep. These latter institutions were placed under the supervision of the boards of social welfare, and were to be inspected once a week. The Empress also drafted a plan for the construction and administration of prisons in which men and women were to be kept separate, and those who had not yet been tried were not to be held together with the convicted. Provision was to be made for medical care and, again, corporal punishment was nowhere mentioned. Infringement of prison discipline was to be punished by confinement in a punishment cell. This plan was never implemented, but some of its provisions were incorporated in the new prison buildings erected in St Petersburg, which were later visited, and on the whole approved of, by John Howard, the English eighteenth-century prison reformer.

Though the implementation of the reform of 1775 took time, and suffered from many unexpected hitches, and though there is as so often with Catherine II a chasm between intention and fulfilment, yet the Statute constitutes one of her major claims to fame. The solidity of the reform is proved by the fact that the division of the Russian provinces she laid down lasted in broad lines until the October Revolution in 1917 and the general structure of the administration lasted until the reforms of Alexander II in 1864. Russian society was given a legal framework within which it could develop, and the Russian state for the first time in its history penetrated to the local level, laid down channels of communication between all classes and the centre and opened up the possibility of inspiring further reform and maintaining law and order.

CHAPTER 7

The Armed Neutrality and the Annexation of the Crimea

From 1774 to 1787 Russia enjoyed internal and external peace. There were no recruit levies in 1774 and 1775, and only one man in 500 was called up between 1776 and 1781. Yet the peace with Turkey was precarious, largely because the Turks were not at heart reconciled to the independence of the Crimea and to the opening of the Black Sea and the Mediterranean to Russian merchant ships. They feared, and rightly, that the establishment of diplomatic relations with Russia and the arrival of a large Russian embassy in Constantinople would open up Turkish territory to Russian espionage, and that the merchant ships would be warships in disguise.

There were moments when war seemed imminent. Disturbances in the Crimea led Catherine to order the reoccupation of the peninsula in November 1776, and she imposed a khan of her choice. But he aroused great opposition among his subjects by his arbitrary methods and the Crimeans revolted in 1778 against him. Russian troops again occupied the peninsula in 1778, and restored their own candidate on the throne. At that time the Turks were not yet prepared to intervene. But the European situation became more complex when a dispute broke out late in 1778 between Austria and Prussia over the succession to the Electorate of Bavaria. If the dispute were to lead to war between Austria and Prussia, Russia, as the ally of Prussia, might be drawn in. This would make her more vulnerable to pressure from the Turks over the Crimea.

However, Turkey's traditional ally, France, was unwilling to encourage her to go to war with Russia, for France was already involved in the first stages of the dispute with England arising from the revolt of the American colonies, which was going to lead to the outbreak of war between France and England in June 1778. The French Foreign Minister, Comte de Vergennes, was determined that this time – in contrast to the Seven Years War – England should find no continental ally to force France to fight on land in Europe as well as on the high seas. So Vergennes worked hard to reconcile the differences between Russia and the Turks and, with the help of Russia, between the Prussians and the Austrians. Almost at the same time, in spring 1779, the convention of Ainalikawak was signed between Russia and Turkey, in March 1779, settling their differences peacefully for the time being, as a result of which Russia agreed to evacuate the Crimean peninsula; in May 1779, the peace of Teschen was signed between Prussia and Austria, and the threat of war passed from the continent of Europe, as Vergennes had planned. Britain soon had to fight both France and Spain, not in Europe, but on the high seas and in America.

However, Britain did not give up hope of finding a continental ally; some time before the outbreak of war with France she had turned to Russia in the hope of hiring Russian troops to fight in the American continent, and of hiring Russian ships to fight under British command at sea. The first demand was turned down flat by Catherine when it was made in 1775; indeed she considered it to be highly insulting that Russia should be asked to hire out her troops as mercenaries, like some minor German principality. It had, moreover, still proved difficult in the early 1770s for a formal agreement to be concluded between Britain and Russia. The two countries were united by their common interest in the trade in naval stores. Russia was one of the major producers of these commodities, which were to a great extent forest products. Large quantities of timber were exported from Archangel in the White Sea, but even more from Riga in the Baltic. The great masts from the Russian and Polish forests were floated down the Dvina river and loaded mainly on to British and Dutch ships for export to the European maritime powers. Anglo-Russian trade had last been regulated in a commercial treaty of 1766. But the stumbling-block to a closer political alliance continued to be the so-called Turkey clause. Russia demanded British assistance against the Turks in the event of war, but Britain was still unwilling to grant it for fear of jeopardizing the extensive trade which she carried on in the Near East. (The British Ambassador in Constantinople was in fact on the payroll of the British Levant Company, not of the British government.)

With the outbreak of war with France, in June 1778, joined by Spain in June 1779, Britain's need for naval reinforcements became ever greater, and she made renewed efforts, going so far as to agree to assist Russia at least with financial subsidies in the event of a war with Turkey. But Catherine had no desire to drag Russia into the British conflict with the Bourbon powers and America, which was of very little concern to her. She felt a certain good-natured contempt for the way George III had handled his relations with the Americans. She did not fear a reduction in Britain's power and she need not fear France as long as she was allied with one of the major German powers in Central Europe, Prussia or Austria. On the contrary, the peculiar nature of the War of American Independence, which took place entirely at sea, operations on land being limited to the American continent, offered Catherine the opportunity of achieving a dominant position for Russia in European affairs owing to the existence of her navy, powerful at least in terms of numbers if not necessarily in terms of its seaworthiness or the skill of Russian sailors.

It had always been British practice in wartime to detain neutral ships on the high seas, and to confiscate the cargo if it was enemy (in this case French, American, or Spanish) property or if it was contraband of war, that is military or naval supplies, and sometimes even food. The ship would be confiscated as well as a penalty for dealing in enemy property. Similarly Britain confiscated all neutral cargo on board a captured enemy ship on the grounds that it became contaminated. The British position in this matter was invariably contested by the major maritime trading powers, namely the Dutch, Danes, Swedes and any other powers which happened to be neutral at the time. The neutrals accepted that enemy property might sometimes be confiscated and that contraband of war, according to very specific definitions, might also be confiscated, but not the neutral ship in which the cargo was loaded. Russia now decided to put herself forward as the champion of the neutral powers and to use her navy to defend their trade (and her own, of course). What attracted Catherine to play this part was the opening the war offered for increasing the Russian export trade in naval stores.

When war broke out, Britain proceeded to detain and condemn as 'good prize' neutral ships, including even Russian ships, carrying naval stores to the enemy powers, France and Spain. Both the Dutch and the Russians protested at the detention of their ships and the condemnation of their cargoes on the grounds that they were entitled by treaty to carry on such trade even in time of war. (The Swedes and the Danes protested too, though they had no such clear treaty rights.) The Dutch relied on the Anglo-Dutch trade treaty of 1674; the Russians on the Anglo-Russian trade treaty of 1766. In order not to appear to be too anti-British, Catherine seized on the detention of a Russian ship by Spain to issue a declaration of 'Armed Neutrality', in March 1780, setting out the principles which were to govern neutral trade and protect goods from seizure by either belligerent in the war. The principles she proclaimed were known in general as 'the flag covers the goods', that is to say it does not matter whose property the goods are, if they are on a neutral ship then they are neutral and cannot be condemned as enemy stores. Similarly Catherine extended and made applicable to all neutrals the definition of what was contraband included in the Russian commercial treaty with Britain, which specifically allowed trade in naval stores.

The advantages of this policy for Russia were twofold. First, the principal exporter of naval stores from Russia (apart from England), namely the Dutch, would be able to continue to come to Russian ports and load up with naval stores for sale to France and Spain. And, secondly, other nations might be encouraged to register their ships under the Russian flag, and the Russian merchant navy would increase as a result. The initial members of the Neutral League, set up in March 1780, were Russia, Sweden, Denmark–Norway. France and Spain both declared that they would accept the principles laid down for the treatment of neutral ships, and Austria, Prussia and Portugal eventually also joined the Neutral League. The first two powers could hope to benefit from the protection of the naval patrols which Russia, Sweden and Denmark inaugurated in the North Sea, the Prussians by transferring their shipping to the Dutch register, and the Austrians by welcoming ships to register in Ostend and fly the flag of the Austrian Netherlands.

England also reacted in two ways. First, she renewed her attempts to attract Russia into an alliance, agreeing even to offer assistance in a Russo-Turkish war, and going so far as to offer the island of Menorca to Russia – British since the peace of Utrecht of 1713, though shortly to be British no longer. (It fell to the Franco-Spanish expeditionary force in 1782.) And, secondly, she found a pretext to declare war on the Dutch in December 1780. The Dutch were the most dangerous member of the Neutral League from Britain's point of view because of the size of their merchant navy. As a member of the Neutral League, the Dutch would be able to enjoy the protection of the Russian naval patrols in order to carry on trade in naval stores with France and Spain. Catherine, however, had never had the slightest intention of being drawn into the war, and she evaded her obligation to come to the defence of the Dutch on the ground that they had adhered to the treaty of Armed Neutrality in St Petersburg in December 1780 when they were already at war with Britain (though the news had not yet reached Russia) and therefore were no longer neutral.

However, by then Catherine's foreign policy was already taking a new direction, closely linked with her victories in 1774 and the acquisition of a toehold on the Black Sea. Encouraged by her initial success she began to dwell on what came to be known as the 'Greek Project'. This was nothing less than driving the Turks out of Europe. Much of the population in the territory ruled by the Ottoman Empire in Europe practised the Orthodox religion, notably in many of the lands which form part of modern Yugoslavia, modern Greece and the Aegean islands, modern Bulgaria and modern Romania. The Churches and the peoples tended to look to Russia for financial assistance and religious leadership.

But the Greek Project involved more than just freeing the Orthodox peoples from the Moslem yoke. It involved recovering Constantinople for Orthodox Christianity, creating a throne for Catherine's second grandson, suitably christened Constantine, and possibly a kingdom of Dacia, carved out of the Danubian principalities of Moldavia and Wallachia for her lover G.A. Potemkin. For such a policy the existing Russian alliance with Prussia was useless, and Catherine began to entertain hopes of switching to an alliance with Austria, particularly after the Emperor Joseph II paid her a visit in May 1780, during which both rulers laid the foundations of a future understanding. Joseph II of Austria had always hoped to wean Russia from her alliance with Prussia, but as long as his mother, the Empress Queen Maria Theresia, was alive, he did not have sole charge of Austrian foreign policy. Catherine II was well aware that as long as she was allied to one of the Germanic powers she did not need to fear the other one. And, clearly, if she contemplated a renewal of war with Turkey and further expansion in the south, then Austria who had territorial ambitions and a common frontier with the Turks, was a better partner than Prussia.

The death of the Empress Maria Theresia in November 1780 freed Joseph from the restraints his mother had imposed on him, and an agreement was reached with Russia by June 1781 to co-operate in the event of war with Turkey. This agreement – which remained secret until June 1783 – greatly strengthened Catherine's hand, when she began to plan for her next acquisition, namely the annexation of the Crimean peninsula. It was important to achieve this major change in the balance of power while France and Britain were still at war with each other, and therefore unable or unwilling to interfere. Catherine and Joseph II had been invited to act as mediators between the belligerent powers, France and Spain on the one hand, and Britain on the other. But no one took this mediation seriously, and Catherine made her plans in the autumn of 1782; in April 1783 Potemkin was ordered to march into the Crimean peninsula. By July the Russian occupation had been completed.

It now remained to ensure that the Turks, outraged by this Russian aggression, would not declare war. Catherine brought pressure to bear on her Austrian ally. Joseph II, caught in the dilemma of forcing Catherine to give up the Crimea and losing his Russian ally, or accepting the Russian annexation without any corresponding compensation for himself, chose the latter course. No other power was in a position to protest openly, for though the preliminaries of peace had been signed between France and England in January 1783, the final peace treaty was not signed until September 1783. It was impossible for the two powers to put their enmity behind them and act together to hold Russia in check.

The annexation of the khanate of Crimea was a major acquisition for Russia. It included not only the peninsula itself but an extensive hinterland which now linked the strip of territory acquired in 1774 to the River Don and the Kuban', as a result of which the Sea of Azov became a Russian lake. Whereas the Cossack lands had been very thinly settled and there were no towns, in the Crimea, now renamed the Tauride province (because of its associations with classical Greece – it was supposed to be the place where Iphigenia, Agamemnon's daughter, had taken refuge), there were several well-established old urban centres, as well as the magnificent Bay of Akhtiar, where the great naval base of Sebastopol was soon established. At the time of the Russian annexation there was much vacant land in the Crimea, for very large numbers of Christian Crimeans had emigrated to Russia in 1778, while Moslem Tartars, variously estimated at 150,000 to 300,000, had emigrated to Turkish territory in the years between the treaty of Kutschuk Kainardzhi in 1774 and the Russian annexation in 1783. In spite of the efforts made by the Russian authorities to treat the native Tartar elite with some consideration, by absorbing the Tartar nobles into the Russian nobility, extending the Russian system of local administration as laid down in the Statute of 1775 with its elective component, and granting complete freedom of worship to the Moslem Tartars, large numbers continued to emigrate to Turkey and were replaced by Russians.

The economic development of the south now proceeded apace. New Russia and the lands of the Zaporozhian Host were united in the new province of Yekaterinoslav (Glory of Catherine) of which Prince G.A. Potemkin was the Governor-General. Since the border was now secure the need for military settlers vanished, and huge tracts of uninhabited land were given away or sold to Russian magnates and nobles, even to Tartar princes, or to anyone likely to prove capable of organizing the colonization of the area. Potemkin welcomed refugee serfs without inquiring closely into their origins, and would even have welcomed English convicts, now that they could no longer be transported to the American colonies. (The first convoy to Botany Bay in Australia only sailed in 1787.) There was trouble at first when incoming Russian landowners attempted to impose Russian serfdom on the native Tartar peasants, but the Russian government opposed this policy. In 1796, in response to pressure from Russian landowners, the government agreed to enforce the requirement that peasants should not be able to move away from the villages where they were registered without permission. But, according to modern Soviet scholarship, this reversal of what had been Potemkin's policy of welcoming free and fugitive settlers did not imply the loss of personal freedom, nor the full range of serfdom.

Not only did Potemkin build towns; he built a navy, what Catherine, remembering the relationship between Venice and the Adriatic Sea, described as 'the wedding of the Russian navy with the Black Sea'. The main naval base was at first at Kherson, on the estuary of the Dnieper, but it was unsuitable as a port and was unprotected from the guns of the Turkish fort of Ochakov. Operations were therefore transferred to Sebastopol in 1784. By 1783 the Russian Black Sea fleet consisted of forty-one large and eighteen small ships, with some eight more sixty-six-gun ships of the line in construction, and many more sloops, cutters and unarmed small vessels. Even so, the Russian fleet was outnumbered by the Turkish navy. Supplies of raw materials for the construction of towns and the fleet enlivened the economy of Belorussia, the area which had been annexed by Russia at the first partition of Poland, the trade of which made use of the Dnieper waterways. Potemkin himself had an interest in this trade since he conducted a thriving business in naval stores from his Belorussian estates in Krichov, which were managed at the time for him by Samuel Bentham.

It should not be imagined that Catherine's forward policy in the south met with universal approval in political circles in Russia. It is clear that there was a current of disapproval for the Greek Project, for the acquisition of 'useless deserts' in the south, and for the annexation of the Crimea, which many thought likely to lead to a renewal of war with the Turks. Count Nikita Panin, who had dominated the shaping of foreign policy at Catherine's side since she had seized power in 1762, and who was deeply committed to the alliance of Russia with Prussia, which he had himself brought about in 1764, fought tooth and nail to prevent the conclusion of the secret agreement with Austria in 1781. Issues of foreign policy became entangled with personal rivalry for influence over the Empress. Panin, as the spokesman of the Prussian orientation of the Russian court, was at daggers drawn with Potemkin, who entered enthusiastically into the Empress's new Greek Project. The climax came in September 1781, when Catherine dismissed Panin from his post as senior member of the College of Foreign Affairs, namely the man in charge of foreign policy, and replaced him with Count A.A. Bezborodko, who had been her secretary, and who was to stay in that office until her death. From now until Catherine's death, alliance with Austria was to remain a fundamental element in her foreign policy.

Both policy and natural curiosity drove Catherine to visit her new acquisition. She had already made several journeys within Russia, to acquaint herself with the condition of the people and to provide occasions for demonstrations of loyalty and allegiance. She had visited the Baltic provinces in 1764 and been much impressed with their orderliness; in 1767, she travelled down the Volga as far as Kazan', a city which was far more oriental in atmosphere than any she had previously seen and which attracted her by its exoticism and its prosperity. She lodged in the house of a rich merchant, which to her amazement had nine rooms one after the other all hung with silk, and furnished with gilt sofas and armchairs. Her occasional visits to Moscow enabled her to note improvements in the countryside. On her journey from St Petersburg to Moscow in 1775, she contrasted conditions with what she had seen eight years before. 'Years ago,' she wrote to one of her regular correspondents abroad, 'one could see little children running barefoot in the villages in the snow; now they all have a suit, a coat and boots. The houses are still built of wood, but they are bigger and most of them have two storeys.' In 1780 she toured northern Russia and Belorussia, inspecting the new institutions established under the Statute of 1775. In

1785 she visited the Vyshniy Volochok canal system, which formed part of the link between Moscow and the Volga and St Petersburg, travelling partly in carriages, partly on richly furnished galleys. Confident of her welcome by the people, Catherine had invited the French, English and Austrian ambassadors to accompany her on the journey. The French Ambassador, the Comte de Ségur, has left a vivid description of the peasants approaching Catherine, calling her 'Little Mother' and talking to her without fear or reserve, and of the huge flotilla of small boats which surrounded the galleys on Lake Ilmen, crowded with peasants playing various instruments and, as dusk fell, singing their melancholy songs.

Potemkin had been pressing Catherine to visit the south of her Empire for some time, and finally in January 1787 she set forth, escorted again by the English, the French and the Austrian ambassadors, before whom the achievements of her chosen favourite were to be displayed. Starting in winter made travel in luxurious sledges much easier and more comfortable; the travellers were well wrapped in bearskins and beaver bonnets. After a brief stay in Smolensk, the company proceeded to Kiev, where they boarded a fleet of beautifully fitted galleys to travel down the Dnieper. Progress was slow; the galleys stopped often, and passengers could land and walk on the banks. 'The towns and villages, country houses and rustic cabins', wrote the French Ambassador, 'were so adorned and disguised with wreaths of flowers, elegant architectural decorations, that they created the illusion of superb cities, suddenly erected palaces, gardens produced by magic.' Nearer to the larger towns, troops were drawn up in magnificent order. Below Pereyaslavl, the right bank of the Dnieper belonged to Poland–Lithuania, and here, at Kaniev, Catherine briefly met her ex-lover, whom she had made king of Poland, Stanislas Augustus. Then the party continued on down to Kremenchug, the *de facto* headquarters of Potemkin, as far as Kaydak, shooting the first of the famous Dnieper rapids under the guidance of members of the Society of Dnieper Pilots set up by Potemkin's factotum, M.L. Faleyev, in 1785, and which lasted until 1917.

Ségur pays tribute to the stage-managing of Potemkin, who always arranged that the galley fleet should stop overnight at some picturesquely situated town or village, and who conjured up herds of cattle, crowds of happy singing peasants. Yet, he wrote,

> if one discards all that was artificial in what he had created, one could also recognise reality; when he had taken over this im-

mense province [in 1774] there were only 204,000 inhabitants; under his administration the population, in a very few years, has risen to 800,000. . . . A Frenchman, who has been here for three years, told me that as he travelled about the province every year, he had found flourishing new villages in places he had left before as deserts. From Kaydak to Kherson, there extended a vast green plain, covered with herds of cattle, horses and sheep.

At Kaydak news reached the convoy that Joseph II had already arrived in Kherson, and was on his way to meet the Empress by land. Not to be outdone in politeness, Catherine hastened to meet her noble guest. Soon afterwards, in the presence of the Emperor, Catherine laid the foundation stone of the new city of Yekaterinoslav (today Dniepropetrovsk), for which Potemkin had drawn up elaborate plans, including a university, a theatre, a huge church and a city laid out according to the latest Russian ideas of town planning.

Ségur was very impressed with what had been achieved in a bare nine years in Kherson. The fort was nearly finished, there were barracks for 24,000 men, a dockyard, two warships and a frigate about to be launched, public buildings and noble churches, 2,000 houses, shops full of goods from west and east, and some 200 ships at anchor in the port. The disadvantages were the shallowness of the draught, which rendered it necessary for ships to unload before sailing up the Dnieper, and the unhealthy, marshy situation. Only the arrival of a squadron of Turkish ships which anchored on the opposite shore of the estuary of the Dnieper at Ochakov prevented Catherine from attempting to visit the Russian fort of Kinburn.

At the end of June a smaller company entered Crimea. The Empress was escorted by a company of 1,200 Tartar cavalry, and proceeded to Bakhchisarai, where the court lodged in the palace of the Tartar Khans. Thus an honorary Romanov now replaced the last ruler of the house of Genghis Khan. From the mountains above the Bay of Sebastopol a splendid view of the twenty-five warships in the new Russian fleet roused the interest and the alarm of both Joseph II and the French Ambassador. Catherine reviewed her navy by sea, then showed her guests the new dockyard and magazines, two hospitals, and the facilities for the garrison and the administration of the new city. Ségur was astonished that so much could have been achieved in barely four years. Catherine was full of pride and admiration, for the achievements of Potemkin gave the lie not only to the critical gossip at court, but to the malicious quip which had been going the rounds, to the effect that his villages were made of painted cardboard, and his happy peasants were the same people who were merely being driven from place to place to reappear before the Empress and her guests. In Russian the expression 'Potemkin villages' has come to mean any surface fake designed to conceal the true poverty beneath. It is of course true that Potemkin showed Catherine his new lands in their best light but his achievements were only too real, as the comments of the French Ambassador reveal, and as later Soviet scholarship has confirmed; and the Turks were certainly not deceived about the strength of his new fleet, which, though smaller than theirs, was anchored only two days' sailing from the heart of the Turkish Empire.

Indeed the Turks had been watching with growing concern the large troop concentration Potemkin had organized for the Empress's visit, and they were increasingly perturbed at his forward policy, which seemed to proclaim the Russian purpose of driving the Turks from Europe – an aim which was *not* shared either by Russia's ally, Joseph II, or by France. The time seemed more than ripe for a preventive war. The King of Sweden too was on the lookout for a pretext to declare war on Russia when she should also be engaged with the Turks. His minister in St Petersburg had not been invited to accompany the Empress on her journey to the south, and spent his time feeding Gustavus with malicious gossip about the allegedly fraudulent nature of Potemkin's achievements. The King of Sweden hoped that Turkey would declare war while Catherine was still in the south, for he placed his hopes in a *coup d'état* in St Petersburg, leading to a revolution in the state, even to the overthrow of the Empress, if she were absent from the capital. On the other hand the Turks wanted to postpone their declaration of war until Catherine had gone north again, far from the actual theatre of operations. So they waited until she reached St Petersburg, in August 1787, then sent for the Russian Envoy and locked him up in the fort of the Seven Towers – the usual Turkish way of declaring war.

CHAPTER 8

Catherine's Influence on Russian Cultural Life

A feature common to the evolution of absolute monarchies was the concentration of cultural life around the court. This was noticeable even in England, where royal absolutism was checked by the revolution of 1688. But until then, under the Tudors and the Stuarts, poets, dramatists, musicians and actors were employed by the court, or by magnates in attendance on the court, and accounted for a good deal of the Crown's expenditure. The accession of the Hanoverians led to a partial decline of the cultural role of the court in England (though George I was astute enough to make use of it when he could derive political benefit from doing so) at a time when elsewhere in Europe the model created by Louis XIV of France was being assiduously imitated, to a greater degree indeed than is usually stated, by Peter I himself.

By Catherine's accession in 1762 the seventeenth-century French model was on the wane in Europe as a whole, either for reasons of economy as in the case of Frederick II of Prussia or the Emperor Joseph II, or because of the increasing desire of European royalty for privacy and domestic comfort. But Catherine had been brought up to admire the brilliant and orderly court life so conspicuously lacking in her native Stettin, or in the ramshackle courts of her predecessors, the Empress Elizabeth and Peter III. Moreover the Russian court in St Petersburg or Moscow was still almost the only provider of theatrical performances, music, ballet, opera and so on, unlike for instance Paris or London, or Venice or Madrid, where a thriving private entertainment industry catered for the tastes of the aristocracy and the common people. Catherine therefore immediately set about restoring the central function of the court. She revised the ranks and the rules, organized suitable entertainments, subsidized the public French and Russian theatres, as well as operas and ballets. Eventually she built her own private theatre, in the Hermitage

Palace, next to the Winter Palace in St Petersburg, to which admission was free to courtiers and officers and their ladies, and even to servants as long as they were not in livery.

Catherine's own personal passion for putting pen to paper was first publicly manifested in her Instruction. But barely had the plenary sessions of the Legislative Commission been abandoned on the outbreak of war with Turkey than she launched out anonymously on another enterprise, destined to leave its mark on the intellectual life of her adoptive country.

Early in 1769 the first number of a short, weekly satirical periodical was published, entitled *Vsyakaya vsyachina* (*All Sorts of Things*). Other periodicals had of course been published before, but none so specifically modelled on the English genre of *The Tatler* or *The Spectator*, in which gentle satire was aimed at general vices and defects rather than at specific persons. What induced Catherine to promote this kind of public criticism of the defects of Russian society (ignorance, superstition, corruption, inhumane treatment of peasants, worship of all things French) at this particular moment, when she had just been thrust into war, has never been satisfactorily explained. It was only discovered in the middle of the nineteenth century, when some unpublished snippets that she evidently wrote for *All Sorts of Things* were found, that she had a close connection with the journal. As a result historians have assumed that her participation in *All Sorts of Things* was common knowledge in the eighteenth century. Looking back, however, this seems unlikely, for it would have been regarded as far too risky and beneath her dignity for the Empress herself to descend into the arena of journalism.

It was in fact assumed that *All Sorts of Things* was edited by a high-ranking official, one of the Empress's secretaries, G. Kozitsky. This was enough to suggest to the general public that she viewed it with favour. In the name of 'Granny', the editor invited children and grandchildren to come forward in imitation of the new trend she had launched, and the children and grandchildren responded. A number of satirical periodicals sprang up at once in 1769, the best known of which were *Truten'* (*The Drone*), edited by N.I. Novikov, *Adskaya Pochta* (*Hell's Post*), edited by the novelist F. Emin, and modelled to some extent on the French *Dialogue entre le diable boiteux et le diable borgne*, and *Smes'* (*Miscellany*), of which the editor has still not been definitely identified. Much of the content of these satirical journals was reprinted from *The Spectator*, *The Rambler* and *The Tatler*, which circulated widely in Europe in the form of collections translated into

French and German. The very names of the Russian journals, such as *The Drone* or *The Painter*, which suggest that the editor stands outside events and describes what is going on without taking part, echo the titles and the editorial approach of the English originals.

The journals also published items specially written for them and more relevant to Russian conditions, such as *The Drone*'s attacks on 'gallomania', the passion of young, foppish courtiers to be taken for Frenchmen, or the equally biting attacks the journal punished on bad serf-owners who exploited and ill-treated their serfs. Again, to this day the actual authorship of some of these pieces is uncertain; they have been attributed to Novikov himself, or to the playwright Denis Fonvizin, or to the writer A. Radishchev. The journals also attacked each other in most virulent terms, and inevitably also their common ancestor, *All Sorts of Things*. In the nineteenth century, when it was generally assumed that the Empress's participation in *All Sorts of Things* was widely known at the time, attacks on it were interpreted as signs of an open opposition to the Empress's policies and her absolute government, and they were particularly associated with Novikov, largely because twenty years later he was charged with and imprisoned for a quite different offence (see Chapter 15). For a long time it was even believed that Catherine closed down Novikov's *The Drone* in 1770 because of its critical and allegedly 'oppositional' attitude. It is true that Catherine disagreed with Novikov on the proper form of satire. She preferred the gentle type of satire directed at 'vice' in general (as defined in *The Spectator*) to the more virulent type of attack on recognizable individuals. At any rate there is no evidence that she closed down any of the periodicals. The sheer number of them which appeared all at once was too much for the very small reading public in Russia at that time, which was in any case much reduced by the absence of many officers on active service with the armed forces in the war against the Turks. As a result the journals all tended to fold after a year or so, including *All Sorts of Things*. Novikov referred indeed to the declining support he was receiving when *The Drone* ceased publication after one year. But he immediately started up a new review, *Zhivopisets* (*The Painter*), for which he received an initial subsidy of 200 rubles from Catherine II. This evidence of her continuing patronage of Novikov has only recently been published and it casts a quite different light on the portrait, which has been traditionally painted by historians, of a young, radical writer (Novikov was only twenty-five years old) challenging an ageing and dissolute ruler (Catherine was forty in

1769 and had been living with her lover Count G. Orlov for the previous nine years). Many of the journals, including Novikov's *The Drone* and *The Painter*, were republished in book form in later years and found a ready sale without any interference from a very lax censorship.

Indeed censorship, in the form it is known today, exercised by a central office applying the same ideological and political norms throughout the country, did not exist. In the 1760s there were no private printing presses in Russia, not because they were specifically forbidden by law, but because no one had ever thought of starting one up. The printing presses belonged to institutions such as the Senate, the Holy Synod (which officially had the monopoly of the publication of religious works, both in the modernized Cyrillic script introduced by Peter I and in the Old Church Slavonic script used for liturgical works in the Russian Orthodox Church), the Cadet Corps, the Engineering School, the University of Moscow and some other institutions, the most important of which was the Academy of Sciences. These printing presses were all self-censoring, in the sense that they did not have to submit original or translated works they proposed to publish to any outside censor or censorship body, but decided, each for itself, whether such works satisfied general criteria which could be broadly summed up as 'inoffensive to authority, decency and religion'. On rare occasions the Empress herself was known to have intervened to tone down personal attacks on individuals, on the grounds that since the presses were all official she might be associated with the attack. It was a power rarely used, but of course Catherine had a residual power to prevent the publication or dissemination of anything she considered subversive to government or morality (for instance libels, or false laws), and to prohibit the importation and distribution of literature which offended against 'authority, decency and religion'.

At one of the sessions of the Senate Catherine attended in 1763 she had made use of this power to ban the sale of the French edition of Jean-Jacques Rousseau's treatise on education, *Émile* (which had already been banned in France), together with a French account of the life of her murdered husband, Peter III. In all probability however the ban did not result from Rousseau's educational theories, which Catherine eventually grew to dislike, but from his views on religion as expressed in *Émile*, in the long passage entitled 'The profession of faith of the Savoyard vicar'. This was a most daring exposition of religious belief founded not on Christian revelation as expounded by an established Church but on the natural intuition of the individual, and it was condemned by the established Christian Churches everywhere. However, when Catherine was more securely established on the throne she could afford to take a more relaxed view and translations of parts of *Émile* including the profession of faith of the Savoyard vicar, and of most of Rousseau's other works, appeared in Russian in the following years, while even his most important political treatise, the *Social Contract*, appeared in a German translation published in Riga, the headquarters of the intellectual life of the Baltic provinces and of German-speaking Russians.

In the search to bring enlightenment to those Russians who could not read either French or German, Catherine also launched a Society for the Translation of Foreign Books, which lasted until 1783. She subsidized this body to the tune of 5,000 rubles a year, a really considerable sum. Many of the established writers and the young intellectuals of the period, whether noble or non-noble, could make a little money by translating the Greek and Latin poets or historians, works of philosophy and political economy, and literary works. Great court magnates took part in this programme, whether by sharing with Catherine herself in the translation of *Bélisaire* by the French *philosophe* Marmontel, in 1767, or by working on their own, like General Paul Potemkin, who translated Rousseau's novel *La nouvelle Héloise*. Intellectual pursuits became fashionable at court and helped to swell the programme of subsidized translations. In the course of fifteen years, 112 translations were published, and a further 129 were in hand in 1783, when the whole programme was transferred to the newly founded Russian Academy of the Language (see p. 98). The choice of books which Catherine sponsored reflects her own tastes and opinions, and her partiality to English literature; there was a good deal of classical history (Livy, Tacitus) and literature (Homer, Cicero) and of contemporary history (Robertson, Hume) and French literature (Corneille, Voltaire). Political and administrative science, such as *De L'Esprit des lois* of Montesquieu or the *Commentaries on the Laws of England* by William Blackstone, loomed large. Fielding's *Joseph Andrews* and Swift's *Gulliver's Travels* reflect Catherine's own taste. There was no theology.

One must not forget that there was a large German-speaking population in the Russian reading public at this time. In spite of the attraction of French culture, and the general knowledge of the French language among the aristocracy and the upper classes, German was still strongly represented in Russia. People as socially different as Prince A.A. Vyazemsky and the leading playwright Denis Fonvizin both spoke German before they learnt French. This happened because in the reigns of Peter I and Anna Ivanovna German influence was strong at court and many Russians were brought up to be German-speaking; and because of the large German colony in St Petersburg, composed of both native Germans and Baltic Germans in Russian service, who to some extent gravitated around the Lutheran church and school of St Peter. Many Russians studied at German universities, and many Germans were employed in the University of Moscow and the Academy of Sciences – indeed Germans played a far bigger part than Frenchmen in cultural life within Russia. The frequently repeated assertion that the Russian court in Catherine's reign spoke French rather than Russian is not true. It is based on the attacks by the satirical journals, or by Denis Fonvizin in his play *The Brigadier*, on gallomania. But such attacks were commonplace in most countries at this time, regardless of the actual reality. Moreover, out of courtesy, leading Russian statesmen and courtiers spoke French to visiting foreigners, who could not be expected to know Russian. But the private and the official correspondence between Catherine and her leading ministers and officials (and her lovers) at this time is – with a few exceptions – written in Russian. In addition this period saw not only the multiplication of translations into Russian, but the flowering of literary works such as the plays of Sumarokov, Knyazhnin and Fonvizin, the poetry of Kheraskov and Derzhavin, and the literary, historical and scientific works of Lomonosov, all written in Russian.

Catherine herself wrote most of her literary works in Russian, and some in French. She did not know English, though there are occasional suggestions that she could read it. At any rate she did not correspond directly with any English man of letters, though she corresponded regularly with Voltaire and Diderot, occasionally with d'Alembert, and from 1774 to her death with Baron Melchior von Grimm. The *Great Encyclopaedia* published by Diderot and d'Alembert had been among Catherine's favourite works as Grand Duchess, and when the editors were refused a licence to publish in Paris, she offered to continue printing and publication in Russia. In the event the editors preferred not to accept her invitation, and d'Alembert also refused her offer to come to Russia as tutor to the Grand Duke Paul. In October 1773 Diderot did visit Russia, impelled by gratitude for the generous financial support he had received from Catherine. He stayed some six months, and saw Catherine very frequently. For his discussions with her he prepared memoranda on political and social subjects which have survived and which give a very vivid impression of the wide-ranging conversations between the ruler and the *philosophe*. Catherine found him impractical and theoretical, as she later explained, but she enjoyed his company and provided generously for his comfort and his travel expenses. On his return to France Diderot also proved helpful in fulfilling Catherine's artistic and literary commissions, though her main correspondent and agent was Baron Grimm. Catherine did not encourage Voltaire to visit her. 'Tell him,' she wrote to Grimm in 1778, 'that Kate looks better from a distance.'

The official presses attached to government institutions seemed to have served Russian literature well. Thus the first request to set up an independent press came from a member of the German colony in 1771, who hoped to establish a publishing business in German for the German inhabitants of St Petersburg, instead of having to rely on works printed in Riga or imported from Germany. Permission was granted, and a few more private presses obtained the right to function, but the situation changed radically when Catherine issued one of the most important decrees affecting Russian cultural development. On 15 January 1783 she published an edict which allowed anyone, anywhere, of any social estate, to set up a printing press providing only that it was registered with the local chief of police. Historians have found difficulty in explaining this decree, which seemed on the surface to liberalize intellectual life to a dangerous degree by abandoning state control and manipulation of the programme of original and translated publications into the hands of potentially subversive elements. It is hard to argue that Catherine's regime was intellectually oppressive, as many of her detractors have done, in the face of such a clear example of her confidence in the response of society to her rule. It may well be that her real motive was a purely commercial one, for both private and government publishing enterprises were at this time losing money, owing to the smallness of the market, and Catherine may have been only too happy to shift the cost of printing her programme of translations on to private enterprise.

Censorship was also formalized in the decree of 1783 by placing it in the hands of the local chiefs of police, who were supposed to read manuscripts submitted for publication on private presses for anything likely to offend against the person of the ruler, the Orthodox

Christian faith and public decency. These guidelines are fairly wide since in an absolute regime it is possible to interpret any discussion of the form of government as 'an offence against the person of the ruler'. Nevertheless they were interpreted in a fairly lax and easy-going manner, thus allowing the publication of some frank attacks on tyrannical government – in the past, or elsewhere.

Taken together, the permission to print and publish and the very lax censorhip seem to represent a basic principle of Catherine's personal outlook, namely her desire to encourage social forces to be active and show enterprise in as many fields as possible, rather than to maintain state control and subsidy. She was at this stage in her reign completely confident in the exercise of her authority, in the general acceptance of her government by the bulk of the people of the Russian Empire, and therefore she did not fear that the general permission to publish would be abused and lead to a flood of seditious literature. We are today so accustomed in democracies to the concepts of government and opposition that it is difficult to conceive of regimes in which 'opposition' in the shape of systematic criticism of the form of government (whether absolute monarchy, oligarchy, republic or 'the Crown in Parliament' as in the United Kingdom), or of *all* the policies of a government because it *is* the government (alliances, wars, taxes, tariffs on imports and exports, welfare) did not exist.

The ukaz of 1783 led to a proliferation of printing presses throughout Russia, some run by nobles on their estates, some run by peasants or townspeople, some attached to the new boards of social welfare in the provinces. Combined with the reforms of 1775 the new presses served to enliven life in the provinces. A new journal was published in distant Tobol'sk (which also boasted a theatre), enterprising governors encouraged publication by local talent, including women writers, and it is at this time that the first efforts were made to provide written alphabets for some of the languages of Russia such as Mordvin or Cheremiss.

The Russian Academy of the Language was also founded in 1783, and here again Catherine showed a degree of originality in her appointment of a director most unusual in eighteenth-century Europe. She had already appointed a woman, Princess Catherine Dashkova, her fervent collaborator in the seizure of power in 1762, to direct the Russian Academy of Sciences, a fairly startling choice. Dashkova was not herself a scientist but she was extremely well connected, had travelled widely, and was acquainted with the leading intellectuals of France, England, Scotland and Germany. An energetic and enterprising woman, she galvanized the Academy of Sciences, and became the obvious choice to head the new Academy of the Language when this was founded. She set about organizing the setting down of the rules of Russian grammar and spelling, and she co-opted the leading Russian writers of the day to work with her in preparing the first dictionary of the Russian language, which began to appear in 1788.

Catherine herself was extremely interested in the development of language and in the relationship between different languages. Her studies in comparative etymologies tended to lead her to make somewhat odd deductions, such as the existence of a Slavonic influence in practically all languages. Thus she saw a similarity between the Russian Gatimalo, and Guatemala in Central America. She surrounded herself with dictionaries of Finnish, Cheremiss and Votyak, she ordered her ambassadors in foreign countries to provide her with glossaries of the meaning of various words, and she hoped soon to prove that the names of most of the rivers and valleys in France, Spain and Scotland were Slavonic in origin. One of the qualities she praised in the Grand Duchess Olga of Kiev, who had ruled in the tenth century, was that she had brought the Slavonic language into general use. 'For it is well known', wrote Catherine, 'that peoples and their languages thrive by the wisdom and care of the supreme rulers.'

The Academy of the Language also sponsored periodicals, to which Catherine herself contributed long essays on Russian history, which by the 1780s had become one of her major interests. Her historical writings are conscientious in the effort to distinguish facts from legend, and they are intended for the general public, even children, rather than for specialists. They are nevertheless extremely naive, and follow the well-worn track of justifying absolute government.

Catherine had also used the theatre as a means of educating the public. She patronized the court theatre, which put on plays by Molière, Voltaire, Diderot, Sheridan and other contemporary European authors, as well as the tragedies and comedies of Russian authors such as Sumarokov. The satirical play *The Brigadier* (1769), which Denis Fonvizin was invited to read aloud to the Empress, to the Grand Duke and in salons all over St Petersburg, and the even more satirical *The Minor*, which received its première in Moscow in 1782, were repeatedly performed. Alexander Vorontsov's serf theatre played *The Minor* in the 1790s, and the Englishman John Parkinson saw a performance of *The Brigadier* in distant Tobol'sk in 1792. Catherine herself wrote plays in Russian with a clearly didactic purpose, which were published and performed anonymously but were generally known to be by her. She remodelled plays by others (the German Christian Gellert, for instance, or even Shakespeare's *The Merry Wives of Windsor*), or she devised the plots herself. She satirized superstition, gossipy old ladies and in the 1780s freemasonry, which had entered Russia in the eighteenth century and had become fashionable among a select group of the aristocracy and the nobility, mainly in the armed forces, but also to some extent among non-noble authors and playwrights.

Music was also cultivated at court, where Catherine wrote the librettos for a number of operas, which were set to music by visiting composers such as the Spaniard Martin y Soler, or the Italians Sarti and Paisiello, or by native Russian or Ukrainian musicians such as Pashkevich and Sokolovsky. Russian choral and instrumental music of the late eighteenth century has a beautiful and distinctive character as a result of the combination of Italian style with elements of Russian church or folk music.

Education was in Catherine's opinion one of the most effective ways of reforming individual human beings (and hence society as a whole). Her educational policy went through various phases (see Chapter 9) but she also published extensively on the subject. She wrote a *Russian Primer for the Instruction of Youth* (*Rossiiskaya azbuka*) in 1781, which sold 20,000 copies in two weeks; its tone was totally secular. In the 210 moral maxims of which it is composed, God is mentioned only twice, and while Plato, Aristotle and Confucius are quoted as authorities, Jesus Christ is not. Catherine also wrote tales for her grandchildren, the first works specifically written for children ever to be published in Russia, one of which was to be the first Russian work to be translated into English.

Catherine's patronage also had a considerable influence on the development of Russian art and architecture. She was well informed about artistic trends in other countries, and during her reign many Russian architects and painters studied abroad, while at the same time she attempted to recruit foreign artists to work in Russia. In architecture she preferred something less florid than the rococo style patronized by the Empress Elizabeth, namely the neo-classical style based on Palladio. Russia and Great Britain are in fact the two countries in which the style associated with the Adam brothers was most widely appreciated and adopted. Catherine had first invited the French architect Charles Louis Clérisseau to Russia. He had made drawings for the Adam brothers in Rome, and though he did not in fact build anything for Catherine his drawings of Roman remains and Roman decorative art influenced her taste. The foreign architect most closely associated with Catherine is Charles Cameron, a Jacobite who had studied in Rome and who came to Russia in 1779. For Catherine he built the Cameron Gallery at Tsarskoye Selo, and the set of rooms specially designed for her own use; he also built the palace of Pavlovsk, which she had granted to the Grand Duke Paul. Another exponent of the neo-classical style was Giacomo Quarenghi, who arrived in 1780. Catherine was very pleased with him, as she wrote to her agent in France, Baron Grimm:

> This Quarenghi is producing delightful things; the whole town is stuffed with his buildings; he is building the Bank, the Exchange, lots of stores and shops and private houses, and his buildings are the very best. He is building a theatre for me at the Hermitage, which will be finished in a fortnight, and which is charming to look at within. . . .

Among many distinguished Russian architects the most outstanding was perhaps E.I. Starov, who built the splendid Tauride Palace for Prince Potemkin, which served as a model for many Russian country houses later on. The appearance of St Petersburg became more and more splendid, and the systematic lining of the banks of the Neva and of the various canals with granite slabs greatly increased the elegance and comfort of the capital.

Catherine herself was not responsible for much building in Moscow. The plan for a vast new palace inside the Kremlin by the talented Russian architect V.I. Bazhenov was never carried out – which is perhaps just as well since much of the medieval Kremlin would have been destroyed to make way for it. But many magnates built sumptuous palaces, of which today the Pashkov Palace (part of the Lenin Public Library in Moscow) is perhaps the most outstanding.

All these buildings needed to be furnished and decorated, and Catherine's reign saw an enormous development of the decorative arts, mirrors, furniture, bronzes, china, tapestries and wall-hangings of brocade, and so on. Catherine herself imported china and had a dinner service specially designed for her by Josiah Wedgwood in 1774, the so-called 'frog service' of over 900 pieces, each with a medallion of a frog on it, made for a palace with the appropriate name of Kekereksinsky. Here again, the English model was popular and frequently copied. In 1774 the Englishman Francis Gardner established his own porcelain factory in Russia, and designed dinner services for the Russian orders of knighthood, St Andrew and St George.

In one field perhaps more than any other was English influence overwhelming, and that was in the laying out of gardens. The formal French style was completely abandoned by Catherine in favour of the lawns, trees and vistas of English taste. For many years her principal gardener was John Bush, who had owned a nursery in Hackney, and who was succeeded in 1795 by his son Joseph. It is some indication of the social status at court of these distinguished landscape gardeners that Baroness Dimsdale noted in the journal she kept of her visit to Russia in 1781: 'I was much entertained one day with dining at Mr Bushes to meet Prince Potemkin and his two neices. . . . Sir James Harris [the British Ambassador] the Imperial and the Portugal Ministers . . . were of the Party, a most excellent Dinner we had in the English Taste. . . .' Bush, in common with other distinguished gardeners, was responsible for the maintenance of the enormous glasshouses in which Russians grew peaches, nectarines and grapes and above all oranges and lemons, in spite of the climate.

The Empress also patronized painting and sculpture. She bought up foreign collections when they came on the market, including the collection which had once belonged to Sir Robert Walpole, and laid the foundations of the collection now displayed in the Hermitage Museum in the Winter Palace in St Petersburg. She was also responsible for one of the landmarks of the capital, namely the great statue of Peter the Great, the bronze horseman of Pushkin's poem. A French sculptor, Falconet, was recommended to her, and worked on it for a number of years. The huge granite pedestal was brought from Finland, and finally in 1781 the statue was unveiled with its austere dedication: 'To Peter I from Catherine II'. The demand for portraits and busts of the Empress, her courtiers and her military leaders provided work for an increasing number of foreign and Russian sculptors and painters – many of the Russians of serf origin.

Russia remained herself in the way of life, the social habits, the food, the clothing of the people. But in Catherine's reign visitors to Russia found much in upper-class life that was familar to them from other European capitals. The same fashions prevailed, the same topics were discussed, the same books were read, the same plays and operas were performed, though the setting was unique. The gulf which had separated Russia from western Europe at the beginning of the eighteenth century was being rapidly bridged.

CHAPTER 9

Catherine's Educational Policy

That society could be improved by means of education was one of the central tenets of the enlightenment. Catherine II was no exception in attaching great importance to education, which in Russia was faced with a number of specific difficulties. In the first place the Orthodox Church had never regarded it as part of its duties to educate lay people, and it had confined itself to the education of monks and to some extent of priests. There were no great Russian religious teaching orders like the Benedictines, the Jesuits, the Augustinians, or the Catholic teaching orders for women. Nor were there any great schools, originally royal or Church foundations, like Eton and Winchester. Nor was there any university in the seventeenth century. Education spread at that time from the Ukraine, finally annexed by Russia with the city of Kiev in 1667. The first Greek and Slavonic Academy had been founded in Kiev in 1632, when Kiev still formed part of Poland, partly in order to train Orthodox monks and priests to enable them to defend their standpoint in theological debates with Catholics. Its basic educational principles, modelled on those of the Jesuit grammar schools, were taken over in the first Muscovite Slavonic–Latin–Greek Academy, which was founded in 1687 in Moscow. At the same time, as a consequence of the religious schism associated with Patriarch Nikon, there was a revival of interest in the study of classical languages and efforts began to be made to educate members of the elite for the posts they were eventually to fill. In comparison with other countries however there was very little private initiative, and on the whole at this time very little state initiative.

The state stepped in when Peter the Great realized Russia's need for experts in the technology of the period, both military and civil, and founded a number of specialist and elementary schools designed to train up his new cadres. Not all his experiments were successful or long lasting, but the groundwork was laid on which others could build. In 1755 the University of Moscow was founded, a totally secular institution in which there was no theological faculty and where lectures were given in Latin or German since most of the teachers were non-Russians. By the middle of the century there was a considerable interest in contemporary educational theorists (Comenius, Montaigne, Locke, Fénelon, Rousseau, La Chalotais), some of whose works had been translated into Russian, and most of whose works could be read in French by educated Russians. There was of course no one single 'enlightenment' theory of education; the most extreme, that of Rousseau, was the one least suited to form the base of a state education system, since it depended on a ratio of one teacher to one child. But at the beginning of her reign Catherine was more concerned with individual schools than with a system of education.

Interest in education was joined in Catherine and her main collaborator in this field, Ivan I. Betskoy, with the conviction of the desirability of increasing the membership of the third estate, that is to say not only merchants and traders, but lawyers, doctors, architects, apothecaries and so on, and with the 'populationist' theories which linked the strength and prosperity of a state with the number of its inhabitants. The first manifestation of this policy in the educational field was the publication in 1764 of a work drafted by Betskoy, setting out the general principles of education which Catherine proposed to adopt, entitled *General Plan for the Education of Young People of Both Sexes*. The object aimed at was the creation of 'a new kind of people'. This could only be achieved by isolating children from all corrupting home influences from the age of five, and by new methods of teaching. Betskoy opposed a narrow, specialized, vocational education (for women as well) and favoured a general curriculum, taught by arousing the child's interest rather than by forcing him to learn by heart. The mind, the heart and the body were all to be educated, and above all pupils were to be imbued with a high moral sense of duty to society and to their fellow men.

The first concrete application of these principles was tried in the Foundling Homes which Catherine and Betskoy set up in Moscow in 1764 and in St Petersburg in 1770. Attached to the Homes were lying-in hospitals to which destitute women were admitted with no questions asked. The Homes were authorized to accept abandoned and illegitimate children; indeed Betskoy even offered payment to those who brought in babies, in the hope that he could bring them up to form his 'new kind of men', morally enlightened and dutiful citizens, skilled in a variety of important crafts, who would fulfil their roles in society in the place to which God had called them. All children graduating from the Homes, whatever their social origins, were to be free (unless it could be proved that a serf child had been falsely entered – and in such cases Betskoy fought hard to keep his foundlings). Unfortunately for Betskoy, his Foundling Homes suffered from the same disastrous mortality which overtook such homes in other countries. They were not equipped to take in infants who – if they survived their arrival – had to be sent away to peasant wet-nurses or foster mothers in the countryside. However, later descriptions by travellers of many different nationalities show that the Homes surmounted some of their initial difficulties and that the children – of both sexes – were healthy and happy, and to this extent grew up to provide an infinitesimal increase in the Russian third estate.

The next major departure in the educational field in Russia was the establishment of an institution to create the new Russian woman. Modelled in general on the school of St Cyr founded by Madame de Maintenon in France, a boarding school for noble girls was set up in the Smol'nyy Convent and attached to it was a school for girls of the lower orders. Here, too, girls were entered at a very early age, and kept for twelve years, protected from the ignorance and brutality of family life. The same educational principles were applied as in the Foundling Homes, though there were differences between the curricula taught to noble and non-noble girls. The boarding school for noble girls survived until the October Revolution of 1917, though the teaching imparted changed with the changing fashions in education. In the Foundling Homes and in the Smol'nyy Institute, schools directly under Betskoy's control, corporal punishment was strictly forbidden, and even the servants were not to be subjected to corporal punishment so that the children should not be brutalized by the spectacle of pain being inflicted on other human beings.

The Foundling Homes were charitable foundations which lived on private donations and on a number of special financial privileges such as running a savings bank and a pawnshop, or the monopoly of the sale of playing cards, as well as their own workshops and enterprises. Though under the overall patronage of the Empress, they were autonomous institutions, and did not come under any government department. Similarly the Smol'nyy Institute was funded directly by the Empress, who paid for the education of many poor noble and non-noble girls, as did Betskoy. Catherine's intention was to educate not 'prudes or coquettes, but pleasant and capable women, able to bring up their own children and manage a household'. At the same time she wished them to be women of the world, with a knowledge of etiquette, polite behaviour and languages.

Private boarding schools, specialist schools (such as the merchants' school in Moscow) and a few major educational establishments such as the schools attached to the Academy of Sciences and to Moscow University, and the gymnasium in Kazan', provided educational opportunities in the 1760s and early 1770s. Once the war with Turkey was over, and Catherine embarked on her reorganization of provincial government, education again came to the forefront, though there was not as yet any systematic national policy. But the Statute of 1775 charged the boards of social welfare with establishing schools in the towns of each province, to be financed out of the interest on the sum of 15,000 rubles granted to each board for welfare purposes. The Statute also laid down that the proceeds of fines levied for a number of offences should be paid to the schools. There was no provision for village schools.

The general encouragement given to education led to further private and public developments. The most notable private foundations were the two schools of St Alexander and St Catherine founded in St Petersburg on the initiative of a group of freemasons, of whom N.I. Novikov was one, which were to be free to poor children in the capital and were to be subsidized by private gifts and by the profits which Novikov expected to make from the sale of a new periodical he had started to edit, *Morning Light*. The schools were extremely successful in collecting gifts from the charitable, including the imperial family, to such an extent that in the event the schools subsidized the periodical, rather than the other way round.

Energetic governors in other provinces achieved good results. Jacob Sievers, Catherine's adviser when preparing the Statute of 1775, who had been appointed governor-general of the two new provinces of Novgorod and Tver', succeeded in setting up schools in all the eleven towns of Tver' province by 1779. Even if the schools did not have their own buildings, and were housed in rooms in government offices, some children were now being taught reading, writing, arithmetic and the catechism. In Pskov the nobles had provided money for a school, but not enough for a building. Catherine, who visited the area in 1780, supplied money for the school and for a seminary, an orphanage and an almshouse. In accordance with the principles laid down by Betskoy in 1764, corporal punishment was forbidden in all these schools. However, there was as yet no general educational policy for the Empire as a whole. Too much depended on individual initiative. A rich merchant or a wealthy state peasant might here and there found a school; most notable was the initiative of the Moscow merchant, Larin, who put up 50,000 rubles to found a school in the court peasant village which was his birthplace – a school also generously supported by Catherine. But otherwise the townsmen in the tiny, shabby overgrown villages which counted as towns in Russia were often uninterested in education beyond the reading, writing and arithmetic necessary for elementary business operations.

Catherine's own views on education are nowhere more clearly expounded than in the instruction she prepared in 1784 for Count N.I. Saltykov, the newly appointed governor of her grandchildren Alexander, then seven years old, and Constantine, five. It is a long document of some thirty pages, which cannot be summarized here. But some of the Empress's ideas are worthy of note because of their basic common sense, their understanding of children and their humaneness. She dwelt more on the moral education of her grandchildren, and the development of virtue and good qualities, than on the acquisition of knowledge. Good health was essential and here Catherine's ideas were very modern: early to bed in rooms kept at a moderate temperature; no feather beds, no night caps; the bedrooms were to be aired twice a day. The children were to bathe their feet in cold water to avoid colds and corns, to wash regularly and to go to the Russian steam baths at least once in four or five weeks. In summer they should bathe in cold water and learn to swim.

The children were to be encouraged to play, and to 'learn while playing', for 'children's play is not play but their most useful occupation'. Food was to be simple and plain; snacks between meals should consist of bread only. Breakfast in summer could be fruit of all kinds. Corporal punishment was of course forbidden, and punishment should consist above all in making the child feel ashamed of his misdeeds. Rebukes should be delivered in private, while praise should be given in public. Catherine goes into less detail over the content of the learning to be imparted to the children, but it is interesting to note that the textbooks for the study of Russian civil law included her Instruction to the Legislative Commission of 1767, and the Statute of Local Administration of 1775 (presumably the charters of 1785 were added later). The children were to be taught the Russian language in order to speak and write their native language properly (though this did not stop Alexander I from using French for most of his life), and Russian was to be the language of teaching. They were to be brought up to be courteous to their elders and betters, and to servants.

We do not know exactly what led Catherine to take up the problem of education on a nationwide scale in 1782. It may have been information about the policies carried on in Prussia, Poland and above all Austria, about which she had heard directly from the Emperor Joseph II when he visited Russia in 1780. She may have been dissatisfied with the lack of response from Russian society to the opportunities offered by the Statute of 1775. She may have realized that a national school system could be introduced in Russia only by the state. She may have paid more attention than has generally been assumed to the advice of Diderot: 'It is necessary to set up in each large town one single school; or if it is necessary to have several schools they should all be formed on the same plan.' And since the schools were intended to form good citizens, all parents should be compelled by law to send their children there, added Diderot. But his ideas were not always so much in harmony with modern thought: he argued that gymnastics, singing, dancing, music and the theatre should be banned in all state schools. In the event, Catherine sought the advice of a leading mathematician at the Academy of Sciences who had once been the tutor of the Grand Duke Paul (and was the expert in cracking foreign cyphers), F.U.T. Aepinus, who came down strongly in favour of the Austrian system, which had been introduced in 1774 after the expulsion of the Jesuits. The Austrian system, based on that of the Augustinian Abbot Felbiger, who had worked for Frederick II in Silesia, comprised three levels of schools: normal schools, high schools and elementary schools. New methods were used, such as teaching all children in a class the same thing at the same time, using techniques to train the memory, and the question-and-answer system to maintain the children's interest in the subject taught. In addition the new theories stressed learning by play, a relaxed relationship between teacher and taught instead of the more usual adversarial attitude, and the elimination of corporal punishment.

Impressed by Aepinus's recommendations, Catherine set up a Commission on National Education in 1782, and asked Joseph II to send her a specialist in the Felbiger method who would be Orthodox by religion and speak a Slavonic language. He sent her F. Jankovič of

Mirievo, an Orthodox Serbian, who became her principal adviser on educational policy. Everything had to be started from scratch. There were no teachers, so the first thing was to set up a teacher-training institute, which recruited students from the religious seminaries in order to teach them the subjects which they were going to have to teach in the schools. There were no textbooks, so Jankovič set about writing them himself, translating them or commissioning them from competent Russian specialists. Buildings had to be selected and prepared, and the status of teachers in a status-oriented society established. All this was done at full speed by the Commission on National Education, which was chaired by Catherine's ex-lover, P.V. Zavadovsky.

The Statute of National Schools was finally issued in August 1786, and the Commission became the Main Administration of Schools. Under this title it continued until the reign of Alexander I, when it became the nucleus of the new Ministry of Education, with Zavadovsky as the first Minister. It provided for the establishment of a high school in each provincial capital and a primary school in each district town. The education was to be modern and broad. The language of tuition was Russian (though it appears that Tartar and Turkic languages were used where relevant). The curriculum included useful subjects such as mathematics, natural sciences, history, geography, classical languages in the south, Turkic or Chinese in areas bordering on Central Asia or China. Though religion was taught, priests played no part in the teaching. The schools were co-educational, and children of all classes were admitted, though the children of serfs could only attend with the permission of their landowners. Attendance was free, but not compulsory. The boards of social welfare were to provide grants of 2,500 rubles per annum for the high schools and 500 rubles for the primary schools. Teachers were given a place in the Table of Ranks which enabled a high-school teacher to claim hereditary nobility after serving for twenty-two years. (This was how Lenin's father rose to be a noble.) The salary of 200–250 rubles a year was the same as that of a captain in the army.

Among the numerous teaching aids provided was a *Guide to Teachers*, based on a textbook prepared for the Austrian educational reform, which was the first teaching manual to be published in Russian and set out the way to conduct a class composed of several children instead of dealing only with individual children. It explained the system to be used for memorizing information, and the question-and-answer method. The teacher was also instructed on how to behave to childen: he must realize that the task of instructing children to become useful members of society was also carried out by personal example. He must therefore be dignified, just, patient, caring and impartial. He must watch his own behaviour in order to be sure that he did not give a bad example. Similarly, a special textbook was prepared to provide the fundamental moral base of the education dispensed in the primary and secondary schools. This was the work entitled *The Duties of Man and Citizen*. It was an adaptation of a work originally written for use in Prussia and the Habsburg Empire. It urged children to obey the ruler, to respect their parents, to live a clean and healthy life, to be content with their situation in life. These principles were supported with quotations from the New, and particularly the Old Testament, but the flavour of the work is almost entirely secular (Jesus Christ is not mentioned once) and its discussion of the nature of the different kinds of government – monarchy or republic – under which people lived, remarkably liberal. The book went through eleven editions and was finally banned in 1819 both for its political content and for its lack of religious content. However, in thirty years it had undoubtedly been widely influential in schools.

The effort which went into this educational reform was considerable. In the course of fourteen years, between 1784 and 1798, over 400 new teachers were trained; by the end of the century, there were 315 schools, with 790 teachers, and nearly 20,000 pupils of whom some 2,000 were girls. The publication of textbooks was controlled by the Commission on National Schools, which contracted with individual publishers: some forty-four textbooks were produced between 1784 and 1800, at an overall cost to the state of 12,000 rubles a year. The print runs for these books, which had a captive market, were also very much larger than the usual 600 for publications for the general market. The primer produced by Jankovic had a print run of over 100,000.

The 'Universalnormalschulmeisterin' (universal normal schoolmistress) as Grimm called Catherine was not content to leave the schools which had existed before she introduced the national schools to continue in their old way. She turned her attention to the two Cadet Corps, which trained officers for the army and the navy, to the other specialized schools such as the engineering and artillery schools, to the merchant schools, to the various schools which had sprung up after the Statute of 1775, such as St Alexander and St Catherine in St Petersburg, founded by Novikov and his masonic friends, and the boarding houses or *pansiony* (from the French word *pension*), of which there were by the 1780s some eighteen in St Petersburg alone, to the German Lutheran School in St Petersburg, to the Smol'nyy Institute for girls. The curricula were modernized and the teaching rendered more efficient in the specialized schools. The quality of the education and the premises was given a thorough overhaul in all the primary and secondary schools for Russian children (which were in any case now placed under the supervision of the boards of social welfare). The schools were made to adopt the curriculum and teaching methods outlined in the Statute of 1786. Russia had really become the country where one knew at any time of day what subject the children were studying in all schools throughout the land.

The foreign-language schools were allowed a little more latitude, but they were made to use the textbooks approved by the National Commission and their teachers had to be examined for competence. German remained the language of tuition in the Baltic provinces, though Russian was now added to the curriculum. No new *pansion* or boarding school could be opened without the permission of the boards of social welfare.

The introduction of the reform into the Ukraine caused different problems. In the eighteenth century the general standard of education had been higher in the Ukraine than in the rest of Russia. There were many parish schools, and the clergy were on the whole better educated. There were Ukrainian grammar schools where Latin was taught, on the basis of a Jesuit manual, and many Poles came to study at the Kievan Academy. Many of the best recruits to the teacher-training course in St Petersburg were drawn from the Kievan Academy. The Khar'kov Collegium, originally founded as a seminary, but open throughout the century to secular study, numbered as many as 700 students at a time. It was against this background that the new educational programme, more modern in that it gave less space to the old concept of the 'humanities', but more 'Russian', was introduced into the Ukraine, more or less at the same time as the new institutions of local administration of the Statute of 1775.

The Statute of National Schools gives the impression of a well-thought-out programme, steadfastly applied over a number of years. But what happened on the ground? This is where the historian is faced with the problem of the lack of evidence of what the schools were actually like in real life. Numbers were small, particularly in the high schools, where parents often took away their children as soon as they were qualified to work as clerks. The lack of trained personnel in Russia affected not only government service but teaching as well. In small towns which had been unable to produce enough educated people to staff the institutions of local government, the attitude of local communities to the schools was often negative, and since the local boards of social welfare, composed of both appointed and elected members, were responsible for their administration, under the overall supervision of the governors, they were likely to show little enthusiasm for what seemed to them sheer waste of money. Of the twelve district towns in the province of Smolensk three at least had barely any literate merchants, let alone peasants. The boards did not have enough money for all the welfare work they were supposed to do, and school premises were often unsuitable. It is also very unlikely that the injunction against the use of corporal punishment was observed in an age and in a society where brutal punishment was commonly inflicted by the state, by landowners, by parents and by husbands. S.T. Aksakov's description of his first visit to the national school at Ufa in the late 1790s illustrates the arbitrary use of corporal punishment only too well. Drunkenness was reported to be the besetting sin of the new teachers.

On the other hand senior officials attempted at first at any rate to arouse support for education by organizing graduation ceremonies and publicizing school achievements. Zavadovsky, the chairman of the Commission, twice attended graduating ceremonies in Chernigov, and the English parson, John Parkinson, who was bear-leading a young English noble around Russia in 1790 describes the ceremony in Astrakhan as follows:

> We were present this morning at the public examination of the young persons who are educated in the schools of Astracan. I was surprised to see four girls in the first class. The Governor and a great crowd of people attended. . . . They are about two hundred in number and divided into four classes, of which the first said their catechism, the second was examined in Arithmetic and Grammar, the third in Geography and ancient history, and the fourth in Geometry, Fractions, Algebra and Fortification. To those who were raised to a higher class the Governor distributed the proper books. . . . This examination takes place twice a year and not only in the capital but wherever schools are established. The Masters dined afterwards at the Governor's.

In April 1793 the national school in Yekaterinoslav was solemnly opened in the presence of the Governor-General, V.V. Kakhovskoy. The party of senior officials inspected the 'school library, the architectural plans, the globes, the maps, and the drawings and models for the teaching of natural history. At the same time the director registered the children who had been presented to be educated, who on this occasion numbered 25.'

Nineteenth-century historians were very critical of Catherine's educational programme for a number of different and sometimes contradictory reasons. Conservative historians condemned its secular tone, the fact the nowhere in the Statute was the Church mentioned and that priests were not even allowed to teach the catechism. Liberal historians condemned it on the grounds that by concentrating everything in the hands of the state, and imposing her own philosophy of education, Catherine signified her determination to prevent social forces from showing any independent initiative. She has also been criticized in more recent times for failing to introduce compulsory education as Frederick II did (though there is some doubt as to how effective the compulsion actually was), and for failing to extend education to the peasantry.

The first charge must be regarded as proven. Catherine would probably in any case have kept the priesthood out of the schools, but there was all the more reason to do so in Russia because of the low level of education and the low social status of the parish priest. The other charges are more complex. It must be said that until the promulgation of the Statute of 1775, and more particularly the Statute on National Schools of 1786, Russian society had done very little to introduce education in the towns. Some of the richer nobles set up schools for some of their serfs on their estates (there were many on estates belonging to the Empress). But the nobility had on the whole very little incentive to set up schools in the capitals, since most nobles of any family were educated in the special schools such as the Cadet Corps, or privately. It was the poor provincial nobles who needed help, and they were not in a position to show much initiative until active governors came to their rescue in the years after 1775. The merchant class was also indifferent to general education; as far as was necessary their own children were taught by parish priests, or in unregistered schools run by officers' widows or retired sergeants. The real point at issue in this criticism is that Catherine took over the few existing private schools and forced them into the state mould in 1786, including the two schools, St Alexander and St Catherine founded by Novikov and his masonic friends in St Petersburg. This, together with an instruction in 1785 to examine whatever schools Novikov might have set up in Moscow where he was then living and working, is regarded as a deliberate persecution by the Empress of 'private initiative' manifested by a social group whose ideas were alien to her, in whom she sensed an underlying criticism and whose activities she therefore wished to curtail.

It is therefore necessary to discuss briefly the exact nature of Catherine's relations with Novikov at this time. He had left St Petersburg in 1779, when his masonic friends procured for him a ten-year lease of Moscow University Press. This enabled him to embark on a considerable publishing programme, of a general and educational kind. At the same time Novikov was drawn into a particular branch of freemasonry, namely Rosicrucianism, with strongly mystical and alchemical overtones (see pp. 197–200). Rosicrucian masonry was propagated in Moscow by a certain I.G. Schwartz, with whom Novikov set up a special group of students at the University under the name of the Friendly Learning Society, from whom he drew the translators and authors he needed for the publications of his press. A close Rosicrucian friend, I.V. Lopukhin, set up a secret press which Novikov was able to use for masonic works, and Novikov himself set up a Typographical Company which he could use in addition to the Moscow University Press. Novikov operated on a very large scale by contemporary standards, and disposed of hundreds of thousands of rubles as a result.

Yet it was not Novikov's masonic activities which attracted Catherine's attention in 1784, but the fact that he had published two of the books specially prepared for the Commission on National Schools, which owned the copyright. A number of other publishers who had also transgressed against the Commission's very lucrative monopoly of the textbooks suffered too and their stocks as well as those of Novikov were confiscated (though Novikov was subsequently compensated for his loss). There was therefore no specific attack on Novikov himself. But in December 1785 Catherine also heard that Novikov was publishing masonic and devotional books, and she ordered the Governor and the Archbishop of Moscow to inquire into Novikov's publications and into his beliefs. Novikov's beliefs proved quite sound, but not so his books. The Archbishop was particularly critical of the large number of works representative of modern enlightened thought, and drew up a list of twenty-three books which he thought might undermine religious belief. Of these

Catherine banned only six, all of which were masonic in content. All the others were released. Thus her judgment proved less restrictive than that of the Archbishop, and she was concerned to ban only what she regarded as nonsensical 'lucubrations', likely to deceive ignorant people.

Perhaps not entirely convinced of the innocence of Novikov's dealings, Catherine, probably in connection with the school reform programme, asked the Moscow Chief of Police in 1786 to investigate a report of the existence of a hospital and schools allegedly set up by the Moscow masons. The Chief of Police reported that there were no such schools, and there was no hospital. There was therefore no question of closing them down in order to bring Novikov's educational initiatives to an end, as has frequently been asserted by historians, who have taken Catherine's request for information as evidence that these institutions existed. But a year later, in 1787, Catherine's attention was again drawn to the number of books of a religious character which Novikov was publishing, this time in breach of the monopoly of the press of the Holy Synod. Catherine then issued an order in July 1787 forbidding the publication of religious works except by the Holy Synod and the Commission on National Schools (which printed the catechism for schools), and she ordered a list to be made of all such books which had been published in Moscow by Novikov and in several other presses in St Petersburg and the provinces. Of these, 313 titles were listed for Moscow alone, and a year later Catherine ordered that 299 of these should be returned to their publishers, and fourteen should be banned. The fourteen books were banned because they were either masonic (some had been banned before) or because they were offensive to the Christian religion. In future, Catherine decreed, all religious works should be submitted before publication to the Synod.

To sum up, there is no evidence of any educational activity by Novikov in Moscow in these years which might have aroused Catherine's suspicions, and insofar as books were banned it was not because they were by Voltaire, but because they were by alchemists like Paracelsus.

Finally something must be said on the question of Catherine's failure to introduce compulsory education, and to extend it to the villages. This criticism seems to be based on a failure to grasp what sort of means Catherine disposed of in order to enforce a policy. In the small Russian towns compulsion might have been theoretically possible, yet not advisable where the willing co-operation of the inhabitants is needed for the smooth functioning of so much of the administration. As for the villages, here the problems were of a different kind. Leaving aside the political impossibility of intruding between the landowners and the serfs, even on state peasant or court peasant villages it would have been very difficult to introduce schools since distances were sometimes so great that the children would have had to leave home, travel to a larger village and live there throughout the winter months when schools would be open. Parents would be deprived of the labour of their children and would have to pay for their keep. Moreover, there were barely enough teachers to staff the high schools and the primary schools. There can be no comparison here with Prussia or Austria, countries which disposed of trained teachers in the religious orders, and of moderately well-educated Catholic and Lutheran parish priests.

In the long run, the new schools do seem to have served the people they were intended for. They were free, and they were open to all social groups, which again is a rather striking departure from the usual pattern of strict division into nobles, non-nobles and peasants of Russian society. The largest single group of the children enrolled, in 1801, were nobles (33 per cent); townspeople made up 26 per cent, soldiers' children 11 per cent, serfs and household serfs 11 per cent, other peasants 5.5 per cent, clerks and people of no status 8 per cent, and priests' children 2 per cent (4 per cent others).

Nothing was done in Catherine's reign to establish new universities. It was often indeed difficult to persuade enough students to attend Moscow University. But the Empress subsidized large numbers of students who were sent to study in Germany, Holland, France (mainly in Protestant Strasbourg), England and Scotland.

The total number of children attending state educational institutions in Russia at the end of the eighteenth century was still very small, between 60,000 and 70,000. Nineteenth-century historians were often very critical of the slowness with which Catherine's educational programme was put into effect. In the twentieth century, when so many Third World countries with backward economies have found how difficult it is to eradicate illiteracy, it is possible to be more appreciative of what was achieved in a bare fifteen years. Catherine laid the foundations on which Alexander I was later able to build.

CHAPTER 10

Catherine's Social Policy

Catherine was neither a liberal nor a democrat, and certainly not an egalitarian. She believed in the kind of social structure that existed nearly everywhere in Europe throughout her reign, according to which each individual person belonged in law to a specific social group or 'estate' and enjoyed the rights and performed the duties attached to that estate. However, Old Regime society before the French Revolution was much more mobile than this description of people each bound to a particular status suggests.

There were three ways in which a man might rise in Russia: courage, skill and luck. Soldiers, even sometimes of serf origin, could be promoted to non-commissioned rank on the battlefield, and very rarely to the rank of officer, though not usually above the lowest commissioned rank. Clerks in government offices, writers, poets, playwrights, architects and physicians could be promoted by the grant of a rank in the Table of Ranks to personal nobility, or even to hereditary nobility, which enabled them to buy an estate with serfs. G.N. Teplov, for instance, whose father was a stoker, became a high government official and a hereditary noble under the Empress Elizabeth, a privy councillor and senator under Catherine II. The scientist, poet, historian and grammarian, M.V. Lomonosov, the son of a prosperous state peasant from Archangel, who became a leading member of the Academy of Sciences and one of the founders of Moscow University, was classed as a runaway peasant in 1748, and by 1753 had been raised to the hereditary nobility and granted an estate of 211 serfs. Gavriil Dobrynin was the son of a priest and rose in the bureaucracy; he records in his diary with tremendous satisfaction the day he finally reached the rank which gave hime hereditary nobility. There are cases of peasant traders like Savva Yakovlev, who made a fortune out of contracts for the government and became a noble; non-noble entrepreneurs in Siberia, owners of mines or foundries, rose to the nobility. Catherine herself favoured ennobling very rich merchants. She viewed them as 'fish too big for the pond they were swimming in' if they remained in the merchantry. When the Academy of Arts was founded in 1764, the professors of painting, sculpture and architecture were established at rank 8, which gave them hereditary nobility, two notches higher than professors in the Academy of Sciences. Foreign medical doctors, like Dr Rogerson, who was Catherine's personal physician, were regarded in Russia as nobles, while Dr Dimsdale, who had inoculated the Empress against smallpox in 1768, was made a baron of the Russian Empire. It was sheer good luck which led to the ennoblement of the young peasant lad chosen to provide the matter for Catherine's inoculation.

The concept of class in use today is very misleading when applied to Old Regime society. In modern political science it is used either in the Marxist sense to describe relations of production: thus the owners of labour are called working class, and are regarded as exploited by the bourgeoisie, who are owners of capital. Or the concept of class is used in a wider sense to express different income and cultural levels and styles of life (upper class, middle class, lower-middle class and so on). In the eighteenth century people initially belonged by law to the class they were born into, however rich or poor they might be. Thus in Russia there were princes descended from the original medieval rulers of Russia who were as poor as church mice. In Novgorod, during Catherine's reign there were nobles who ploughed their own land, owned no serfs and indeed did not have the clothes necessary to present themselves for government service. There were nobles who owned no land at all. Yet in law all of them were entitled to the same privileges as the wealthiest and highest-ranking nobles.

These privileges were not merely social. They included access to specific educational establishments such as the Cadet Corps for officers, or the Smol'nyy Institute for the Education of Noble Girls. Nobles were often enrolled as children in the Guards Regiments, so as not to have to serve in the ranks when they grew up; after the regulation number of years they were promoted and emerged as officers – a system not unlike that operated by Scottish sea-captains in the British navy, who enrolled their relatives as midshipmen and enabled them to achieve more rapid promotion to the coveted rank of first lieutenant. There were in addition certain jobs specifically reserved for nobles, in local government and the central bureaucracy. These privileges were of particular importance to the growing number of poor or landless hereditary nobles who occupied the lower levels of the Table of Ranks or to those who were promoted only to personal nobility from non-noble backgrounds (ninth to fourteenth ranks).

Yet if the law was more important than wealth in the formal organization of the Russian social hierarchy, in Russia, as elsewhere, money did matter. A rich noble was more likely to rise in the Table of Ranks, to acquire a good education, to secure well-paid jobs, to attract notice at court, to marry into a rich and well-connected family, than a poor noble. A rich noble would be treated with greater consideration by officials, whom he was in a better position to bribe. Thus though all nobles were equal in law, they were not equal in society, where wealth could to some extent modify even the rigid hierarchy which the Table of Ranks imposed and ease the life of the unprivileged. But in Russia rank and title, privilege and social prestige could not in general be bought. There was nothing similar to the purchase of office which existed in France and Spain (and even in England), which made the post of judge in a law court in France, for instance, a piece of private property, to be handed on from father to son. In theory, in Russia everyone began at the bottom of the Table of Ranks; in practice the rich and well-born started higher up. Thus 'legal class' was ultimately more important than 'economic class' at this time, though money helped. In modern terminology, there was more than one economic class in a legal class, and more than one legal class in an economic class. The existence of this order of society was taken for granted and assumed to be the strongest foundation for social stability.

Catherine did not tinker with this pyramid. But in her efforts to modernize Russian administration and to draw upon the social classes to co-operate in the reforms outlined in the Statute of Local Administration in 1775, she attempted to organize and give corporate form to the various social estates and to codify the laws setting out their rights and duties. She was faced with the problem of noble rights at her accession, for one of the very few measures passed by Peter III which had won him popularity was the Manifesto on the Freedom of the Nobility from Service which he had issued in February 1762 (see Chapter 2).

Catherine had at first caused some apprehension among the nobles because she did not at once confirm Peter III's Manifesto. Instead, in 1763, she set up a Commission to examine the whole question, and then shelved its report. However, she issued orders to the Senate to act upon the Manifesto, so that nobles were no longer in fact compelled to serve and after the end of the Seven Years War many nobles left the armed forces and returned to their estates, where for the first time in the history of the Russian nobility they could live the lives of gentlemen of leisure.

The first stage in Catherine's organization of the noble estate occurred in connection with the elections to the Legislative Commission in 1767. She had ordered the nobles in each district to meet in an assembly and elect a 'marshal of the nobility' to organize the election of a deputy to the Legislative Commission. The marshal continued in office for three years, when a new marshal was elected. Thus by the time Catherine issued the Statute of 1775, the idea of a marshal of the nobility and of a local assembly had already taken root, even if their functions were still very vague. The Statute of 1775 did however give them specific duties, such as arranging for the election of officials to take part in the new local government institutions, the law courts and the welfare bodies which it set up.

The coping stone of Catherine's programme of giving corporate status to the social estates was the twin charters issued to the nobles and to the towns respectively in 1785. A great deal of work went into these laws, which therefore had taken some years to prepare. Both documents set out the personal civil rights of the members of the corresponding estates, as well as a very limited range of corporate political rights belonging to the estate as a whole. But the Charter to the Towns also introduced an elaborate system of urban self-government, which complemented and amplified the Statute of 1775, and regulations for the urban craft guilds.

The Charter to the Nobility confirmed a number of personal civil rights which the nobles had enjoyed in practice since the middle of the century but which had never been spelled out in one single law before. They could not be deprived of their lives, their rank in the Table of Ranks, their 'estate' (that is to say their quality of nobility), their property or their honour without trial, and they must be tried by their equals or peers (that is to say, other nobles). Trial of nobles by their peers had of course always existed in Russia since all judges were in fact nobles; but the new law courts set up by the Statute of 1775 enabled nobles to elect 'assessors' to the courts, who would ensure that the nobles were treated fairly. In addition the Charter laid down that nobles could not be subjected to corporal punishment. The nobles' freedom from the poll-tax and the obligation to billet soldiers was restated. Freedom from compulsory service in the armed forces or the bureaucracy was confirmed, as well as the right to travel abroad and to enter foreign service. The Charter also confirmed a number of property rights, such as the right of nobles to establish manufactures on their estates and to the free exploitation of the forests and the subsoil on their lands (such as mines and quarries). Their right to 'buy villages', that is to say to own and acquire serfs, was also confirmed. The implication of this particular clause was to grant to the nobles the *exclusive* right to own serfs, though this is not spelled out, and in fact non-nobles continued to own, and at times even to acquire, serf labour for industry. But the nobles' power over the serfs was not altered in any way, contrary to what is often stated. Moreover the nobles' property rights over their serf villages still suffered from two restrictions in law: nobles were responsible to the state for the payment of the poll-tax by their serfs, and they were also legally bound to look after those who were unable to work and not to allow them to wander around the countryside begging.

The nobles were also granted certain corporate rights, that is to say rights granted to the noble estate as a whole, or to the noble assemblies set up not only in districts as previously, but in the provinces as well, where they elected a provincial marshal of the nobility. All the nobles registered as belonging to a particular province, because they owned an estate there, had the right to attend the provincial assembly but only nobles who had reached the rank of officers (the fourteenth) in service could vote or be elected, and nobles with an income of less than 100 rubles per annum from their villages could not be elected. These qualifications underlined again the importance of service and fortune in the life of a noble. A noble who had never served in the army or the bureaucracy could play no part in the corporate self-government of the noble estate, nor could young men who had not yet inherited a share of the ancestral property. The most significant 'political' right granted to the nobility was the right to 'make representations', that is to address petitions about local needs and grievances directly to the Empress in person, without going through any intermediate channels.

One of the principal functions of the provincial noble assembly as a corporate body was to keep the register of the nobility in the province. This was a new departure in Russia. Previously the records of the nobles had been kept in the Herald Master's Office, a department of the Senate, in the capital, so that nobles could be posted to serve in a regiment or an office when they grew up. After the abolition of compulsory service in 1762, the Herald Master's Office continued to keep the service records of nobles so as to show who was still available, who had resigned and retired from service, who wanted to return to service. It was often quite difficult to determine whether a man who claimed to be a noble was actually entitled to that status, and the records of the Herald Master's Office illustrate the lengthy process of collecting evidence about ancestry, economic status, landownership, way of life and so on of claimants.

Until 1785 the Russian nobility had all been regarded as equal in law if not in public esteem, where precedence was based on rank in the Table of Ranks. Now, alongside the hierarchy established by the Table of Ranks, new distinctions were introduced, for the Charter divided the nobility into six different groups, according to whether they were titled, very ancient, foreign, had received patents of nobility directly from Catherine or other rulers or had merely been promoted as members of the armed forces, or as civilians, in the Table of Ranks. While remaining a service caste, the nobility now more closely resembled the west European nobility, for a record based on birth, as well as service, was required in order to achieve recognition of nobility.

In the Baltic provinces of the Russian Empire the register of nobles or *matricula* had always been kept by the local *Landtag* or Assembly of the Nobility, and it was this noble corporation which decided who was a genuine noble and who was not, and not a bureaucratic body like the Herald Master's Office. The same system was extended by the Charter throughout the Russian Empire, and the provincial noble assemblies were kept very busy in the 1780s sorting out the claims to nobility which flooded in upon them. Some of these claims were very dubious, particularly those arising in parts of the Russian Empire with different social traditions like the Ukraine or the parts of Poland annexed in the partitions. Many of these claims were not finally decided until the reign of Nicholas I (1825–55).

Very little is known about the way the noble assemblies actually functioned. They certainly met regularly to elect local officials, and there is evidence that, at any rate in the earlier years, quite high-ranking nobles were elected to the post of marshal of the nobility or accepted service in the local administrative institutions. The assemblies also played a useful part during the Napoleonic wars as centres for the mobilization of the defence against the French. But they do not seem to have made use of their right to petition the Empress directly, and as political institutions they seem to have been a complete failure. It is difficult to tell whether this arose as a result of apathy among the nobles or pressure from the government.

The 'layered' structure of the towns, divided between the merchantry, the townsmen and the unregistered dwellers, was to some extent modified by Catherine when she issued the regulations for the elections to the Legislative Commission in 1767. All town-dwellers who owned house property in the town were entitled to vote, regardless of the social group they belonged to, and to elect in the first place a 'town chief', (*gorodskoy golova*) parallel to the marshal of the nobility. The merchantry had petitioned in the past to be granted certain rights which would recognize their personal dignity and worth, and they voiced these demands in the sessions of the Legislative Commission which discussed draft statements of their rights. Their demands included immunity from corporal punishment, which had come to be regarded not only as painful but as degrading; replacement of the poll-tax by some other form of tax, since the poll-tax too, as a personal tax levied on all non-noble Russians, was regarded as degrading; and the right to wear swords, which was the external sign of belonging to a 'gently born' social class. There is nothing surprising in these social aspirations. In sixteenth-century England, Shakespeare, the son of a dealer in wool, procured a coat of arms to attest that he was a gentleman, and at the other end of Europe, in the 1760s in the Spain of Charles III, the newly elected municipal councillors promptly demanded the right to wear wigs and swords.

Catherine developed her policy towards the urban estate further in the Manifesto of 17 March 1775, issued on the occasion of the end of the war with the Ottoman Empire and of the repression of the Pugachev Revolt. The manifesto included a number of articles which redefined the structure of the town population and met some of the merchantry's demands. The new structure was obviously intended to bring the law closer to the reality and to prepare the townspeople to participate in the new institutions of local government which were already being worked out. The criteria Catherine adopted in defining the various classes in a town were purely financial. The status of merchant or *kupets* was now to be granted only to merchants possessing a capital of more than 500 rubles. The merchantry was divided into three guilds according to whether merchants possessed a capital of 500 to 1,000, 1,000 to 10,000 or above 10,000 rubles. The result of this was a drastic overhaul of the merchantry, for of a total of some 222,000 registered merchants throughout the country only

27,000 turned out to possess (or admitted to possessing) more than 500 rubles. The remainder, who were mainly petty tradesmen, craftsmen or even workers on the land, dropped into the class of townspeople or *meshchane*, but if they made money they could rise again into the legal category of the merchants. The gulf between the two groups was further stressed by two additional privileges granted to the merchantry. They were no longer to pay the poll-tax, which was replaced by a tax of 1 per cent on their declared capital, and they were allowed to buy themselves out of the recruit levy or conscription into the armed forces by making a payment instead. The replacement of the poll-tax by a tax on capital was the first breach in the collective responsibility of the town-dwellers for the payment of taxes levied on the community as a whole. It opened the way to individual enterprise. The merchantry's demand to be allowed to wear swords was however rejected by the Empress.

The Charter to the Towns issued in 1785 completed the organization of the urban estate. It listed the personal civil rights and the 'political' rights of the merchantry and the townspeople in almost the same terms as the Charter to the Nobles. Town-dwellers, like the nobles, were divided into six categories but they did not all enjoy the same rights. The first group comprised townspeople who owned houses or land in the town; the second comprised members of the three merchant guilds divided afresh according to their wealth (capital from 1,000 to 5,000 rubles, from 5,000 to 10,000, and from 10,000 to 50,000); the third group comprised registered craftsmen, the fourth foreigners, the fifth a new category of 'distinguished citizens' such as university graduates, artists, architects, painters, musicians, bankers, wholesalers, industrialists, capitalists and shipowners. This category included the top layer of those who belonged to a social group known in Russian by the word *raznochintsy*, or people who did not belong in one of the existing legal categories of nobles, townspeople or peasants. A sixth category swept up all those who did not fit into any of the other five.

As in the case of the nobles, town-dwellers in all six groups could not now be deprived of their status, property, life or reputation without a trial by their peers, that is to say by other merchants or town-dwellers; provision for trial by their peers had been made, as in the case of the nobles, in the Statute of 1775, which set up the urban courts and allowed town-dwellers to elect their own assessors to assist the judge in reaching a decision. In addition merchants belonging to the guilds could still buy themselves out of the recruit levy, and could not be conscripted as previously to perform services for the state (such as tax-collecting); members of the two first guilds and the 'distinguished citizens' were freed from corporal punishment, paid a tax on their capital instead of the poll-tax, and in the third generation could petition to be raised to the nobility. The corporate rights of the urban estate also paralleled those of the nobles; they could meet in an assembly which included *all* the registered citizens to elect a town chief and officials, who must own capital sufficient to provide an income of fifty rubles (that is about 1,000) and be over twenty-five years old. But whereas the noble assembly could address petitions to the Empress in person, the town assembly must address itself to her through the governor of the province. It should be stressed that both in the case of the nobles and in the case of the townspeople the charters represent the first legal enactments of their personal and property rights. Until this date, these rights had never been fully formulated. In this respect they are landmarks in Russian social history. Catherine herself considered that in these charters she had enacted many of the reforms which had been proposed in the meetings of the Legislative Commission.

The Charter to the Towns also set up a complicated system of town government: a town council or duma composed of representatives of the six registered groups was elected every three years by the town assembly. The town duma elected an executive council of six, the six-member duma (one member for each group) whose duty it was to superintend the activities of the urban community in the field of trade, public order and decency, food supply and so on, under the overall direction of the town chief. Finally the Charter to the Towns included detailed regulations for the organization of the craft guilds.

Little is known about how town government, as described above, actually worked in Russia except in relation to the city of Moscow and to a few towns in the province of St Petersburg, neither of which are of course typical of the country as a whole. But in many instances the towns did not have enough citizens who could be fitted into the six categories laid down in the Charter. The towns were too small or too isolated to have rich merchants, or foreigners, or large-scale capitalists; often they did not even have literate merchants, so that the elective posts in the town administration, the law courts and the police simply could not be filled, nor could the six-councillor duma, the real administrative centre, be properly set up with representatives of all six groups. The Charter failed to set out the functions and the powers of the urban institutions clearly enough, and they were usually unable to stand up against encroachments by governors or police officials. Nevertheless, judging by the few detailed studies which have been made, some town dumas were very active, met regularly and dealt with food supply, shops, building regulations, the issuing of passports and a whole lot of questions which were not their concern at all, such as granting permissions to marry. The records of these urban institutions have not been studied extensively enough to enable one to pass a final judgment on their work, let alone the extent of their independence from the nobles or the government.

Catherine was the first ruler of Russia to conceive of the state peasants as a specific social group and to grant them specific rights, as state peasants, in the various bodies set up in 1775. Peasant law courts were established for them, to which they elected assessors, and they elected their own assessors to the conscience courts, to the boards of social welfare and to some other bodies. We have no evidence unfortunately of how these elected peasant bodies worked nor do we know the extent to which peasants elected peasants rather than nobles or educated people with no rank, to act on their behalf. However, oddly enough, the shortage of educated nobles and merchants worked in favour of the peasants. By 1779, Catherine had already authorized the recruitment of sons of priests and of merchants, and of graduates of Moscow University to fill posts in the administration, and state peasants were also recruited, particularly in eastern and north-eastern Russia and Siberia, where there were few nobles. But they were not given a rank in the Table of Ranks.

It is typical of Catherine's somewhat abstract and theoretical approach to administrative reform that she also drafted a plan for the reorganization of the estate of the state peasants. It set up a peasant 'society', parallel to the noble assembly and the town society; village-dwellers were divided into six different groups to correspond to the six groups of nobles and townspeople, and the group of very wealthy rural dwellers was declared in this draft to be free from corporal punishment. Villagers could not be deprived of life, status or property without trial by their peers, that is to say by peasants. Again, as in the case of the nobles and the townspeople, this requirement had been met by the peasant courts set up by the Statute of 1775. This draft Charter for the Free Rural Dwellers was never put into effect, possibly because of the outbreak of the second Turkish war in 1787, possibly because its provisions were unsuited to peasant society, possibly because Catherine was dissuaded by noble opposition from continuing with it. Some of its provisions were carried out in the province of Yekaterinoslav by Prince G.A. Potemkin, but no record of any discussion about this project has ever been published.

The failure of the Emperor Nicholas I to reform or abolish serfdom in the nineteenth century, in spite of the many secret committees he set up to investigate the problem, has been explained by the tales he had been told of the horrors of the Pugachev Revolt. How much more must Catherine have been affected, who had lived through it and was personally acquainted with some of the people murdered by Pugachev's followers. The revolt persuaded Catherine that it was too dangerous to Russian social stability to attempt any major reform of the system of serfdom, or to control relations between masters and serfs by further legislation. The cruelties inflicted by both sides had hardened the lines. Any decrease in the authority of the noble over his peasants might lead to a further terrifying outburst.

As a result Catherine only tinkered with the problem, and this has led the greatest historian of the eighteenth-century peasantry, V.I. Semevsky, to remark that in her reign serfdom increased both in depth and in extent, a remark which has been repeated uncritically ever since, without any fresh examination of the evidence. Yet some of Catherine's efforts to improve the lot of the enserfed peasantry should be noted. The Statute of 1775, for instance, enabled governors of provinces to sequester and appoint guardians to estates where the landowner was reputed to be ill-treating his serfs or ruining the estate, and landowners could be prosecuted for cruelty. Some twenty such prosecutions are known to have taken place in Catherine's reign but there were probably more. For instance, in 1779, the estates of a minor poet, F. Dmitriyev Mamonov, a distant connection of Denis Fonvizin's mother, and of Catherine's later favourite A.D. Dmitriyev Mamonov, were sequestered and handed over to trustees to administer, because of reports of the owner's ill-treatment of his serfs. This incident is reflected in Fonvizin's well-known play, *The Minor*. The English prison reformer, John Howard, who died in Russia in 1791, saw a noble who had been sent to prison in Moscow for whipping his serfs to death. (There was no death penalty for murder in Russia.) In some cases of ill-treatment of serfs which were brought to her notice Catherine quietly arranged for the owners to be bought out.

In other ways Catherine intervened to reduce the number of people entitled to own serfs and the total number of enserfed peasants. The blanket provision in the Manifesto of 17 March 1775 that no serf who had ever been freed could be enserfed again was one of several laws passed during her reign which limited enserfment. The process of enserfment had often been very casual in the past, and it was now stopped. Non-noble industrialists were forbidden to buy serfs for industry in 1762, and the practice of 'assigning' villages of peasants to industrial enterprises also ceased (see Chapters 2 and 5). At different periods laws were passed by Catherine prohibiting the enserfment of orphans by their foster-parents and of non-Christian prisoners of war. Similarly all foundlings taken to the Foundling Homes in Moscow and St Petersburg emerged as free people and were helped to find work. There were a number of cases in which serfs had managed to enrol in the institutions of higher education like the Academy of Arts, without the permission of their owners, who then tried to get them back. These cases were nearly always decided in favour of the serfs.

Finally it is often stated that Catherine II 'enserfed' thousands of otherwise free state peasants by handing them over as gifts or rewards to her favourites or officials, and that she did so in order to conciliate the nobles and make them accept her rule. In the ten years from 1762 to 1772 grants ranging from 200 to 2,000 male serfs, up to a total of 66,125 serfs, had been made to a number of individuals. The sources from which these grants were made were studied more than a hundred years ago, and it is clear that Russian state peasants were not given away. Catherine drew upon the court peasants; upon estates in the Baltic provinces where the peasants were already serfs; on the Chancery of Confiscated Lands, an official body which administered estates confiscated from private owners for political reasons in previous reigns, or which came into government hands as a result of court decisions for bankruptcy or lack of heirs; on lands attached to Cossack regiments in the Ukraine; and she sometimes bought estates in order to make grants.

After the first partition of Poland in 1772 many estates became available which had belonged to the Polish Crown, to Polish Catholic monasteries or to the Catholic Church, or to individual Poles who had refused to take the oath of allegiance to Catherine and had remained in Poland. Between 1772 and 1796 a further 318,000 male peasants were distributed as rewards, most of which came from previously Polish territories. The largest number of individual grants was made in the year 1795 when the third and final partition of Poland had been completed (see Chapter 13). The timing of these grants, the fact that so many were made in what was to prove the last year of Catherine's reign, suggests that the Empress was not driven by the necessity of shoring up her power by buying off potential noble opposition. Indeed at the very beginning of her reign Catherine was severely criticized by some of the nobles for her reluctance to make grants from lands belonging to the state peasantry, but she refused to give in to their pressure. It is a fact that the estates which were taken over from the Church in 1764 remained in the hands of the state. At one time before 1772 there was an absolute shortage of estates considered suitable to be granted as rewards, and the estate of 9,000 serfs granted to Count Nikita Panin in 1773 was bought for him.

However, in judging this policy of granting estates to Russian and Baltic nobles, two further considerations must be borne in mind. It was traditional in the eighteenth century everywhere to reward distinguished service by military or naval leaders with gifts or pensions payable by the Crown on one or more lives. One has only to think of the princely rewards received by the Duke of Marlborough and the Duke of Wellington, and the pension awarded to Lord Nelson, or the enormous expenditure on pensions of the French court. In Russia, an estate took the place of a pension, and an estate without peasants attached to it had little value for the poorer and middling nobles who could not transfer serfs from an existing estate to unpopulated lands. Between 1682 and 1710 Peter the Great had made grants of over 170,000 serfs and many more were given away before his death in 1725. His successors followed the same policy.

Secondly, Catherine's many grants of estates in Poland had a political purpose. The Statute of Local Administration of 1775 was introduced at once in the ex-Polish lands, and it was in Catherine's interest to replace Polish landowners with Russian landowners in order to strengthen Russian control and to balance the remaining Polish landowners with a strong contingent of Russian landowners in the elective institutions which the Statute provided for. Catherine's policy is summed up by Princess Dashkova (who benefited from it) in her memoirs: '[The Empress] had made it a rule never again to give away any Crown lands but desired me to find a suitable piece of land for which she would pay the price.' Eventually Catherine granted the Princess 2,500 peasants in Belorussia because she 'had not restricted her freedom of action in respect of Crown lands in Belorussia, that on the contrary she wanted them to belong to and be administered by Russian gentry . . .'.

CHAPTER 11

How Catherine Governed

Unlike the Empress Elizabeth Petrovna, Catherine was a working ruler. She devoted a great deal of time to reading and drafting papers, and to discussions with her officials and chosen advisers. Her papers show that consultation was genuine; she asked for advice and it was freely given and discussed in a friendly atmosphere. She had set the style of her relationship with her senior officials from the beginning in a letter she wrote to Prince A.A. Vyazemsky, when she appointed him Procurator-General in 1764: 'I am very fond of the truth, and you may tell me the truth fearlessly and argue with me without any danger if it leads to good results in business.'

Once Catherine had found public servants she trusted she kept them in office for years. Vyazemsky worked for her from 1764 to 1792, when he retired because of ill-health; Count Nikita Panin was in charge of foreign affairs from 1763 to 1781, when, after Catherine changed from a Prussian to an Austrian alliance, A.A. Bezborodko, who had been in her service since 1776, took over and remained until her death in charge of foreign policy. S.I. Sheshkovsky, the head of Peter III's Secret Chancery in the Senate, was taken over in 1762 and remained until 1792; Count Alexander Vorontsov was president of the College of Commerce from 1773 until 1793, and there were many others who remained in their posts as long as they wished or until they were promoted. A very few were dismissed, but no one was ever disgraced or exiled, or suffered from the arbitrary confiscation of property common in previous reigns. Government service had now become a safe occupation instead of a highly dangerous one as before. High officials were normally well paid and well rewarded with pensions, grants of land and serfs, orders and titles. The title of count or baron was freely granted, though the title of prince, which in Russia implied hereditary descent from a princely ruling family, such as the first ruler of Russia, Ryurik, or Gedimin, Grand Duke of

Lithuania, or Tartar tsars, could not be granted. Thus for favourites whom Catherine wished to elevate to that rank she procured titles of Prince of the Holy Roman Empire from the Holy Roman Emperor Joseph II.

The vast size of Russia and the difficulties of transport and communication rendered its administration slow and cumbersome. Officials faced problems of much greater complexity than those which confronted Prussian or Austrian officials. It could take eighteen months for an imperial order to reach distant Kamchatka, and another eighteen months for the reply to be received in the capital. In the circumstances it was very difficult to keep a close check on the activities of military or civilian officials, particularly as the number of people employed in the administration was very small in relation to the size of the country and of the population.

The Senate, which was the highest government institution, was charged with co-ordinating the administration, that is to say the work of the various colleges and of the governors and governors-general of the provinces. At the same time the Senate acted as the supreme court of appeal in civil and criminal cases. This role was considerably increased with the reform of 1775, since appeals against the verdicts of criminal or civil chambers throughout the provinces now came before the Senate. The Senate had a total staff of 193 people after the reorganization which Catherine decreed in 1764, which increased to 274 by the end of her reign. The Senate also had its own printing press, which was supposed to cover its costs.

Though the Senate had existed since 1711, Catherine had frequent occasion to be dissatisfied with the way it conducted its business. Russians educated in the first half of the eighteenth century were not accustomed to the discipline needed for the efficient performance of administrative duties. As early as 3 August 1763, Catherine wrote to the Senate complaining that the senators had failed to carry out oral and written edicts and she attached a list of 148 of her personal orders which had not been fulfilled. She ordered the senators to attend their office not only from 8.30 a.m. to 12.30, but also three times a week in the afternoons until the backlog had been cleared up. As late as 1792, Catherine was still rebuking the Senate for its delays, and she deprived one of the departments of the Senate of its holidays in 1794 because of the accumulation of undecided cases. Similarly, when preparing her administrative reforms at the beginning of her reign Catherine found that the Senators did not know how many towns there were in Russia and had no proper maps, a deficiency which she set about remedying. (Excellent maps were in fact produced throughout her reign and were one of the hallmarks of her administration.)

In 1768, on the outbreak of the Turkish war, Catherine set up a small Council of State, composed of her closest advisers and officials, who were also her personal friends, to co-ordinate the military effort, define the Russian war aims and lay down the general lines of foreign policy. The Council was a completely *ad hoc* body which only discussed whatever matters Catherine, who frequently attended its meetings, put before it. It was not concerned with the general administration of the country, and none of Catherine's great domestic reforms were discussed with the Council as a council, though its members could well be consulted privately. But it was consulted on major issues such as how to deal with the Pugachev Revolt, or the financial crisis of the late 1780s and 1790s, and of course the second Turkish war (though not the partitions of Poland until very late in the day). Some of the members of this informal Council were presidents of colleges, some were appointed as reliable advisers. It continued in being until the end of Catherine's reign, though the membership naturally changed as a result of the retirement or death of its members.

The colleges set up by Peter I to deal with internal matters had reflected his overwhelming concern with the economic development of Russia. He had established a College of Mining, a College of Manufactures and a College of Commerce as well as a College of Justice to deal with appeals, and an Estate College which held the records of landed estates. There were also three financial colleges or chambers, the College of Revenue, which dealt with income, the College of Expenditures, and the College of Audit. There was also a central college for the urban estate as a whole, the Glavnyy Magistrat or Main Council, which combined administrative and judicial duties. Disputes between local town councils, or appeals from decisions taken by town law courts in cases involving members of the urban estate, would be sent to the Glavnyy Magistrat for decision.

However, as a result of the decentralization of government which Catherine had introduced with the local government reform of 1775, some of the colleges began to seem superfluous. Catherine and the Procurator-General, Prince A.A. Vyazemsky, therefore put through a major reorganization of the central government administration in the 1780s which further increased the Procurator-General's power, since the Senate, of which he was the principal official, inherited most of the remaining central functions of the colleges which were abolished. With his own network of agents throughout the country, responsible directly to him, the Procurator-General was moreover in a very strong position. He could be supplied with better information and could advise more effectively on policy than the heads of colleges.

The establishment of the new network of law courts from which appeal lay to the Senate led to the abolition of the College of Justice, and to the gradual phasing out of the urban Main Council, which disappeared by 1782. The College of Manufactures was abolished in 1779 and the College of Mining, which had supervised prospecting on state and privately owned land and had regulated conditions in state-owned mines, was abolished now that landowners had been given absolute property rights in the subsoil of their estates by a law of 1782. The central colleges dealing with the collection and expenditure of revenue were also abolished (see Chapter 14). The old College of Estates was also abolished because lawsuits over property and over boundaries would now be dealt with by the local courts; there was no longer any need to refer every case to St Petersburg, and only appeals from the decisions of the highest provincial courts would be heard by the Senate. As a result of the reform the Procurator-General became in fact the Minister of the Interior, the Minister of Finance and the Minister of Justice. Unlike Catherine's reform of the local administration, which proved lasting, her reform of the central government was considered by her son Paul I to have gone too far, and some of the central colleges were restored in his reign.

A new department was also set up under Vyazemsky in the Senate to oversee one of the most important, yet undramatic, policies put into effect by Catherine. This was the General Land Survey. A periodic land survey had been necessary in pre-Petrine times because the state allotted estates with serfs in exchange for military or civilian service, and had therefore to know how much land and labour it could dispose of and to control the disposal of lands which fell in as the result of the death of the land-user. Once Peter I had introduced salaries for officers and officials in 1714 instead of the grant of estates, the whole mechanism of the land survey fell into disuse, with the result that in many parts of Russia neither the state nor private individuals had any idea of the boundaries of their lands, and the areas attached to towns and villages were not delimited. Landowners of course took advantage of the situation to encroach on to vacant state lands or neighbouring state peasant villages, and peasants too were involved in frequently violent disputes over boundaries.

The government had become aware of the problem already in the reign of Elizabeth, but the survey projected at that time was too complex and advanced too slowly. Catherine in 1765 simplified the planned survey, which was now to delimit state land, and lands attached to specific towns and villages. The actual ownership of lands within villages and settlements, and the boundaries of private estates, were to be decided on the evidence by agreement between the owners and at their expense. Landowners who had encroached on state lands were to be allowed to buy what they wanted to keep at the going rate.

The Office of the Land Survey formed part of the Senate, and surveyors were eventually attached to the new Treasury Chambers of local administration in each province. The survey in fact took a long time to complete; it was still being carried on in the reign of Nicholas I. But it served several useful purposes. It reduced the illegality and violence in the countryside, since disputes over land could now be dealt with before a local law court, and it allowed large quantities of unused land to come into cultivation. To some extent it satisfied noble acquisitiveness by enabling nobles to acquire legal title to lands they were already using.

Anyone studying Catherine's statecraft will be struck by her passion for uniformity. Once she had devised the new social and administrative institutions for the Russian part of the Empire, it was not long before she decided that the Statute of 1775 and the two charters of 1785 should be introduced in the non-Russian areas 'living under their own laws' of the Empire as well. This formula applied specifically to the two Baltic provinces of Livonia and Estonia, on whose administrative and legal practice she had to a great extent drawn for the reform in Russia, and to the small strip of land between Russia and Swedish Finland, known as Russian Finland; and also to that part of Left-Bank Ukraine known as Little Russia (as distinct from Slobodska Ukraine, which had formed part of Russia since it was first settled in the seventeenth century).

In Livonia and Estonia, the mainly German nobles had preserved the ancient social structure. All nobles were entitled to attend a *Landtag* or noble assembly, which elected a number of councillors and those who manned the various law courts; the towns had similar well-preserved privileges. In many respects the rights and privileges of nobles in Livonia were more extensive than in Russia but Catherine was convinced that the best way to integrate these provinces into the Empire was to introduce uniform institutions. She also believed that her own laws, which were, as she put it, based on her Instruction of 1767, were far superior to and more humane than the Livonian and Estonian laws, which were based on 'Justinian's Code', that is on Roman law, which admitted torture and the death penalty.

At the end of 1782 the Governor-General of the two Baltic provinces, a picturesque Irishman called George Browne, first appointed in 1762 and who remained in office until his death in 1793 at the age of ninety-four, was ordered to divide up the provinces into 'districts' on the Russian model of 1775; on 3 May 1783 the Russian poll-tax was introduced, thus completely altering the basis of taxation which had previously prevailed and which was based on land. At the same time the landowners were given a privilege they had long been clamouring for: the distinction between land held on a feudal tenure and land held in outright property was abolished, so that the German barons became absolute owners of all their lands.

The next stage was the introduction of the two charters into the Baltic provinces. Here, too, Catherine's policy met with considerable resistance among the German barons, but it was supported by a group of non-noble landowners who, as landowners, would be accepted as nobles according to the Russian Charter to the Nobility. By August 1786 the social and political institutions of Livonia and Estonia had been totally remodelled in accordance with Catherine's new policy. The traditional *Landtag* of the nobles, and the high courts of the cities which the Baltic barons and the citizens had preserved against the Swedes and Peter the Great, crumbled before Catherine's onslaught.

The Empress showed a similar determination with regard to Little Russia. This area of the Ukraine had formed part of the Russian state only since 1654, but it had kept much of its freer organization. Though serfdom as such existed, the Little Russian peasants had preserved a degree of freedom of movement until 1760, when peasants had to obtain the landowners' permission before they moved from one estate to another. But they did not pay the poll-tax, and the Ukraine contributed nothing to the imperial Treasury.

The first sign that Little Russia was to be integrated into the Russian Empire was its division into three provinces in 1782; Kiev, Chernigov and Novgorod Seversk, which were made into separate provinces of the Empire and ceased to be united to each other in any particular way. This was followed by the introduction of the poll-tax in May 1783. This is usually described as the extension of serfdom to the Ukraine. It was rather a change in the nature of the serfdom which already existed. What it implied was complete loss of mobility, since the poll-tax payer had to be registered to a given locality in which he paid the tax. This was followed by the restructuring of the Little Russian towns, which lost all the remnants of the urban rights they had maintained under Polish suzerainty, and the elimination of all the Ukrainian or Cossack titles and ranks of legal and administrative offices which had been in use and their replacement by the titles and ranks in the Statute of 1775. Noble assemblies were promptly set up in accordance with the Charter of 1785, and they were kept extremely busy deciding who was a noble, since in Little Russia many Cossack officers or officials claimed to be noble on somewhat tenuous grounds.

On the whole, Cossack officers and Little Russian nobles benefited from the integration with Russia since many of them were granted official Russian military titles which implied hereditary nobility in the Empire, and they could also be elected to the posts reserved for nobles in local administration. But the peasantry and the run-of-the-mill Cossacks lamented the final loss of their previous freedom, the much prized right to move, even if the landowners' permission had to be secured. Some of the nobles too were angered at the loss of the elements of legal and administrative autonomy which Little Russia had succeeded in preserving until then, and expressed their feelings in clandestine verse and nationalist historical writing. The birth of the modern Ukrainian nationalist movement can be dated from Catherine's ruthless crushing of Ukrainian aspirations to autonomy in the eighteenth century.

With the assimilation of the Baltic provinces and Little Russia into the centralized Russian administration under the Senate, two more colleges could be dispensed with: the Little Russian College and the College of Livonian, Estonian and Finnish Affairs.

The Procurator-General and his network of procurators were also entrusted with an important role in the implementation of Catherine's attempt to reduce, if possible to eliminate completely, the use of torture in Russian civil and military criminal procedure, and particularly in the Secret Chancery, which investigated accusations of treason and sedition (see p. 10). The staff of the Secret Chancery was surprisingly small by today's standards, and in the 1730s its annual budget was less than 5,000 rubles. One of the most popular actions of Peter III in his brief reign was the abolition of the Secret Chancery and the whole procedure of 'Word and business of the lord' in 1762, and the transfer of the security service to a secret department within the Senate, which was kept on by Catherine and eventually placed under the Procurator-General.

On her accession Catherine issued secret instructions ordering local authorities not to use torture where the accused had already confessed to a crime, and in any case only after reference to the local governor. She also included a strong denunciation of torture in her Instruction of 1767, but she did not dare to abolish it publicly and at once, since public opinion as expressed in many of the sessions of the Legislative Commission was clearly in favour of maintaining it. 'But I ask you', wrote Catherine, commenting on one well-known political trial in the reign of the Empress Anna, 'how can any sensible person believe in what has been said under torture and rely on it with a good conscience?' Thus, in November 1767, she issued a further edict, ordering the authorities to follow the policy laid down in Chapter 10 of her Instruction, in cases where the existing law allowed torture. Chapter 10 of the Instruction is a very detailed analysis of the proper procedure to be followed for arrest, trial and conviction, and includes the statement: '*that the Innocent ought not to be tortured*; and in the Eye of the Law, every Person is innocent whose crime is not yet *proved*' (art. 194). Evidently it proved difficult to interpret the law of November 1767 since a whole volume of correspondence about its application has survived. Nevertheless Catherine held her own and repeated it in November 1774, extending it to military courts in 1782. Judging by her private letters and the constant pressure she exercised behind the scenes in this field, this was no hypocritical pretence on her part, and torture was certainly not used on the accused in any of the major political trials of her reign.

The suggestion that torture was used in the Secret Department of the Senate has often been made by historians, but little evidence – mainly gossip – has been brought forward to support it. However, whether Catherine was really successful in eliminating the brutal treatment of the accused remains doubtful. There is some evidence that General A.I. Bibikov, when he was investigating prisoners taken during the Pugachev Revolt, deliberately concealed his methods from the Empress. In general, the greater the distance from the capital, the more likely were cruelty and brutality to survive, and the higher the social status of the accused the less likely was torture to be used.

By the mid-1780s Catherine had completed a major reorganization of the central government, local administration and the social structure of the Russian Empire. But she continued to turn over in her mind further plans for the reform of what might be called Russia's constitutional structure. Among the notes which she took while she was reading William Blackstone's *Commentaries on the Laws of England* are drafts for a body to be called a High Court of Justice (see pp. 207–8).

In general Catherine's outlook was characterized by a total lack of religious (or political) fanaticism, and by belief in the use of the very minimum amount of force or coercion to achieve her ends. She never issued a general edict of religious toleration, but her approach was realistic. 'We need to make our huge deserts swarm with people,' she wrote while still Grand Duchess. 'To succeed in this I don't think it would be advisable to force our peoples who are not Christian to embrace our religion; a plurality of wives serves population better.' Thus her reign saw the gradual dismantling of the whole apparatus of religious persecution which had existed in Russia, as elsewhere (even in Great Britain), in the eighteenth century. As late as 1738 a Jew had been burnt alive on religious grounds in St Petersburg for converting a non-Jew (who was also executed). However, in lawless and distant Kamchatka a witch seems to have been burnt alive as late as the 1780s. (One must remember that women were still being burnt alive in Great Britain for the murder of their husbands in the eighteenth century.)

The Old Believers were the first to benefit from the new religious climate. Peter III had already introduced some measures designed to alleviate their position. Catherine, always concerned to increase the population of Russia, had confirmed his decrees which enabled fugitive Old Believers to return to Russia, and guaranteed them against persecution. Potemkin, who was well disposed towards the Old Believers, helped also to lighten their burdens, and as a result the double poll-tax they paid was lifted in 1782, and in 1785 their right to elect and to be elected to posts in urban administration was established. After the decree of 1783 authorizing the setting up of printing presses, the Old Believers, who until then had indulged in clandestine printing, mainly in Poland, set up an authorized printing press in the village of Klintsy in the province of Starodub to produce their own liturgical texts. An effort was made to conciliate the priested Old Believers, those who accepted the services of priests consecrated by Orthodox bishops, by setting up within the Orthodox Church a movement entitled *edinoveriye* or united faith, which would allow the Old Believers to keep their own Old Ritual while accepting the authority of Orthodox bishops. The experiment was successful only on a local scale and for a short time, and the problem, which involved delicate negotiations with the hierarchy of the Orthodox Church, was not solved in Catherine's reign.

If Catherine was tolerant, she nevertheless kept a strict control over the non-Orthodox religious communities, whether Christian or not. The forcible conversion of the Moslem Tartars and Turkic tribes ceased to be official policy – though it was not always possible to control what individual ecclesiastical authorities did in distant and understaffed provinces – and a special regime for the administration of the Moslem peoples of the Russian Empire was established in 1788–9. A Moslem Spiritual Assembly was set up, charged with the spiritual welfare of all Moslems, and the oversight of mosques and schools for Moslem children. School books were published in both Russian and Tartar, which was recognized as the official language of the Moslems. The Spiritual Assembly dealt with matters of faith, marriage and divorce, but otherwise Moslem lawsuits came before the ordinary Russian state courts. Senior Moslem officials were given noble status and allowed to own land and Moslem, but not Christian serfs. In general terms the settlement of the Moslem religious question in the eighteenth century lasted until the Bolshevik Revolution of 1917.

Catherine's approach to the Jews was similar, yet took account of their specific characteristics. They were not after all nomadic in background as were some of the Moslem tribes, but were mainly engaged in urban and rural commerce and in rural administration. The problem of how to govern large numbers of Jews only arose after the first partition of Poland in 1772 which brought under Russian control areas of territory with some 40,000 Jewish inhabitants mainly in Belorussia. Until then Jews had not been officially allowed to settle in Russia, though there were some small settlements in the Ukraine. The next major increase in the Jewish population came only in 1793 with the second and in 1795 with the third partitions of Poland, which raised the Jewish population of Russia to some 400,000.

Approaching the subject in the light of enlightened thought, that is to say without religious prejudice but deeply imbued with social prejudice against a totally alien culture and way of life, Catherine took over the existing decentralized Jewish organization based on the kahal, or self-governing Jewish community, which had grown up in

Poland. But, unlike in the case of the Moslems, her ultimate aim was to integrate the Jewish population into the urban estate, to make them participate fully in its duties and responsibilities, and in its privileges (regardless of the fact that many Jewish communities were rural rather than urban). Thus in the 1780s Jews were allowed to register in towns and pay town taxes as members of the urban estate, and to take part in the election of urban officials and to be elected to posts in town administration. After 1785, they also came under the official Russian judicial authorities, and not under the kahal, which was confined to matters of religion, marriage, wills and so on. In 1786 Catherine issued a formal definition of the rights of the Jewish population of the Russian Empire, giving them legal equality with other citizens of the Empire and leaving only religious matters to be decided by the kahals.

Catherine's tolerant policy towards the Jews derived not only from her lack of religious fanaticism but from her belief in the importance of developing the third estate in Russia. Her reign provided a breathing space for the Jews in the Russian Empire during which their communities achieved the highest degree of legal security and social acceptance in Russian history – in theory at any rate. For the facts did not always live up to the laws. It was difficult to ensure that the liberal provisions of the laws were actually carried out in provincial and district towns, where prejudice remained rife, particularly those laws concerning the election of Jewish members of the third estate to posts in town government, which, in some areas of Belorussia, might have led to Jewish majorities. Moreover, most of the Jews were poor and lived not in towns but in the countryside, where they were engaged not in trade but in such activities as keeping taverns, distilling, and acting as agents for landowners.

Yet, in spite of the broadly tolerant character of Catherine's legislation, one of the most repressive features of nineteenth-century Russian policy towards the Jewish community dates from her reign. This was the setting up of the so-called Pale of Settlement. In order to cut short Jewish economic competition with Moscow merchants, Catherine in 1791 issued an order restricting the areas in which Jews could settle. The territory was in fact very large, comprising eventually the lands taken from Poland in the partitions, Little Russia, the Crimea and the lands conquered from the Turks in the two Turkish wars. At the time the law was not regarded as a form of racial or religious discrimination so much as a means of directing settlement towards underpopulated lands. It was only in the nineteenth century that the Pale became restrictive as population pressure increased. Nevertheless, the legal status of Jews was never perfectly clear in Catherine's reign, partly it may be said because the laws issuing from the centre, though well intentioned, were contradictory, badly drafted and therefore difficult to interpret. Moreover, in 1794 Catherine, at a time of great financial stringency, introduced the first discrimination against Jews when they were ordered to pay taxes twice as high as those levied on the Christian population in the same areas. (The double taxation of religious minorities was of course not confined to Russia: in the reign of George I in England Roman Catholic landowners had to pay a double land tax.) Polish and Ukrainian racial as distinct from religious anti-semitism also began to extend among Russians, who for the first time came into contact with large Jewish settlements in the ex-Polish territories.

Protestantism had been officially tolerated in Russia since the days when Peter the Great invited foreigners to assist in his planned modernization of the state. The various Lutheran communities remained independent of each other, and were allowed to recruit their own clergy mainly from Germany. Catholicism too was tolerated though it was less favourably treated than Protestantism since it was not a disunited and fragmented Church but a strong political organization under one head, the Pope, and relying for proselytising activities on seasoned campaigners like the Jesuits. In 1769 Catherine laid down the regulations for the conduct of the small Catholic community in Russia. The state would not interfere in matters of dogma but it exercised the right to set up a council of administration composed of both priests and laymen to supervise Church property and the school for Catholic children.

The first partition of Poland brought a large number of Catholics into the Russian Empire. They were both Roman Catholics and Uniates, namely those Catholics who followed the Orthodox liturgy and Church organization, but accepted the supreme authority of the Pope. In the following year, 1773, the Pope was finally induced to suppress the Jesuit order, and this faced Catherine with the problem of what to do with the Jesuit establishments in ex-Polish territory, which included many educational institutions, some of great reputation. At the time of the annexation of Polish territories, Catherine had undertaken to respect the religion of the inhabitants. She intepreted this as allowing her to organize Catholic religious life, and the relations between the Catholic community and the state, as long as she did not interfere in matters of faith and dogma. Without consulting the Papacy she therefore established new Catholic and Uniate dioceses, appointed bishops and arranged for the conciliar system introduced in 1769 in Russia to be applied to Catholic Church property in ex-Polish lands. At the same time she decided that the role of the Jesuits in education was too important for them to be disbanded, and she did not therefore promulgate the papal bull dissolving the order in the Russian Empire. The Jesuits were even allowed to set up a Jesuit noviciate, which accepted new recruits, thus securing the continuity of the order. The Pope was reduced to accepting Catherine's policy on pain of further Russian encroachments on Catholic life. After the third partition of Poland had enormously increased the number of Catholics and Uniates in the Russian Empire Catherine extended to them her system of administration of religious matters, again riding roughshod over the protests of the Pope at her unilateral decisions.

When Catherine seized the throne in 1762, there were many who feared that her reign might see the development of the influence of unaccountable or unworthy favourites on the government, leading to corruption and bribery by foreign powers. Russia had been ruled by Prince A.D. Menshikov under Peter the Great's widow, Catherine I; the German Biron, raised to Duke of Courland by the Empress Anna, had left a sinister memory. The Empress Elizabeth's favourites, the Ukrainian peasant lad who became Count Aleksey Razumovsky, and I.I. Shuvalov, who helped to found the University of Moscow, had exercised a more beneficent influence, but thanks to Elizabeth's own lack of order the government had suffered from outside interference. Favouritism was not unknown in other countries, and under other names. Don Luis de Haro or the Count Duke of Olivares were the *validos* of Philip III and Philip IV of Spain respectively; Buckingham was the favourite of James I and Charles I; Cardinal Mazarin was the favourite of Anne of Austria as regent for her son, Louis XIV. Absolute rulers seemed to feel the need to delegate some of the tasks of government to trustworthy people who could also act as lightning conductors behind whom the ruler could shelter from the full impact of public criticism, people who could indeed be disgraced if it became politically necessary.

But whatever the fears of her senior officials may have been, favouritism, as a permanent feature of the political system, developed only gradually in Catherine's reign. When she came to power, her lover was the twenty-nine-year-old Guards officer, Grigory Orlov. She appointed him to a senior position in the armed forces as chief of the artillery, which was probably higher in rank than he deserved, but not outrageously offensive to more senior men. He also became a member of Catherine's Council of State in 1768.

It was natural for Catherine to appoint her next important lover, G.A. Potemkin, to high office. He had distinguished himself on the battlefield against the Turks and had reached the rank of lieutenant-general on active service in the army. By 1774 she had appointed him vice-president of the College of War (there was no president at the time), in fact the Minister of War, in charge of all the land forces of the Empire. He ceased to be Catherine's lover in 1776. His successor, P.V. Zavadovsky was also an educated man, who went on to a career in the field of education and finance. Nevertheless, from about 1778 onwards, 'favouritism' did open up channels of access to the Empress for the distribution of rewards and promotions, if not for genuine influence on policy. Otherwise only Catherine's last lover exercised real influence on public affairs. After the death of the mighty Potemkin in 1791 the young Platon Zubov, who had become Catherine's lover in 1789, gradually inherited many of the posts held by the dead man, though not that of head of the College of War. He did however become governor general of New Russia and the southern lands, and was extremely influential in foreign policy, pushing Catherine towards the final partition of Poland. More than anyone else among Catherine's favourites he came to stand for the corrupt influence which could be exercised behind the scenes on an ageing woman.

CHAPTER 12

How the People Lived

The life of the people throughout Russia was marked by startling contrasts between wealth and poverty, comfort and squalor, starvation and abundance. The climate, however, affected both rich and poor, who had to suffer the extremes of temperature, which in St Petersburg could freeze the breath, dropping to 17 degrees centigrade below zero in winter (when everyone stayed at home and all outside work ceased), and rising to stifling heat in summer.

Those who suffered least were inevitably the richest, notably the wealthy magnates who lived in the capital cities and on their country estates, and also the rich merchants. Most foreign visitors to Russia were astounded by the beauty of St Petersburg, built on the islands and on both banks of the wide Neva, linked in summer by a bridge of boats, and intersected by many canals, traversed by elegant bridges. Apart from the palaces of the imperial family, the Winter Palace and Catherine's Hermitage next door, many of the magnates had built their own often very beautiful palaces, some of which survive in disguise to this day. The Anichkov Palace is the headquarters of the Leningrad Young Pioneers, the Yusupov Palace now belongs to the Union of Workers in Education, the great Tauride Palace, which was built for Potemkin and was briefly the seat of the Russian Duma, became the Leningrad Communist Party High School. Most of the few remaining private palaces now belong to official organizations and cannot be visited, including the lovely Stroganov Palace. Almost all of the private houses of the more important courtiers, built in the neo-classical style, which lined the road from St Petersburg to Peterhof or Tsarskoye Selo, where Catherine usually spent the summer, have vanished. In Moscow, the great assembly hall of the nobility became the headquarters of the trade unions.

Catherine, who loved St Petersburg (and detested dirty, untidy and ramshackle Moscow), set up a commission soon after she came to power, charged with its systematic improvement (and that of Moscow). Little by little the canals were lined with stone embankments, manufactories were banned within the city, building lines were laid down and precautions were taken against fire – the most serious threat to Russian urban centres because of the many wooden buildings.

The magnates who lived in the great palaces had vast retinues of servants, grooms, coachmen. In winter huge braziers were lit in the streets so that servants waiting to take their masters home from the ball or the theatre should not freeze to death. People dashed around on horse-driven sledges, or carriages on runners, which circulated not only on land but on the frozen canals and rivers. In summer, there were numberless little boats with awnings, performing the function of the gondola in Venice. In accordance with the social conceptions of the time, the number of horses which could be harnessed to a carriage, and indeed the kind of carriage which could be used, was strictly laid down according to rank, ranging from six horses and a carriage for a man in the first rank of the Table of Ranks, to a one-horse coach for a merchant. Clothing was also regulated by sumptuary rules. Only the nobles could wear gold and silver brocade, velvet, gold and silver thread. Foreigners commented on the quantity of jewellery, particularly diamonds, worn by both men and women. As she grew older, Catherine liked to be comfortable, and in 1782 she introduced regulations governing the dress to be worn at court. On major festivals, gala suits or dresses in gold or silver brocade were to be worn by men and women; but for festivals of lesser importance she introduced the traditional loose Russian gown, falling from the shoulders, the *sarafan*, together with a not-too-high, traditional Russian headdress, or *kokoshnik*. The rules forcing everyone to wear 'European' dress once issued by Peter the Great had been completely abandoned; the merchants and their wives usually reverted to the traditional Russian garb when they wished, and only the nobility and the so-called *raznochintsy* (see p. 125) wore wigs and were usually clean-shaven.

Though Catherine and her senior officials maintained a constant interest in town-planning (frequent fires gave many opportunities to indulge in the reconstruction of towns), and attempting to keep them clean and orderly, one problem does not seem to have been solved. As John Parkinson commented when he paid a formal visit to the Vice-Chancellor, Count I.A. Osterman, 'in entering we were almost poisoned by the Stench of the necessary'. Privies did not seem to exist in Russian houses, not even in the palace. 'In winter, from being froze, the inconvenience is not conceived; but in Spring, particularly when it begins to thaw, the Nuisance is insufferable,' wrote Parkinson. The houses of the rich, in St Petersburg and Moscow and in the major provincial towns, and on their country estates, were elegantly – even lavishly – furnished in accordance with the taste of the time. The walls were adorned with tapestries and mirrors – very large mirrors, commented the young Irish visitor, Catherine Wilmot. The habits of the nobility are indeed very well illustrated in the diaries and letters of Martha and Catherine Wilmot, two young Irish women who stayed with Princess Dashkova, the former for five years, from 1803 to 1808. Though she arrived seven years after the death of Catherine, the Russia which Martha Wilmot saw would not have changed very much. The comments of the sisters are particularly valuable, because though they criticize the political and social system, comparing it unfavourably with that of England, they compare the state of the peasantry with that of the peasants in their native Ireland.

Some of the rich magnates were men of education and taste, who had travelled abroad, corresponded with their opposite numbers in France and England, visited Voltaire, translated Rousseau. They had well-stocked libraries, open to visitors, and kept open tables at which anyone, once introduced, was welcome to dine. Many had their own private theatres in their country estates, notably Count Sheremet'yev, the richest landowner in Russia (over 100,000 serfs), Count Alexander Vorontsov and his sister Princess Dashkova. Foreigners also commented on the great musical gifts of Russian peasants. Servants in private houses were called on for part singing and for dancing to entertain guests; peasants sang while at work, and soldiers while at ease. Many serfs played musical instruments and formed small orchestras for private balls and theatricals in their masters' houses. But most nobles serving, as officers or officials, lived much more modestly.

Nobles did not pay the poll-tax. This is frequently regarded as one of the most striking examples of privilege, but it should be seen in context. It was a social, not a financial privilege. The poll-tax amounted, during most of the century, to seventy kopeks, on peasants, and one ruble twenty on townspeople per annum. There were approximately 50,000 male nobles, who together would have contributed not much over 50,000 rubles to the Treasury had they paid the poll-tax. But one must also remember the origins of the poll-tax. When Peter I introduced it in 1721, the revenue was to be devoted entirely to the upkeep of the armed forces. There was no point therefore in asking a noble to pay a tax which was in fact at that time used to pay for his upkeep. (Soldiers did not pay the poll-tax either.) Nobles did pay other taxes: for instance, the tax on baths introduced by Peter; the duties on imported luxury goods, and the quite heavy taxes on promotion in the Table of Ranks and the granting of titles, ranging from 50 rubles for an ennoblement or a captaincy to 100 rubles for the title of count, and 500 rubles for the rank of field marshal.

After 1762, when nobles were freed from compulsory service, many landowners returned for a time or forever to live on their land. But their expenses could still be considerable for they had to pay for foreign tutors to educate their children if they were to make any kind of career, or procure a place for them (and their serf attendant) in one of the state educational institutions such as the Cadet Corps, the school attached to Moscow University, or in private boarding schools. The ordinary middling noble then entered the army (more rarely the navy), sometimes the bureaucracy, and if he were very poor even the clerical grade, at a very young age. In 1789, of 119 junior clerks employed in the bureaucracy in the province of St Petersburg, 15 were nobles by birth.

One of the reasons for the increasing impoverishment of the nobles was the system of inheritance which prevailed in Russia. In the seventeenth century, when a young man reached the age to serve, he would be granted a *pomest'ye* or estate by the Crown (hence the name *pomeshchik* – a landowner). In 1714 Peter I ceased to grant estates in service tenure, as a result of which a noble family did not automatically acquire more land as its sons grew up. On the other hand, the Russian legal tradition imposed the equal division of an inherited family estate among all the sons, leaving one-seventh as the portion for the widow. (A landowner was free to bequeath as he wished land which he had acquired himself, by purchase or imperial grant.) However, equal division did not mean that, if there were four villages, each one of four sons would receive one village; each son received one-quarter of each village, that is to say one-quarter of the serf households, one-quarter of the ploughland, one-quarter of the meadowland, one-quarter of forest land and so on. There was no possibility of consolidating an estate into a manageable size, and estates became smaller and smaller in each generation, which explains why so many nobles owned only four or five serfs. Decisions about what to plant and where, when so many people had to be consulted, took a long time to be reached and, in such cases, families often did not bother to divide the property, but ran it as one enterprise, merely dividing the income. (This may explain incidentally why it seemed natural to the land commissar that Jeremy Bentham should pay the debts of his brother Samuel – see p. 76.)

At the beginning of Catherine's reign only 1 per cent of noble heads of household (out of a total estimated 20,000 heads of household), or some two hundred great nobles, owned more than 1,000 serfs; 2 per cent, or some four hundred noble heads of household, owned between 500 and 1,000; and 51 per cent, or about 11,000 noble heads of household, owned less than twenty serfs. The average income in money dues is estimated at about two rubles per serf in the 1760s, two and a half rubles per serf in the 1770s, four rubles per serf in the 1780s and five rubles per serf in the 1790s. In the 1760s the income of over 80 per cent of households amounted to less than 300 rubles a year rising to 500 rubles in 1795. Peasants had also to make deliveries in kind. If a serf was engaged in some form of craft, or was allowed to seek work away from the estate, he might have to pay more.

In the circumstances the life of the owner of a small estate in the provinces was dull and primitive. He had few occupations, other than visiting his neighbours, lawsuits, hunting, and family and Church festivals. Provincial women were almost totally uneducated, though there were some notable exceptions. In one respect however, Russian noblewomen were better placed than their sisters in many other countries. They were entitled to own property, and did not lose control of it to their husbands on marriage. If they died childless, landed property reverted to their own families. As a result many women were capable estate managers, and some proved to be among the most ruthless and cruel to their serfs.

Most of what is known about the life of the Russian nobles comes from descriptions of how the great magnates lived, written by foreign diplomats, foreign visitors or foreigners employed about the Russian court. Very little is known about how the middling or poor nobles lived in the eighteenth century, since contemporary novels dealt mainly with romantic adventures. Only perhaps the plays of Fonvizin and the memoirs of one or two noble authors are really enlightening. But, seeing how poor most of them were, it is not surprising that most nobles served for a number of years in the army or the bureaucracy before retiring to live on their lands (sometimes with a pension) and that nearly all young nobles needed to serve in the armed forces or the civilian bureaucracy until they inherited a share of the family property. It has been argued that the costs of 'westernization', that is to say the consumption of imported luxury goods (wines, furniture and clothing, certain foodstuffs and so on) amounted in 1795 to some 225 roubles, or the income from forty-five serfs per household. To this had to be added the costs of education – up to 150 for a boarding school, 100 if the child lived at home, or at least 300 if a resident tutor was employed. Clearly the majority of the nobles simply could not afford any western luxuries, and were unaffected by the pressure to increase their income in order to satisfy new demands.

It was again the wealthy nobles, with capital to spare, who invested in manufacturing or attempted to increase the productivity of agriculture. The whole subject, however, must still be dealt with very tentatively, for there are very few, if any, studies of the exploitation of small estates or of state peasant communities. Owners of small private estates, which were divided up further in each generation, were careless about record-keeping, and as far as is known little evidence of how management problems were dealt with has survived, whereas the large estates of the magnates were serviced by an army of officials, serf or free, who maintained a regular correspondence with the owner or his agent. The codes of practice laid down by great landowners also provide much detail about the general administration and the economic operations of the estate. But generalizations about the noble way of life are not yet possible.

In the nineteenth century Russian writers began to write about life in the Russian countryside as a subject deserving attention in its own right, or as a background to novels and short stories. But in eighteenth-century Russian literature there is little reflection of the real life of the modest noble or of the peasantry. All the more striking therefore is the beautifully written, psychologically deeply perceptive and factually accurate – even if the characters are somewhat fictionalized – *Family Chronicle* by S.T. Aksakov. Born in Ufa in 1791, he gives a portrait of his grandfather based partly on his own recollection, partly on what he has been told, which illustrates all the best and the worst of serfdom. The grandfather's patriarchal attitude to his little kingdom, immense kindness of heart, simplicity and generosity, coupled with tyranny, brutality and abuse of power, is portrayed with a great understanding of the harm it does to both master and servant. As in slave societies in North and South America, the absence of any social pressure on the masters to compel them to control evil or cruel impulses allows them only too easily to degenerate into monsters. That they did not do so, as a general rule, is a tribute to their basic humanity. Yet even the best, like Aksakov's grandfather, could overstep the bounds. And what could be more revealing than the classic phrase in the play, *The Minor*, by Denis Fonvizin, pronounced by the elderly, illiterate noblewoman: 'What is the use of the nobility being free if we are not free to beat our serfs!'

In comparison with the nobles and the merchantry, the peasants were poor. They were poor not because of serfdom (after all, the state peasants were poor too), but because almost all peasants in all countries were poor. Indeed until the twentieth century peasants have been poor in a great part of Europe, and most of them remain very poor in the Third World. There were, it is true, some who made a fairly good living out of farming, such as the yeomen farmers of England or the *laboureurs* of parts of France or the wealthier peasants in Russia. But nearly everywhere peasants had to supplement the meagre earnings they obtained from the land by the use of some additional skills.

There were several reasons for the poverty of the Russian countryside. The first was of course the climate, the long winter, during which animals had to be kept indoors, and the short growing season. The second was the soil. The communal structure of the village, and the methods of cultivation which this imposed on the peasants, also hindered the modernization of agriculture. Fields and meadows were divided up into strips, which were allocated to peasant households according to the number of males in them, and cultivated collectively. (Often these peasant strips were intermingled with strips belonging to the landowner). It was thus difficult for a hardworking family with many sons to consolidate its own separate holding, though peasant families could rent more land, sometimes even from the landowner. In most villages a traditional egalitarian spirit led to the practice of redistributing the land between households every so many years, in order to ensure that all had enough land to be able to feed themselves and pay their dues to the landowner and their taxes to the state. Redistribution thus suited some at least of the peasants, the landowner and the state.

In many areas, such as in central and north-eastern Russia, agriculture was not productive enough to maintain the peasants on the land; many of them left the villages (with the permission of the landowners in the case of serfs, of the commune in the case of state peasants) to work in manufacturing or other industrial enterprises in towns or to secure jobs as drivers, porters, carriers, servants and so on. They also supplemented their earnings from agriculture by working in a well-developed cottage industry, and marketing their production in the nearest town.

It is very difficult to assess the standard of living and the degree of poverty of Russian peasants, whether serfs or state peasants, in relation to other countries at the same period, though all the evidence goes to show that they lived better in the late eighteenth century, when the balance between population and natural resources was more favourable, than in the nineteenth century. The Russian climate rendered it essential for the peasants to live in solid wooden houses, or *izbas*, with large brick or clay stoves in which they baked their bread and on which they slept. But they lived in close proximity to their animals in conditions of real squalor. Food depended very much on the area in which they lived. The average annual per-capita food consumption was high in meat (194 kg) and fish (290 kg), milk (251 lit.) and butter (29.5 kg), because in the more fertile Black Earth zones there was a productive balance between plough-land and animal husbandry, at any rate until the late 1780s. Bread at 125 kg was less important than in the west. In the poorer areas the diet was more monotonous. It was based on rye bread and other grains and pulses; Russia also produced isinglass, used for the preservation of eggs. Diet was very much affected by the Orthodox Church, which imposed very severe fasts on up to 200 days in the year which were religiously observed. On such fast days, neither meat, milk, butter nor any milk products, nor eggs nor poultry could be eaten. On ordinary days rye bread, porridges of various kinds, pulses, cabbage and cucumbers, berries and mushrooms, apples, pears, cherries, watermelons in season, meat, fish and some kinds of game, some poultry and eggs and milk products (though oddly enough not cheese, as Catherine II noted with some surprise) made up the diet in varying amounts. Russians were well acquainted with the practice of the deep freeze; noble houses had ice-cellars dug into the ground, while peasants kept game and meat in the snow. The meat market in St Petersburg was a curious sight in winter, Baroness Dimsdale was told (she was there in August), with vast stacks of 'whole Hogs, Sheep, Fish and other Animals piled up in the Market for Sale all froze'. Landowners could enforce whatever game laws they wished on their own land, but on the whole there were no restrictions, and peasants could shoot wild fowl freely, and preserve it in the snow through the winter. Count Sievers had proposed importing potatoes

11 *The village commune.*

12 *The St Petersburg frozen meat market.*

13 *The interior of a peasant hut.*

14 *The Russian bath: a practice popular with all classes of society.*

15 *Russian monks.*

16 *A carriage on sledges.*

17 *A merchant's lady in winter dress.*

from Ireland in the 1760s but as elsewhere the potato met with strong resistance among the peasants, always very conservative about their diet. However, Potemkin, with his usual enterprise, exported substantial quantities from his estate in Belorussia for sale in Kremeuchug.

Contemporary descriptions do not suggest that the Russian peasant suffered from the grinding poverty typical of the southern European and Mediterranean peasantry. In France at this same period, the number of urban and rural poor has been assessed at between 30 and 50 per cent of the population; they suffered from more or less permanent undernourishment and lived in squalid conditions. Farm labourers, both in England and in France, eked out a precarious existence. Martha Wilmot in 1805 described a scene on the estate of Princess Dashkova in Kaluga province as follows:

> There is a Small Meadow opposite to my Windows in which 150 Mowers are mowing this moment, Men and Women. All the Men are clothed . . . in white trowsers and a Shirt border'd at bottom with the scarlet work of the peasants and likewise on the Shoulders, girdled round the waist with a gaudy girdle. . . . those who imagine the Russ peasantry sunk in sloth and misery imagine a strange falsehood. Wou'd to God our Paddys . . . were half as well clothed or fed the year round as are the Russians. There is *for* and *against* in every state but take the two Nations to Robt's touchstones, 'Have they enough to eat, to drink?' 'Have they Houses, firing and a bed to lie on? and trust me the *Bears* would triumph, oh, beyond comparison. . . .

Journeying through Tver' province, Martha Wilmot again comments on the excellence of the milk and brown bread, the only provisions travellers would buy from the peasants.

> The Peasants one and all pleased me from the frolicksome Variety of their Dresses. . . . Here and there you will see a country girl with a head dress of gold and earrings necklace etc of tinsel. . . . I think the Men handsomer than the Women in general, but I give you my word both are as superior to Irish people of the same class as one nation can well be to another.

Princess Dashkova was undoubtedly among the better landowners, and the Wilmot sisters did not visit the poorest parts of Russia, but they were quite shrewd observers, and noted with disgust the prevalence of corporal punishment among domestic serfs, who could not, as Martha Wilmot explains, be sacked for incompetence, and the general tyranny of the nobles.

It is instructive to compare foreigners' impressions of Russia with Russian impressions of other countries. Denis Fonvizin, travelling in France in 1778, was shocked at the crowd of beggars which flocked around his carriage. The French might be free, he commented, but they seemed free to starve rather than to live. Russian peasants in fertile areas were infinitely better off than French peasants, who were ground down by taxes. In turn Princess Dashkova, travelling in Scotland in 1777, remarked that the hovels of the peasants were horrible, without flooring, with a hole in the middle to make a fire, and built of loose stones not held together by mortar. Soviet economic historians have divided villages into rich, middling and poor peasants, but these are relative terms. Wealth can be measured by the capacity of a peasant household to produce a surplus of corn for sale, and by the number of horses, cows, sheep, pigs and so on. In the province of Kursk, the land surveyors counted as rich some 20 per cent of the peasant households which had 10 horses, 120 cows, 10 sheep and 50 pigs per household. Kursk was a relatively prosperous part of Russia, but the number of cattle per head in the really rich Black Earth zone was much higher.

It is also probable that the standard of living of the peasantry rose in the last quarter of the eighteenth century. The opening up of the new Black Earth lands led to an increase in the land under cultivation and a rise in prices, from which both landowner and peasant benefited. In spite of wars, and mounting inflation from 1788 onwards, the poll-tax remained the same, seventy kopeks, per head, until 1794 when it was raised to one ruble. With all due caution, owing to the unreliability of the figures available, the economic historian A. Kahan argues that the real burden of taxes and dues on the peasants and serfs declined in the last quarter of the eighteenth century. Taking 1730 as 100, Kahan esimates the total tax burden weighing on the peasants in the 1790s as 76.2.

If membership of the commune, and communal cultivatio ı of the land, by both serfs and state peasants, was economically restrictive and hampered agricultural innovation (new methods and new crops), it was socially supportive. Unlike the French, the Irish or the English peasant, the Russian peasant had a safety net. He was *entitled* to land, and the possibility therefore of making an income. If he died, his widow and young children would become the responsibility of the commune and ultimately of the landowner if he was a serf, and would not be cast out on the world, though they might suffer great poverty. In the event of famine the landowner was bound in law to supply his peasants. The real hardship of the peasant serf lay not in his poverty but in his vulnerability. One bad season could bring famine with all its attendant horrors. And always there hovered above him and his family the threat implicit in his servile status, of being taken off the land, sold, sent into the army, or to settlement in Siberia, brutally punished, whether innocent or guilty, abused, beaten or even killed. With a good landlord, life might be quite bearable. But even a good landlord could be unjust, and a change of owner could lead to the introduction of new customs, new demands, fear and distrust.

What possibility was there for the serf to escape from his condition? A serf conscripted into the armed forces was free if he survived the twenty-five-year term of service introduced in the 1790s. But he could not easily return to his village, whether serf or state peasant, since he no longer fitted into the community. Usually he was simply kept in the army and employed on light garrison duties. Thus the army only very rarely provided an avenue of escape from serfdom into another social estate. But by the end of the eighteenth century, not only were there many peasants, both serfs and state peasants, making money in trade and manufacturing, there was also the nucleus of what Soviet historians call a serf intelligentsia.

Landowners had long found it necessary to train a certain number of serfs to act as bailiffs, surveyors, agents of various kinds. Sometimes parish priests taught a few of the children of the richer serfs. Sometimes landowners set up schools to teach children reading, writing and arithmetic. Prince Alexander Kurakin, who owned over 5,000 serfs in six provinces, founded schools in all six of his estates, some with twelve, some with twenty pupils. However, they tended to be the children of house serfs, not of peasants, who usually hated being taken from the land to work in 'the big house'. The schools prepared the children to act as clerks and stewards, but they were often taught to read Church books and to sing. Most of the magnates, the Sheremet'yevs, Golitsyns, Yusupovs, Orlovs, Rumyantsevs and many others, set up schools at which some of their peasants received an elementary education. Prince D.M. Golitsyn, who built the handsome hospital in Moscow, set up two schools on his estates in 1781, mainly for the children of household serfs but also for peasants. He built stone houses, supplied furniture and crockery, and arranged for village women to cook and clean. To encourage children to continue with their studies, he created a small library with works on agriculture. The teachers were not serfs, but were paid 150 rubles a year, together with allowances in kind. Sometimes children were paid to attend school, at other times they were supplied with food, clothes, books. Many schools taught painting and drawing, and some court schools specialized in icon-painting. After the setting up of the national schools in 1786, some of the large landowners sent their serf children to these schools. Nothing is known about the education of serf children on small estates, but seeing that so many landowners, and particularly so many noblewomen, were nearly illiterate, schools for serfs probably did not have a high priority.

Education did not however always make the life of the serf any easier. Those who were employed as bailiffs and stewards were caught between the demands of the landowners and the complaints of the peasants, and were subjected to much ill-treatment if they failed to deliver the dues or the produce required to their owners. But those who were trained for more refined occupations such as architects, painters, musicians, dancers, actors and singers were frequently placed in unbearably humiliating situations. They were often taught by the best masters, some of them serfs, some of them leading foreign architects like Quarenghi, or leading foreign musicians like the court composer, Sarti. Some serfs even went abroad to study – and returned! Members of a serf theatre were given better food and living accommodation than household serfs; they were even sometimes paid salaries. But they could be flogged if they forgot their lines. Count P.B. Sheremet'yev married one of his serf actresses; but when he disbanded his company he sent many to work as lackeys and footmen. A serf painter, known in St Petersburg for his many portraits of nobles, was sent by his owner back to service, and could be seen standing on the footboard behind his master's carriage.

What rendered the serf's situation particularly galling was that he had no right to buy his freedom for a fixed sum, as a slave could, for instance, in Spanish America. Sometimes a landowners agreed to free a serf; this often happened to household serfs on the death of their masters. But often he refused to allow a serf to go even for a very substantial sum of money, 12,000 rubles in one case. Purchasing one's freedom seems to have become more common in the first part of the nineteenth century, when 28,900 cases have been recorded, for sums as low as 139 rubles and as high as between 1,000 and 5,000. But little is known about the eighteenth century.

In general the worst part of serfdom, whether for peasants or entrepreneurs or the serf intelligentsia, was the arbitrary power wielded over them by the landowners and, in their name, by officials. In practice serfs had no rights. When the crunch came they could be deprived of their property, sent to work on the land, raped, married off, tortured and beaten. If they went to law, in all likelihood they would be disbelieved and sent back to their owner. Moreover, in a society in which husbands – whether nobles or peasants – beat their wives, and parents their sons and their daughters, it took a very long time to train masters to accept the idea that corporal punishment should not be inflicted except after the sentence of a court.

Much less is known about the way of life of the merchant class and the townspeople in general, which included not only craftsmen, clerks and officials below the Table of Ranks, but also the social category described as the *raznochintsy*, that is to say those people who had ceased to belong to the estate of their parents, but had not been formally registered in another estate. These were usually people belonging to what eventually came to be known as the liberal professions, people with qualifications of some kind, writers, translators, journalists, solicitors, apothecaries, artists and so on.

It must be borne in mind that many settlements which counted in law as towns were nothing but overgrown villages: streets were narrow and irregular, cows wandered about the streets, grazing on whatever grew, brick houses stood cheek by jowl with wooden hovels, interspersed with meadows, market gardens or even cornfields. Towns were in addition dirty and lawless. Until the reform of 1775 there were often no public buildings, no schools and no local administrative bodies.

It was not easy in Russia to change one's legal status, but if the towns were to grow they had to recruit newcomers from somewhere. The state peasants were best placed to move into the towns and swell the ranks of the townsmen, but they had to continue to pay the poll-tax as state peasants while they were being reregistered as townsmen, so they had to pay the poll-tax both in the towns and in their villages until a new census took place which recorded their change of status.

The number of registered dwellers in a town was far smaller than the actual number of residents, and the number of registered merchants was even smaller. Like the nobles, the merchants fell into two uneven groups, the small number of the very rich and the larger number of middle rank or poor. In Moscow in 1782, there were 4,542 registered merchants, of whom 982 were newly registered state peasants. A smaller number of state peasants registered as ordinary townsmen (*meshchane*). By 1793, there were 11,768 registered merchants in Moscow (by far the largest number in the whole of Russia – Tver' coming next), of whom 620 were still paying the poll-tax in their village as well, while 258 were freed ex-Church peasants and serfs of the nobles. In 1801, in St Petersburg, there were 202,100 inhabitants, of whom 14,300 were registered as merchants and 23,400 were registered as townspeople. There were in addition over 50,000 peasants and nearly 40,000 military personnel. Only the merchants of the first guild were allowed to participate in the wholesale export trade. Merchants of the second guild could participate in wholesale and retail trade in the domestic market.

The merchants of the first guild also included industrialists and factory owners. Many of them had acquired serfs for use in industry when it was still allowed, before 1762. Some continued to acquire serfs by devious means or by special permit. They were employed in making woollen and cotton cloth, silk, paper, building materials, ironware, glassware, leather goods and so on. In theory these serfs were attached to the enterprise and could not be turned into house-serfs, but it is difficult to know what actually happened.

The merchant class has often been described as indifferent to westernization, and hostile to education beyond the basic requirements of commercial life. This verdict should perhaps be modified to some degree. Before the Statute on National Schools was promulgated in 1786, some merchants had already made substantial gifts for the setting up of schools. After 1786, it appears that more voluntary gifts to the schools were made by merchants and townspeople than by any other social group; the eminent citizens of Moscow for instance each gave 500 rubles. The majority of the pupils in the state schools in six of the central provinces, where support for the schools was particularly noticeable, were children of merchants or townspeople. Nobles on the whole did not attend the state schools except when they were very poor, as for instance in Tambov province.

The Wilmot sisters were very impressed by the spectacle of the merchants' families out walking or driving. Martha Wilmot describes them as follows:

> The Merchants' Wives are particularly splendid. Headdresses of pearls and veils of muslin embroidere'd with gold and with silver,

> or silk embroider'd with ditto, their pelises of gold silk lined with the most expensive furs, their faces painted red & white altogether give them a very shewy and handsome appearance.

The men too wore the 'native dress of the country, a Coat of green Velvet with a sort of petticoat skirt reaching to his heels and embroider'd all round with gold, flat crown'd hat which never quitted his head . . .'. The 'native dress' was in fact usually worn by members of the merchantry, as can be observed from contemporary accounts and paintings. The women (except for Old Believers) also painted their faces bright pink and white, a practice common among peasant women too. The parks of the great nobles, for instance at the house of Count Stroganov on Kamennyy Ostrov in St Petersburg, were open to the general public and the merchants were allowed to set up their shops there in fine weather and turn the park into a fair. In Catherine's reign merchants began to be allowed to open shops in their dwelling houses, as distinct from the special bazaars assigned to them, thus rendering the streets more lively.

There was one particular group among the registered merchants or townspeople of most large towns which to a great extent followed its own way of life, namely the Old Believers or *raskol'niki*. They were particularly important in Moscow where, during the great plague epidemic of 1771, the two principal communities, the priested and the priestless, had been allowed to set up their own cemeteries at Rogozhsk and Preobrazhensk. These cemeteries became centres for the communities, with hospitals, almshouses and moneylending facilities. The Old Believer centres in Moscow were linked with their co-religionists throughout Russia, from whom they received substantial funds, which could be used for investment. In turn they could rely on economic and charitable help in the areas, usually around the fringes of Russia, where Old Believers had settled (the north-east, Nizhniy Novgorod, the Volga area, the Urals).

Old Believers presented many of the moral features associated with Calvinists. They were honest, hardworking and thrifty, and often harsh taskmasters. They were particularly prominent among textile manufacturers – the serf millionaires on Count Sheremet'yev's estate at Ivanovo were Old Believers who, on achieving their freedom, registered as first-guild merchants in Moscow. One of them, E. Grachev, a member of the priestless community at Preobrazhensk, built public baths for the use of his co-religionists. An Old Believer serf, F.A. Guchkov, founded his textile works in Moscow at the end of the eighteenth century; his great-grandson Alexander

Guchkov was a deputy to the Duma and a minister in the Provisional Government in 1917.

The Wilmot sisters in 1807 visited one of the leading Old Believers in Moscow:

> The Princess [Dashkova] . . . order'd a Russian entertainment in the House of Elic Alexovitch who is a sort of Patriarch to the Sect of Roscolnics. This Man was born the subject of the Dolgoroukys but purchased his Liberty for £2000 Ster^g^, and is one of the richest Merchants in Moscow. He is quite a portrait of the perfection of Human Nature at the advanced age of 80; simple, cheerful, active and benevolent with the most beautiful features and Silver Beard on a magnificent height of Stature render'd more striking by his Russian attire. In his capacity of Sectarian he amused me more than in that of Merchant, as a gigantic dinner was its only symbol; but as a Sectarian he conducted us to his Churches and Hospitals and Convents and Monasterys which surrounded his dwelling in a very considerable Circle. . . .

Old Believers, like Puritans in England, disapproved of the theatre and other forms of public entertainment like balls and masquerades. But the merchants and town-dwellers in general had long been accustomed to some forms of public entertainment. In St Petersburg, or Moscow, they were received at receptions and masquerades given in the palaces of the imperial family for celebrations of their namedays – indeed the Grand Duke Paul always took his hat off to merchants who were dressed in the old Russian costume; they were allowed to walk in the imperial parks and gardens and attend the imperial theatres as well as the public theatres which were opened in Moscow and St Petersburg. With the establishment of the new provincial institutions after 1775, enterprising governors also set up theatres in the provinces for the entertainment of townspeople.

Like the nobles the merchants divided their inheritance among their descendants. As a result great fortunes seldom lasted beyond three generations. Some merchants declined to the status of second or third guild, or even common townspeople. A few maintained their status as members of the first guild or as eminent citizens; and a small number, particularly among the large industrialists, were ennobled, and usually lost to the world of business. Their children went into the armed forces, and attempted to make the sort of career which would enable them to buy a landed estate. To a great extent the poorer merchants suffered from rivalry with the peasants and particularly the serfs. The latter were encouraged by their masters to bring their craft production to the towns for sale, where they could undercut the merchants since they did not pay town taxes.

It cannot be said that the merchants seized with alacrity on the new opportunities opened up for them in self-administration and in economic activity once they were freed from the burden of government service previously imposed upon them and from the collective responsibility for the towns' payment of taxes by the Charter of 1785. However, most of what is known about the operation of the municipal institutions is based on two studies, one of Moscow, the other of St Petersburg, one published in the nineteenth century, the other in 1909. New research has provided a somewhat different picture. The six-man duma set up by the Charter, where it was actually elected, seems in some cases to have met regularly and to have dealt with a number of issues of importance to the town, even if it did not always have the capacity to stand up to more powerful institutions like the board of local government or the military commandants.

Peter I has often been criticized for allegedly opening up a cultural gulf between the westernized nobility and the peasants – a gulf which only increased under Catherine and her successors. This is one of the statements about Russian history made in the nineteenth century in order to prove a political point of view and which is unsupported by systematic research. There is no evidence that the gulf between the upper class and the common people in Russia was any bigger than it was in France or England. But in Russia, unlike France or England, the army served as a means of linking nobles and ordinary people in a common activity with a common purpose, indoctrinating them with its own ethical and cultural values.

Moreover, as distinct from the slave societies of North America, the fragmented Russian society was nevertheless united by belonging mostly to the same race, and to the same religion. In Christian Russia, all classes attended the same church and shared in the same ritual, particularly the joyous greeting of the Resurrection with the words 'Christ is Risen'. The practice of a common faith could sometimes smooth out the asperities affecting relations between different social classes.

CHAPTER 13

The War with Turkey and Sweden, and the Destruction of Poland

The Turkish declaration of war in August 1787 forced Russia into a war for which she was not in fact prepared, though the many provocations Russia had inflicted on the Turks should have led Catherine to expect it. The annexation of the Crimea in 1783 and the creation of the Russian Black Sea fleet were challenges to Ottoman power which could not be taken lying down. The advantage for Catherine however of the Turkish declaration of war was that it brought into action the secret treaty of 1781 (see Chapter 7) with the Emperor Joseph II, committing him, as ruler of the Habsburg hereditary possessions (though not, of course, as Holy Roman Emperor), to fight the Turks as Russia's ally.

The second Turkish war was to inaugurate a long period of warfare. It lasted four years, and merged with the second partition of Poland in 1792 and the war with the Polish resistance which broke out in 1794. The final partition of Poland in 1795 was followed by preparations for a campaign against revolutionary France and a campaign against Persia which was still being waged when Catherine died in November 1796. All these wars put an end to many projects of reform, and placed an enormous strain on the financial resources of the country, as well as on its manpower. The war was to prove far more difficult and complex than Catherine's first Turkish war (which had however lasted six years). Moreover, though Russia now had the advantage of naval bases on the Black Sea since the peace of Kutschuk Kainardzhi and the annexation of the Crimea, she too had become vulnerable by sea, and had to guard against Turkish naval attack.

The war at first took the form of inconclusive naval operations in the Black Sea. The main Russian effort was directed against the Turkish fort of Ochakov, which controlled the Russian exit from the estuary of the River Dnieper, and defended the Turkish territory between the River Bug and the River Dniester. By February 1788, Joseph II had moved to the attack on land but the Austrian advance across a vast front was slow and sluggish, and Joseph, as a military commander, lacked the military genius which had distinguished his great rival Frederick II.

As in 1769, Catherine planned to send a fleet to the Mediterranean, to supplement the activity of the Black Sea fleet and to act as a focal point from which to encourage revolt among the Christian Orthodox peoples of the Ottoman Empire, such as the Greeks, Serbs, Montenegrins, Moldavians and Wallachians. But almost at once the entirely different diplomatic alignment in Europe put obstacles in her way.

In the first place Britain, since Catherine had launched the policy of the Armed Neutrality in 1780, during the American War, was no longer so friendly and did not offer Russia the use of the naval facilities essential for the long journey around Europe from the Baltic to the eastern Mediterranean. Secondly, Frederick II, her ally in the first Turkish war (even though he played no part in military operations) had died in 1786, and his successor, Frederick William II, had embarked on a policy which was to unsettle Europe for several years. On the one hand he had formed in 1788 with Great Britain and the United Provinces of the Netherlands a Triple Alliance designed primarily to restore the authority of the Stadholder (the title used by the constitutional head of the United Provinces of the Netherlands), who was married to his sister. The Stadholder's position had been challenged by the so-called Patriot Party, a faction which in some ways anticipated the demands for political participation in government by wider social groups typical of the French revolutionary period. At the same time the Prussian Foreign Minister, Count Hertzberg, was launching an extremely complicated plan for exchanges of territory by which Prussia would succeed in extending her frontiers at Poland's expense, leaving other powers to do the fighting. This project greatly alarmed Joseph II, who feared a Prussian attack in his rear, and in any case neither he nor Catherine intended to allow Prussia to benefit from the war they were fighting against the Turks and obtain compensation in Poland for whatever Turkish territory Russia or Austria might annex as a result of a victorious war. Catherine even went so far as to offer an alliance to Poland in 1788, in terms which perpetuated Poland's total political and military dependence on Russia, but defended the integrity of her territory against Prussian designs. The proposed treaty, which

Poland did not sign, alarmed the Prussians, since it made it quite clear that Russia would not allow Prussia to annex Polish territory. So Prussian policy was now directed at forcing Russia to change her Polish policy, and ultimately to ensure, by means of diplomatic or military threats, that Russia should make no territorial gains from Turkey.

This tense diplomatic situation became even more dangerous for Russia when Gustavus III of Sweden declared war on a trumped-up issue in June 1788. Gustavus had been only crown prince at the time of the first Turkish war in 1768. He was now king and he felt that the opportunity to recover some of the lands lost to Russia was too good to miss, seeing that Russia was fully engaged on the Turkish front. He accordingly advanced his troops by land on St Petersburg, in the fond belief that he would soon be dining in the Russian capital. But in one respect he had acted too soon: the Russian fleet destined for the Mediterranean was still in the Baltic. In July 1788 the two fleets met in a severe but inconclusive naval battle.

The war in the Baltic seemed to be about to spread when Denmark, in accordance with her treaty obligations to Russia (treaty of 1767), declared war on Sweden in August 1788. However, the anti-Russian aspects of the Triple Alliance between England, Prussia and the United Provinces of the Netherlands now emerged into the open. British pressure on Denmark forced her in October 1788 to agree to an armistice with Sweden which, under attack from both Denmark and Russia, had by then almost been driven to the wall. However, if Denmark was forced out of the war by British pressure, the Swedish war effort was undermined by the revelation of the existence of a plot against Gustavus among Finnish officers in the Swedish army, who hoped for greater autonomy for Finland, a plot which had been secretly encouraged by Catherine.

On the other hand, Catherine's attempt to draw Poland into her circle of allies collapsed against Prussian and Polish resistance. Prussia would not tolerate any Russian guarantee of Polish territory which might prevent her from annexing Polish lands. And Polish hatred of Russia was too deep to allow of any form of co-operation between the two countries. By December 1788, the only bright spot for Catherine was the capture of the Turkish fort of Ochakov, which opened the way for a Russian advance along the north shore of the Black Sea into Turkish territory. Thanks to the military genius of one of the great Russian commanders, A.V. Suvorov, the operations of the joint Austro-Russian forces in Moldavia were successful in summer 1789, and the Austrians captured Belgrade in September, while the main Russian army advanced from the River Bug to seize the port of Gadzhibey (now Odessa) in September and the fort of Bender in November, thus controlling the course of the River Dniester.

Faced with the conduct of a difficult war on two fronts, against Sweden in the north and the Turks in the south, and with an ally – Austria – with whom military operations were not easily co-ordinated, Catherine would willingly have negotiated peace with the Turks. But the latter were still egging Sweden on and signed a treaty agreeing to subsidize the Swedish war effort in July 1789. The accession of a new Sultan, Selim III, in 1789 signified no change in Turkish policy.

Meanwhile Joseph II was facing increasing internal discontent in the Austrian Netherlands (modern Belgium, then ruled by the Austrian Habsburgs) and in Hungary, where his centralizing policies had aroused the opposition of the ancient corporate bodies. His death, in February 1790, was a serious blow to Catherine, for he had sacrificed Austrian interests to the maintenance of his alliance with her. Joseph's brother and heir, Leopold, Grand Duke of Tuscany, did not share the former's territorial ambitions and had no sympathy for the so-called Greek Project. He gave priority to the restoration of order in the Austrian Netherlands and in Hungary, and surrendered to the pressure of the Triple Alliance, out of fear of the military power of its principal continental member, Prussia. He showed himself willing to abandon the war against Turkey without any annexations or compensations. An armistice between Austria and Turkey was concluded at Reichenbach in June 1790, and Austria took no further part in the war. Peace between Austria and the Turks was concluded in August 1790. This rather put paid to the pet project of Hertzberg, mentioned above, to annex Polish lands in compensation for Austrian acquisitions at the expense of Turkey. But he did not give up his ultimate aim of acquiring the free city of Danzig and the Polish city of Thorn (situated on the River Vistula just south of the 1772 Prussian border with Poland and controlling much of the navigation on that important waterway) as compensation for any acquisitions which Russia might make.

Meanwhile the traditional pattern of international relations in Europe had taken a new twist. The French Revolution of 1789 led to a political vacuum in the heart of Europe. France, though very active in diplomacy, could not, at this juncture, offer military support to her allies, namely Austria, at war with the Turks, and Spain, in 1790, in the crisis over Nootka Sound, an outpost on the Pacific coast of America, to which Britain also laid claim.

The difficulties experienced by revolutionary France were at first regarded with somewhat malicious satisfaction by the crowned heads and political leaders of Europe, particularly England and Russia, since they weakened one of the hitherto strongest European powers traditionally hostile to both of them. The calling of the States General, the formation of the Constitutional Assembly and the drafting of the monarchical constitution of 1791 did not at first alarm the other rulers, who did not for one moment grasp that the revolutionary juggernaut could not be stopped at the borders of France. Hence traditional power politics continued to be played.

The Triple Alliance of England, the United Provinces and Prussia was not however politically united. The Dutch played a negligible part in the formulation of policy, but both Great Britain and Prussia had specific aims. William Pitt, in England, had been seduced by a plan to replace Russia by Poland as the main source of British naval stores. To achieve this aim, Poland had to be preserved from Russian aggression. But since Pitt needed Prussian help to achieve this aim, he was prepared to agree to Prussian demands for the annexation of Danzig and Thorn, as the price for Prussia's support. He was thus agreeing to cut off Poland's control of navigation along the River Vistula to the Baltic, the very route which naval stores exported to England would have to take, and hand it over to Prussia. Prussia in the meantime had signed a treaty of alliance with Poland in March 1790, in which no mention was made of a Prussian acquisition of Danzig and Thorn, but this was merely a postponement of the evil day.

The success of the Triple Alliance in forcing the Emperor Leopold out of the war led Britain and Prussia to attempt the same policy with Catherine. Her position was still critical in the summer of 1790. Swedish guns had rattled the windows in St Petersburg. (Catherine kept up her morale by reading a French translation of Smollett's *Humphry Clinker*, which entertained her so much that she ordered the novel to be translated into Russian.) More and more men were called up to fight, and in order to avoid raising taxes more money was printed, and the gap between income and expenditure rose in 1791 to 25 million rubles. Russia also suffered a disastrous naval defeat in July 1790 at the hands of Sweden. But the Swedish fleet had been decimated in the battle and Gustavus III was anxious for peace. Thus the two powers patched up the peace treaty of Verela in August 1790, which left things between them much as they had been.

Freed at last from the Swedish threat on her northern frontier, Catherine was nevertheless kept on tenterhooks by the Prussian threat in the west, which prevented her commander-in-chief in the south, Potemkin, from committing all his forces to an offensive against the Turks. But the capture of the Turkish fort of Izmail on the Danube in December 1790 strengthened her hand. Thus when Pitt launched his diplomatic offensive in January 1791, issuing ultimatums demanding that Russia should make peace, return Ochakov to the Turks and abandon all her conquests at their expense, under threat of the despatch of a British fleet to the Baltic, she refused to give way. In March 1791 Potemkin, who had arrived in St Petersburg from the Danube front, and who was more alive to the danger from the Prussian army, bullied her into climbing down, at least to the extent of agreeing to negotiate a secret treaty with Prussia, which would allow her to keep her conquests from the Turks, while accepting Prussian annexation of Danzig and Thorn. There are many entries in the diary of Catherine's secretary, A.V. Khrapovitsky, recording the disputes between the Empress and Potemkin, who frequently reduced her to tears. But if Prussia were to agree to such a secret treaty with Russia it would of course imply that the Prussians were abandoning their British ally in order to secure advantages for themselves.

Before her surrender could be communicated to Prussia, Catherine was rescued from her dilemma by British public opinion. Pitt had failed to explain his policy fully in Parliament and had misjudged opinion in the country in pressing his demands on Russia. Even those people who were critical of Russian policy did not think it was worth going to war with Russia over her acquisition of Ochakov. The Russian Ambassador in England, Simon Vorontsov, began to cultivate the leaders of the Opposition like Charles James Fox, and succeeded in launching a widespread press campaign which undermined Pitt's policy by implying that he was acting as a Prussian catspaw, and that Britain had nothing to gain by forcing Russia to give up Ochakov. If a British fleet was sent to the Baltic it might bombard Riga but 'we cannot pluck a single grey hair from the old lady's head', wrote the *Morning Chronicle*. There were meetings in Norwich, Manchester and other cities at which resolutions were passed opposing war with Russia. Pitt was unable to carry either the

Cabinet or Parliament with him, and was forced to withdraw his ultimatum to Catherine and to inform Prussia that his whole policy had collapsed. Catherine's agreement to negotiate with Prussia was thus never communicated officially to the Prussian King and she was able to avoid the humiliation of a climbdown. Pitt sent a special envoy, William Fawkener, to negotiate in Russia and by July 1791 Catherine was assured that Britain had withdrawn her objections to Russian annexation of Turkish territory east of the Dniester river.

Events in Poland were now going to make it possible to make Poland pay for Prussian failure to benefit from the Russio-Turkish war. Profiting from the fact that Russia was deeply engaged in a war on two fronts, the Poles had set about dismantling the apparatus of Russian control in Poland, and had sought the protection of Prussia. On 3 May 1791 NS they adopted a new constitution, establishing a hereditary, limited monarchy, and abolishing the *liberum veto*, the need for unanimity in the Diet. Though they were to some degree inspired by events in France, they were introducing not a radical republic, but a moderate, mixed monarchy which might enable the Polish state to raise enough revenue to pay for its defence.

Both the military and the political aspects of the Polish Revolution were regarded as dangerous by Catherine. She could not easily accept the loss of the dominating Russian position in Poland, and she was outraged by the vociferously anti-Russian Polish speeches and writings, many of them couched in language extremely offensive to her. At the time she had to swallow her anger, but after the collapse of the Anglo-Prussian ultimatum in May–July 1791, she was prepared to work with Prussia to restore the old, unreformed Polish constitution, which she had guaranteed and which would keep Poland weak, and to make Poland pay for her insolence.

In spring and summer 1791 a more active policy against the Turks became possible, now that Sweden and Prussia had both ceased to threaten. The Russian armies inflicted a series of defeats on the Turks by land and sea, which led the latter finally to open peace talks. The preliminary peace was signed on 31 July 1791 and the final treaty was concluded in Jassy on 29 December. The results fell well below the expectations of the Greek Project; the Turks remained in Constantinople, there was no kingdom for the Grand Duke Constantine; but it was a splendid victory for Russia. The annexation of the Crimea was now quietly accepted by the Turks, and the coast between the Bug and the Dniester was ceded to Russia, extending her control of the north shore of the Black Sea, and the important valley of the

River Dniester, which now became the frontier between the Russian and Turkish Empires.

Looked at from a purely Russian point of view, Catherine's wars against the Turks represented the fulfilment of aims which had long been harboured. The treaty of Kutschuk Kainardzhi opened up vast areas for economic development in the south of Russia; the annexation of the Crimea represented the final subordination of the descendants of Genghis Khan and allowed Russia to become a naval power on the Black Sea; the peace of Jassy in 1791 consolidated Russian control of the estuary of the Dnieper and opened the way for the development of other major Black Sea ports, such as Odessa, which were to become the outlets for the grain trade. To this extent therefore, Catherine's achievement was fully in line with traditional Russian aims.

After the conclusion of the peace with the Turks in December 1791 Catherine was free to turn her attention to chastising the Poles. Her policy had been formulated in lengthy discussions with Potemkin, but he was no longer alive to carry it out. The man who had been her constant partner in all her political ventures for seventeen years had died in October 1791, before the conclusion of the final treaty with the Turks. But before his death he had organized a party of his own in Poland, composed of great nobles who did not accept the new constitution of 3 May 1791 NS and hankered after the restoration of the 'glorious liberty' of the nobility which had done so much to reduce Poland to helplessness. These nobles were now to form the nucleus of a 'confederation' which was to proclaim the old constitution, and to invite Russian armies to assist in overthrowing the reformed constitution of 3 May.

Russia could not, however, act in total disregard of the other powers involved. The Emperor Leopold II, who was strongly opposed to any Prussian aggrandizement, exercised a moderating influence, but he died unexpectedly in March 1792. His successor, Francis II, allowed himself to become involved in the wars against revolutionary France, and turned away from annexations in Poland in favour of a long-cherished Austrian aim, the exchange of the Austrian Netherlands for Bavaria. Russia had therefore only Prussia to deal with, only too ready to seize her share of Poland, in spite of the treaty of alliance between Prussia and Poland of 1790, which guaranteed the integrity of Poland. This time, however, Russia had to buy Prussia off for if Russia invaded Poland, ostensibly to restore the old constitution, Prussia might well attack Russia, exhausted after the long Turkish war and unable to count on her Austrian ally. Prussia could then hope to obtain her 'compensation' directly from the Poles as a reward for defending them against Russian attack.

Having forewarned Prussia of her intentions, Catherine's armies invaded Poland on 7/18 May 1792, in the name of the Polish confederates, called after the Polish town, Targowica, in which they first raised their banner. Any anxiety Catherine might have felt regarding Austrian intentions was allayed by the news received a few days earlier that revolutionary France had declared war on Austria and Prussia. Catherine's partisans in Poland immediately proclaimed their 'confederation and restored as much as they could of the old constitution in the territory they controlled, assisted by the Russian forces. Prussia went back on her treaty obligation to defend Polish integrity on the ground that the 3 May constitution had changed the situation. Indeed, after the failure of the campaign of 1792–3 against revolutionary France, Prussia declared that she would not continue the war in the west if she did not receive compensation in Poland to maintain the balance with Austrian expectations of compensation in Bavaria or at the expense of France.

Catherine was anxious to keep the attention of both Austria and Prussia firmly fixed on the war with revolutionary France, so that she could have a free hand in Poland. But, under pressure from the factions in her own court, she finally agreed to solve the Polish problem by a fresh partition. Austria was this time excluded, and Russia and Prussia agreed in January 1793 on a partition which was explained on the ground that it was necessary in order to protect their respective countries from the infection of revolutionary 'Jacobinism' alleged to be rampant in Poland. The Russian portion was this time very large. The rest of Belorussia and almost the whole of Right-Bank Ukraine were annexed, amounting to over 250,000 square kilometres and over three million inhabitants. Prussia acquired the much coveted Danzig and Thorn.

It remained to secure Polish consent to this amputation of their territory and to establish some form of government for the rump of Poland. The deputies to the Polish Diet used what means they could to evade assenting to Russian demands, but in the presence of overwhelming numbers of Russian troops resistance was impossible, and by September 1793 consent to the partition had been extorted from a totally silent Diet, the so-called 'Dumb Diet', silence being taken for consent. By October a Polish treaty with Russia was signed which turned Poland into a Russian protectorate: the Polish army was to be reduced to 15,000 men, and Polish foreign policy was to be controlled by Russia. But it was clear to Russia, Poland and the other powers that this was but a temporary solution.

There were indeed many Poles who did not accept this tame surrender, some of whom hoped to secure support either from Turkey or from France. The reduction of the Polish army to 15,000 men, in accordance with the treaty, sparked off a rising which soon swept the country, and led to full-scale war against the Russian occupying troops. In April 1794 the Poles in Warsaw rose against the Russian garrison and slaughtered or took prisoner more than half of them. Frederick William of Prussia was now forced to divert his energies away from the war against France and sent some 25,000 men against Warsaw. The siege of Warsaw began in earnest in the autumn of 1794 when the troops of Field Marshal A.V. Suvorov advanced on the suburb of Praga, and conquered it in one of the bloodiest and most savage assaults on an unfortified town which Europe had seen for a long time. Some 20,000 men, women and children were massacred indiscriminately, allegedly in reprisal for the earlier slaughter of the Russian garrison of Warsaw by the Poles. Suvorov's conduct on this occasion made his name a byword throughout Europe, and did great harm to the reputation of the Russian army. The city of Warsaw surrendered in order to avoid a similar fate.

The Polish Revolt had been accompanied by some attempts at a political revolution, involving also an improvement in the condition of the Polish serfs, and by much rhetoric in favour of France and the French Revolution. This was enough to convince Catherine and her advisers of the extent to which Poland was now infected by Jacobinism, and of the danger which this presented to her neighbours. The outright annexation of the whole of the rest of Poland was considered by Catherine, but she realized that Prussia would not tolerate this, and in the end she preferred to propose a fresh and final partition, this time including Austria, who had lost all hope of securing compensation in the west as a result of the failure of the Austro-Prussian campaign against the French revolutionary armies. By January 1795 the treaty of partition of Poland with Austria had been signed, to which Prussia later acceded. Russia now acquired Lithuania, what remained of Belorussia and what remained of the Ukraine, about 120,000 square kilometres. She also extended her sovereignty over the Duchy of Courland in the Baltic, which had been a Polish dependency, but had been ruled since the 1760s by Catherine's nominees, the Biron family, descended from the favourite of the Empress Anna.

Russia had now to extend to her newly acquired territories the institutions which had been set up in Russia proper by the Statute of 1775 and the charters of 1785. New Russian provinces were carved out of Polish provinces; where the local inhabitants submitted to Russian occupation, existing landowners and officials were largely left alone. The Orthodox population was now administered from the Metropolitanate of Kiev, while special arrangements were made for Roman Catholics and Uniates (see Chapter 11).

One problem which remains unsolved for historians is whether the second and third partitions of Poland followed inevitably on the first. Of course it was easier to carve up Poland the second time: 'Ce n'est que le premier pas qui coûte.' But the options open to Catherine were to keep Poland intact and under her domination as an effective buffer state, or to share her out, thus increasing the relative strength of her rivals, Austria and Prussia, and bringing their frontiers into immediate contact with her own. It is very probable that until the Polish Revolution of 3 May 1791 NS the former policy predominated. It is also likely to have been supported by Potemkin, who may well have regarded Poland as a place of refuge for himself, in which he could live out his life as a great Polish magnate, in the event of the death of Catherine and the accession of Paul, who hated him. Certainly court gossip in 1787, which reached Catherine through the interception of the dispatches of the British Envoy Alleyne Fitzherbert, said that Potemkin was planning to make of lands he had recently bought in Poland a 'tertium quid', independent of both Poland and Russia, for which Fitzherbert had given him a device: 'nec viget quicquam simile aut secundum'.

But the conjunction of Catherine's repression of the Polish 'Jacobins' with the failure of the Austro-Prussian campaigns against France made it almost inevitable that it should be Poland who would be made to pay to keep Prussia and to a lesser extent Austria in the war against revolutionary France. The final, desperate Polish rising of 1794 was treated in purely military terms, and though Catherine probably would have preferred to annex the whole of Poland, she could not in the circumstances get away with it.

Catherine argued that she had not annexed a single Pole, only Belorussians and Ukrainians, though this is debatable. But her participation, indeed leadership, in the second and third partitions and in the final extinction of a great eastern European state was a blot on Russian foreign policy. Some, including her son Paul I, and even her grandson Alexander I, disapproved of her Polish policy. But they did not restore Polish independence. It seems indeed as though Poland and the Poles brought out the worst in Russians, rather as the Irish do with the English. There is a resentment that the Poles have evaded being Russians by becoming Roman Catholics, that there is something in their very hearts that will never yield or bow to the superior power of Russia. Hence the massacre of Praga, and the fact that ordinary Polish prisoners of war were often treated very brutally.

While Russia had been busy imposing her will on Poland, the war against revolutionary France had continued in the west. From a geographical point of view Russia was not well placed to take an active military part in the war, though of course she could assist by means of the loan of troops and of subsidies. One important Soviet historian has argued that Russia was a leader in the campaign against revolutionary France; but he uses this argument in order to emphasize the reactionary nature of tsarist foreign policy. Yet all the evidence points to the fact that Catherine had no intention of getting bogged down in the war against revolutionary France. She wanted to push Sweden, Austria and Prussia to take an active part in the war in the west, while she concentrated on mopping up 'Jacobinism' just over the border in Poland.

Meanwhile France herself was becoming increasingly 'Jacobin'. The monarchy was overthrown in August 1792, and the Republic was proclaimed. The French victory over the Prussian and Austrian troops at Valmy in September opened the way for the French armies to sweep into Germany, seize Mainz and occupy the Rhineland. By January 1793 the trial and execution of Louis XVI had taken place. Revolutionary France was now exporting the revolution. A combination of political and strategic considerations led Britain to join the war in February 1793, and to organize the first coalition against France.

As early as 1791 Catherine had offered to subsidize Sweden and to defend Swedish possessions in order to drive Gustavus into leading the anti-French crusade. Certainly until the final peace with Turkey in December 1791 and the occupation of Poland preparatory to the second partition, Catherine could not take an active part in the war against France, though she provided Prussia and Austria with a subsidy of 500,000 rubles in the summer of 1792, and she gave some financial help to the French *émigrés*. The execution of Louis XVI led her to break off diplomatic and commercial relations with France. Negotiations with Britain began in 1793 for Russia to join the first coalition, but Catherine deliberately pitched her demands very high, probably in order to ensure a British refusal. No agreement on military co-operation was reached but Russia did put a number of Russian ships at the disposal of Britain (Catherine could not after all use Russian ships in Poland) and conducted a naval campaign against French trade which led to strained relations with Sweden. Swedish policy had become less warlike after the assassination of Gustavus III in March 1792 and the accession of his son Gustav IV Adolf, under the regency of his uncle the Duke of Sudermania.

The war in Poland after the Polish rising of March 1794 turned Catherine even further from the war with France, which was in any case at that time going disastrously for the forces of Prussia and Austria, as the French armies advanced in the Austrian Netherlands, Holland, Germany, Spain. By 1795 most of the powers in the first coalition were making their separate peace with France. Russia did not make peace since she had never declared war; indeed in February 1795 she signed a further agreement with Britain to provide ships for joint operations in the North Sea, and in autumn 1796 she ordered an army of 60,000 men to be assembled to act against the French in the Holy Roman Empiore, but Catherine died before an agreement on military operations with England could be concluded.

Though Catherine's attention might seem to have been fully engaged in these last years with Turkey, Poland and France, she still found time to pursue Russian expansionist aims in the Caucasus. The great mountain range was divided into numerous petty kingdoms, some, like Georgia, Christian, some, like Daghestan, Moslem. The whole area was torn by the efforts of three powers, Russia, Turkey and Persia, to assert their predominance. King Heraclius of Georgia had placed his kingdom under Russian suzerainty by a treaty of 1783 – one of the ultimate causes of the outbreak of war between Turkey and Russia in 1787. A high degree of instability marked the region throughout the second Russo-Turkish war, but the intervention of Persia widened the conflict in 1795.

Armenia too attracted Russian attention in the eighteenth century. It was not semi-independent, like Georgia, but divided between Turkey and Persia; its ancient Christian population was ruled over by Moslem Kurds and many Armenians emigrated to Russia, notably to Astrakhan, where they formed a large merchant community. Discussions were even held in the 1780s between Potemkin, who liked all exotic peoples, and leaders of the Armenian groups seeking to free themselves from Persian and Turkish rule, with the object of setting up an Armenian state with its capital in Erevan. The Persian invasion and devastation of Georgia and Armenia in 1795 played into the hands of the bellicose faction in St Petersburg, associated with the Empress's favourite, Platon Zubov. A corps of some 25,000 Russian soldiers was despatched in winter 1796 under the command of Zubov's younger brother, Valerian, and advanced along the east coast of the Caspian, seizing Derbent and Baku, and preparing to invade Persia proper. The death of Catherine in November 1796 brought the campaign to an end, for the Emperor Paul I reversed his mother's policy and recalled his troops, leaving the Russian conquest of Georgia and Armenia to be undertaken in the nineteenth century.

Chapter 14

Catherine's Economic Policy

Not for nothing was Catherine a disciple of the Encyclopaedists, and even of the Physiocrats, the school of economists associated with Louis XVI's physician, Dr Quesnay, in France, who believed that the land was the source of all wealth. She was attracted by the belief of the latter in economic liberty, and by the importance they attached to agriculture as the foundation of a nation's wealth. It was the Physiocrats also who stressed the importance of population growth, necessary for a flourishing agriculture. Catherine, and her advisers, lived in a period when political economy was all the fashion. Many important French and English works were translated into Russian, and many Russians produced their own proposals for Russian economic development. The extent to which Catherine's economic policy was consciously determined by theoretical considerations must not, however, be exaggerated. It would be more correct to say that she adapted the ideas which she borrowed from political economists and cameralists to what seemed to her Russian requirements and that she improvised as circumstances required.

Though the overwhelming majority of the Russian population consisted of peasants, it was not a country in which agriculture flourished everywhere. In most of central and northern Russia the soil was infertile and difficult to cultivate. The low population density also contributed to make farming a harsh and unrewarding occupation. The severe climate meant that the growing season was short and rendered it necessary to keep cattle indoors in the long winter; manure was scarce. The return on the grain sown was often very poor; the yield might be as low as 1:2 or 1:3 in some northern and central areas, which meant that the peasant had no surplus grain for sale, indeed barely enough to feed himself and his family, and had to buy seed corn in the autumn, when the price was high. Further south, in the rich Black Earth zone of the south, south-east and south-west, yields were better, often reaching 1:7 or 1:8, and the standard crop, rye, could be varied with other grains, notably wheat. Here, too, cattle-raising prospered, oxen were harnessed to heavier ploughs than in the north, and the higher yields on well-manured land enabled the peasants to sell their surplus grain, which eventually found its way, mainly by river transport, to the markets in the towns and cities like Moscow and St Petersburg.

The primacy accorded to agriculture is reflected in one of the earliest policies systematically followed by Catherine, namely the promotion of immigration into hitherto uninhabited lands. This had long been one of the fashionable economic doctrines of the eighteenth century and had been practised by rulers as diverse as Frederick II of Prussia and Charles III of Spain. Thinly populated Prussia indeed relied on immigrants to such an extent that by Frederick II's death in 1786, nearly 20 per cent of the inhabitants of the kingdom of Prussia were immigrants or descended from immigrants. Catherine herself had from the beginning of her reign been aware that Russia was underpopulated. This was the reason why she had no objection to polygamy in Moslem or pagan areas. Soon after her accession she had taken steps to attract foreign settlers. Some of the powerful magnates at Catherine's court shared these ideas and took steps to invite foreign, mainly German, religious colonists, like the Moravian Brethren, to settle on their lands.

But a major programme of immigration and settlement needed government backing, and this was achieved with manifestos of 1762 and 1764, setting out the favourable conditions, such as exemption from taxes for a specified number of years, which would be offered to foreign settlers, and establishing a special department, the Chancery of Guardianship of Foreigners, under Catherine's favourite, Grigory Orlov, to administer their affairs. Such an invitation to foreigners to settle in Russia was necessarily accompanied by toleration of religious diversity among Christians at least. Jews were neither permitted nor excluded by the manifestos, but Catherine took secret steps to encourage Jewish immigration, in her search for colonists. Moslems however were excluded, in all probability because of a tradition of nomadism, because they were unlikely to be so efficient as agriculturalists, tradesmen and entrepreneurs, and because they traded with the east rather than with the west.

In this early period foreign agricultural settlers were primarily directed towards the area around Saratov on the Volga; at the same time a somewhat different regime for military and civilian settlers was introduced in the 1760s into the area known as New Russia, then the southernmost part of the Russian Empire (today in Ukraine), stretching from the River Bug to the River Donets, just north of the territory of the Zaporozhian Cossack Host. The military settlers were liable to perform military service and came under military command. Recruiters were encouraged to bring in settlers not only by favourable economic terms, but by the offer of rank – 300 military settlers for a major's rank (which entailed the status of hereditary noble), 30 for a sergeant's. Whereas the colonies of foreign settlers suffered from many initial hardships and only came into their own with the second generation of settlers, the population in New Russia, which was mainly composed of Great Russians with a smattering of Moldavians, Greeks, Bulgarians, Poles and Ukrainians (most of them Orthodox by religion), grew rapidly, though in absolute terms it was still very small in 1772 – some 162,920 of both sexes.

The treaty of Kutschuk Kainardzhi opened up a period of peace which was to last for thirteen years and which was to allow Russia to embark on the economic development of the south, and to witness a quickening of agricultural and manufacturing production. The destruction of the Zaporozhian Host opened up further great areas of land for colonization on both banks of the Dnieper, now safe from Tartar raids, and offered the promise of trade relations with the Danube basin and the countries of the eastern Mediterranean. (Shortage of land was never a problem in the eighteenth century – it was always shortage of labour.) The Empress's favourite, G.A. Potemkin, was appointed governor-general of New Russia in 1774, and set about building new towns and attracting settlers. Ten towns were founded between 1775 and 1782. The town of Kherson, on the estuary of the Dnieper, was founded in 1778 as the principal naval base. The need to feed the armed forces stationed in the south and the new opportunities for export led to an upsurge in the cultivation of wheat, barley and oats, and millet; a particular kind of hard wheat, which stood up to wind, frost and drought, was to become a major export commodity to Italy where it was used to make pasta. Conditions were also ideal for cattle and horsebreeding, as well as sheepfarming, and the rivers were teeming with fish. Vineyards and wine-making were also introduced.

The annexation of the Crimea and its hinterland in 1783 placed even more land at the disposal of the government. Huge tracts were distributed to favoured courtiers. Potemkin helped himself to some 86,000 desyatinas of land in the Crimean peninsula and on the mainland, on which he proposed to set up a model farm. Many of the military and naval officers on his staff were given land, to which they subsequently moved serfs from other parts of Russia. Leading Tartar nobles were similarly rewarded. But Potemkin also distributed land to people of other social estates, notably to non-noble petty officials, entrepreneurs, horticulturalists and so on. The port of Odessa became the main outlet for the southern grain trade. In 1793 there were 10 inhabitants; in 1799, there were 4,573, apart from the garrison. In 1795, trade turnover was 67,889 rubles; by 1797 it was 208,492. The Land Survey (see Chapter 11) and the opening up of these new lands for cultivation led to the striking increase in agricultural production which marked the last decades of the eighteenth century, which went to feed St Petersburg in its inhospitable marshes, and to feed the alcohol distilleries from which the great nobles drew much of their income and the state an increasing share of its revenue.

In the opinion of W.H. McNeil in his *Europe's Steppe Frontier*, 'Until the invention of steamships and railroads in the nineteenth century opened up . . . the American Middle West, the Argentine pampas, the Canadian prairies . . . to commercial farming this Russian expansion remained unparalleled in the scale, scope, and rapidity with which it was carried through. It still remains unparalleled in respect to the socio-political means that produced so massive an agricultural expansion . . .' – that is to say serfs and state peasants with no agricultural machinery. It was the success of Russia in developing and later in taxing the produce of these new areas which provided the power which saw Russia through the Napoleonic wars.

In the industrial field, following in this respect the policies of Peter III, Catherine from the beginning expressed her disapproval of monopolies, and particularly the monopoly rights granted by the Colleges of Mining and Manufactures to merchants for the production of specific commodities. She wished to free economic enterprise as much as possible by removing the need for members of any social estate to ask for government permission before setting up any workshop or factory. The general principle of the freedom of economic enterprise was proclaimed in the Manifesto of 17 March 1775, and in 1779 a further law ordered the local governors not to interfere in manufactories and enterprises, since these should be regarded as private property which everyone could set up in accordance with existing laws, without asking for permission from anybody.

In the early 1770s Catherine was faced with the economic consequences of two major disasters, namely the plague epidemic in

Moscow and the surrounding territory in 1771 and the destruction of industrial enterprises and factories in the Urals and western Siberia during the Pugachev Revolt (see Chapter 5).

In the course of the plague, Moscow lost about one-fifth of its population and two-fifths of the merchant estate. As in other countries, plague affected the poorer strata of the population much more severely, mainly because of living conditions, such as the crowded wooden houses which harboured huge numbers of the rats which carried the plague-bearing fleas. It is noteworthy that the Foundling Home in Moscow, which was built of brick and stone, suffered almost no casualties. Many houses were burnt down both in Moscow and in the countryside as a means of plague control. In the result, the workforce declined drastically, and much capital and equipment was lost. The large-scale manufactories, particularly textiles, which relied on their own 'possessional' serf labour, suffered particularly heavy losses in manpower, and as the non-noble owners were no longer allowed to buy serf labour they had to compete for hired labour and never succeeded in recovering their previous importance.

The permission, granted to everyone, of whatever social estate, in the Manifesto of 17 March 1775 (see previous page) to set up a work-bench, factory or industrial enterprise anywhere and in any branch of production helped to restore economic activity. It opened the way for serfs, state peasants, merchants and townspeople to branch out into any kind of craft or manufacture, and abolished the previously existing legal monopoly of the urban estate. As a result many new small businesses started up in Moscow, attracting immigrants from the countryside, and helping to repopulate the city. This law reflected Catherine's own preference for small-scale industry over large factories; it also contributed to increasing the number of peasants who left the villages to work (with their masters' permission) in industry, and were lost to agriculture, something which Catherine on the whole did not approve of. It also represented a victory for the standpoint of the nobles, who benefited from the non-agricultural activity of the peasants, and went against the demands of the urban merchants, who had always attempted to preserve their legal monopoly of manufacturing and trade and to prevent the peasants from trading in the towns and undercutting them because they did not have to pay town taxes.

The opportunity was also taken to reform the government of the city of Moscow, to remove large-scale manufactories from the city centre in order to reduce pollution, to clean up slaughterhouses and cemeteries and place them too outside the city, to improve the water supply and clean it up, all in accordance with the recommendations of the German cameralists. A new body, the so-called Plague Commission, was set up to co-ordinate the fight against infection and the reconstruction of the city along more modern lines. The new Catherine Hospital was also founded together with a lunatic asylum.

The increase in production following Catherine's liberalizing policies is reflected in the rise in the number of enterprises from some 600–700 in 1762 to over 2,000 by the end of the reign. Cotton, silk and woollen cloth were mainly produced in larger-sized manufactories owned by merchants and sometimes by nobles, sometimes even by serfs. Cotton was particularly well developed in the village of Ivanovo, belonging to Count Sheremet'yev, where his millionaire serfs ran the industry in his name. There was a flourishing cottage industry, prominent in the linen industry, on the narrow looms used by peasants in their huts; peasants produced such items as handkerchiefs, silk ribbons, hats, shoes, furniture, nails and ironware, cutlery, earthenware, leather goods and soap and dominated the processing of agricultural produce (for example flour-milling, timber production). It is difficult however to measure output produced in such quantities on such a small scale, except when one is dealing with villages which specialized in a particular commodity, such as cutlery in Pavlovo in the province of Nizhniy Novgorod.

Heavy industry, such as large-scale textile production, mining and metallurgy, was usually owned by merchants, though some nobles had acquired large enterprises at below market value in the 1750s, and sold them back at a profit to the state when they proved unable to manage them. Peter III had abolished the practice of allowing non-nobles to buy peasant villages as possessional serfs in 1762 and Catherine repeated his law soon after her accession. There were noble officials, particularly in the College of Manufacturing, who, like the President, D.V. Volkov, believed that it was far better for industry to be manned by 'free hired labour' that is to say salaried state peasants, or serfs seeking work with the permission of their owner, who could be hired and fired by the enterprise (Volkov had probably originally inspired the decree of 1762 forbidding non-nobles to buy serf villages for industry). Catherine shared this opinion, and during her reign the purchase of serfs for industry continued to be forbidden, though it was at times possible to get around the prohibition. The practice of 'assigning' peasant villages to heavy industry also ceased.

In attempting to interpret this policy one is again faced with lack of evidence and with differences of view between historians. There are those who hold that it represents the victory of the nobles, who were able to maintain their exclusive right to buy serfs and to prevent non-nobles from buying serfs allegedly for industry but often in order to 'live like nobles'. There appears to have been an increase in the number of serfs purchased for heavy industry by non-nobles in the late 1740s and 1750s. This may have alarmed nobles, fearful of losing their monopoly of serf-ownership, and thus sparked off the decree of 1762. By 1764 there were some 29,293 male serfs in the iron and copper foundries; by the end of the century, the number had grown to over 48,000 in spite of the ban on purchase (much of the rise was due to natural increase). However, in other industries, such as the textile industry, which were entitled by law to buy a certain quota of serfs until 1762, the purchases were less than half the number the owners of the enterprises were entitled to. In some cases, industrialists entitled to buy over 200 serfs bought only three or four. It appears therefore that in preferring the use of 'free hired labour' the government was endorsing the prevailing view of many non-noble industrialists, and that the demand to purchase serfs was centred around industries like metallurgy which, for geographical reasons, found it more difficult to obtain labour.

Serf labour was also widely engaged in the textile industry by means of the putting-out system, when merchants travelled the country, supplying the peasants with the raw materials, and bought the finished product later in the season. As in other European countries at the time, child labour was extensively used particularly in textiles. Economic historians have frequently commented on the lack of entrepreneurship displayed by the Russian merchant class which led to economic backwardness and increased the role of the government in fostering enterprise. There are many reasons for this characteristic of the Russian economy, among which one might mention lack of education, lack of capital, lack of numbers, difficulties of transport and the material obstacles of the climate, as well as a mentality which was not primarily orientated towards profit-making.

Extensive measures were taken to compensate for the damage caused by the Pugachev Revolt. Copper and iron foundries had been pillaged or destroyed, particularly in Bashkiria, and the total of the damage to industry was estimated at over 2.5 million rubles. Many cities had been burnt, like Kazan', or had suffered damage to public buildings, fortifications, and warehouses. An initial grant of 100,000 rubles served to compensate landowners and their families who had often been left destitute, and in 1775 branches of the Nobles' Bank (see below) were set up, in the areas affected by the revolt, to provide loans at low interest. Catherine herself gave 250,000 rubles for the reconstruction of the city of Kazan'. Nevertheless industry was relatively quickly restored though production, which had declined drastically during the revolt, did not recover until about 1780. Unfortunately the opportunity was not apparently taken to modernize production methods in the foundries and, though Russia still remained one of the largest producers of iron in Europe, its primacy was lost by the end of the century. Revenue from taxation in the ravaged areas also declined severely: in 1772, before the revolt, the poll-tax collected in the province of Orenburg came to 20,055 rubles; this fell to 11,596 in 1773 and 157 in 1774. The town of Orenburg was exempted from the poll-tax for two years after it was freed.

Catherine also took steps in May 1779 to improve the condition of the assigned peasants by defining their duties, increasing their wages and shortening their season of work. This seriously affected the production of precious metals in the great Kolyvan complex, by creating a shortage of labour. In the mid-eighteenth century, until 1771, Russia had been the largest producer of precious metals in Europe, but a combination of factors, some external to Russia, some arising within the industry itself, led to a decline which lasted until the early 1800s.

The abolition of internal customs duties in 1754 had greatly enlivened Russian internal commerce. Again, following the policies of Peter III in this respect, Catherine immediately on her accession issued a decree abolishing most of the remaining commercial monopolies, including the trade in furs, and trade with China. There was a constantly growing demand for foodstuffs in the cities of the north, particularly St Petersburg, which could not be met by the production of local serf estates. More distant parts of Russia such as the region of the Volga were drawn into the market and produced crops for cash. The need to supply the two largest cities in Russia, St Petersburg and Moscow, with supplies of an increasing variety of commodities proved a tremendous incentive for the development of the internal market. There was also an enormous transport industry, horse-drawn for short distances, water-borne for longer distances. In Catherine's reign the network of navigable waterways was considerably extended, and the relative cost of transport declined. But if

Russians played the dominant part in internal trade, they were poorly represented in foreign trade.

St Petersburg was the main Russian port, attracting to it the bulk of goods for export, and with a large colony of foreign merchants, of which the British were the largest and the best established. British, Dutch and other ships often came in ballast and loaded up with timber, iron, hemp, flax, sailcloth, pitch, tar and other goods. Russian imports were mainly silk and woollen cloth, dyes, colonial products, fruit, wines and ale. (Catherine was at one time recommended to drink English porter.) In line with the more liberal commercial trend, the first customs tariff issued in Catherine's reign, in 1766, modified the protectionism of previous customs tariffs. Goods of which the equivalent could be procured in Russia were charged at 30 per cent of the value; goods actually produced in Russia were forbidden or paid duty at 200 per cent. Luxury goods paid between 20 and 100 per cent, while imports of raw materials for processing by Russian industry paid nothing or very little. Duties on Russian exports were decreased, thus rendering them more attractive in foreign markets.

Catherine also hoped that her subjects would make use of the measures of trade protection on the high seas she had embarked on (see Chapter 7) in 1780, and she enacted a code of maritime practice in 1781 for Russian commercial shipping. Though the number of Russian registered merchant ships did increase from some 20 to over 400, the Russians were not natural sailors (most of the ships were in fact manned by people from Livonia and Estonia), nor did they have the capital necessary to maintain long-distance shipping, which remained overwhelmingly in foreign hands.

The revised customs tariff of 1782 has to be seen against the background of the freeing of economic enterprise enacted in the Manifesto of 1775. The abolition of the College of Manufactures in 1779 led to the end of its power to issue licences to manufacture, and this was followed by the permission granted to nobles in 1782 to exploit the raw materials on their estates and set up enterprises in the countryside (see Chapter 12).

The customs tariff of 1782 further reduced the duties on imported and exported goods and raw materials, and maintained the 25 per cent reduction of duties payable on imports and exports through the Black Sea ports which had been enacted in 1775, in order to encourage this new branch of Russian trade. Total foreign trade grew enormously during Catherine's reign, from a turnover of some

20 million rubles in 1762–3 to over 100 million rubles in 1796. The liberal trade policy was abandoned by Catherine in part as a result of the war against revolutionary France. In 1793 trade with France was banned, but the duties on the import of a whole range of other, mainly luxury goods were increased.

Economic historians have endeavoured to assess the extent to which Catherine's tariff policy was motivated by a conscious protectionism of Russian industry in the national interest (regardless of sectional Russian economic interests) rather than by considerations of national revenue, that is to say the amount the state could collect in taxation of foreign trade to supply its own financial needs. As in so many aspects of Russian eighteenth-century history, one must suspend judgment until more evidence is available of the motives which inspired particular policies.

The suggestion that tariff policy was worked out in relation to the state's need for income is not surprising in view of the backwardness of the Russian financial structure. The first Russian banks were set up in 1754, one for the nobles, one known as the Commercial Bank, primarily for merchants. A feature of the Nobles' Bank is that it lent money at the moderate interest rate of 5 or 6 per cent to nobles on the security of landed estates, the value of which was assessed in the numbers of 'souls', that is peasants attached to the land. But, although the bank lent money, it was not empowered until 1770 to receive deposits of money on which it would pay out interest. Other institutions, such as the Foundling Homes, were also authorized to receive deposits and pay interest on them. Since the bank rarely foreclosed on defaulting nobles, bank loans were in the end a form of long-term subsidy to the noble landowners. There were of course moneylenders, but they charged a much higher rate of interest. On the other hand there was no form of investment for capital in government stock which could guarantee an annual income on the lines of the English Consolidated Debt or the French *cens*. Bills of exchange and letters of credit (*vekseli*, from the German *Wechsel*) were widely used for the transfer of money within Russia, and recent research has shown that the Russian money market was closely linked to the great Dutch firm of Hope and Co., in Amsterdam, which discounted Russian bills. Only the existence of St Petersburg, a Russian port city (as distinct from the other Baltic ports, with their long-established German traditions), enabled Russia to begin to participate in her own right in the European money market. There was yet no Russian stock exchange.

One of the most serious deficiencies of the administrative legacy of Peter the Great was the chaos in the financial administration. Catherine took steps to remedy this situation, and 'it is from Catherine's reign, not from that of Peter I, Paul, or Alexander I that the beginnings of an effective centralized state financial administration must be dated'. At Catherine's accession, more than fifty state agencies were empowered to collect revenue and to spend it locally. It was thus almost impossible to obtain a true picture of the total revenue of the state, and of its total expenditure, and therefore to draw up an annual budget. All the financial colleges were understaffed, and quite unable to process the reports and requests for information which came in. Piecemeal attempts at reform were made in the 1760s and the early 1770s, under the impact of the increasing expenditure called for by the Turkish war.

The opportunity for a major reform came with the enactment of the Statute on Local Administration in 1775. The separation of functions which the Statute laid down provided for the setting up in each province and district of Treasury Chambers, placed under the deputy governors, charged with administering the collection of revenue and the disbursement of what was required locally; and with the collection of the special tax (*obrok*) paid by the state peasants and the 'economic' peasants, that is to say those who had been attached to the Church before 1764 and had then come under the jurisdiction of the College of Economy. This college was now abolished and the 'economic' peasants were merged with the state peasants. The new Treasury Chambers collected the poll-tax and supervised the farming of the salt and liquor taxes. (Both these commodities paid an excise at the point of sale, which formed a considerable part of the state's revenue.) They were ordered to provide reports on their revenues directly to a new office set up in the Senate, the Office of State Revenues, under the Procurator-General, A.A. Vyazemsky, who was given the additional post of State Treasurer in the Senate. Though it took twenty years for the institutions of the Statute of 1775 to be introduced throughout the Empire, the Treasury Chambers were set up at once nearly everywhere. Their reports sent to Vyazemsky enabled him to present Catherine with a state budget by 1781, that is agreed expenditure, and estimated revenue. With the establishment of the post of State Treasurer it proved possible to dispense with the previous financial colleges, which were gradually eliminated.

There is general agreement that financial administration if not financial policy improved considerably in Catherine's reign. 'Many of the Catherinian procedures remained in force until the budget reforms of the 1860s,' wrote one of the historians concerned. But historians have rightly been critical of her financial policies. In the first years of her reign, she practised good housekeeping, keeping expenses down and even incurring criticism on the ground of her parsimony. Yet it was at this period that she was faced with the increased cost of the salaries which had now to be paid to officials as a result of the 'little reform' of the bureaucracy of 1764 (see Chapter 3) and amounting to over one million rubles. She paid for them by a miscellaneous series of indirect taxes. The tax on liquor was increased, taxes on wills, mortgages and loans were introduced, and taxes on promotion in the Table of Ranks were laid down. These taxes were specifically intended to provide for the medical care of the officer or official employed in any capacity. In 1775, 9,200 rubles were collected in taxes on promotion in the Table of Ranks.

With the outbreak of war in 1768, expenses shot up. The money due (*obrok*) paid by state, Church and Crown peasants over and above the poll-tax of seventy kopeks was increased to two rubles, and special war taxes, many of which were abolished in 1775, raised some 500,000 rubles. In addition Catherine received subsidies from Prussia, and borrowed money in the United Provinces. She also embarked on the issue of paper money, or *assignats*, and since the operation was carefully conducted and kept to only 5 per cent of the annual revenue, the value of the paper money was maintained at between 102 and 103 kopeks to the silver ruble. The war indemnity paid by the Turks in accordance with the treaty of Kutschuk Kainardzhi was used by Catherine to pay off the loans she had received from the Dutch to finance the war, and she reverted again to good housekeeping.

But with the reforms of the 1780s and the costs of later development in New Russia and the Crimea expenses mounted up again, and Catherine met them by printing more money. The outbreak of war in 1787 raised the Russian deficit to unprecedented heights. Ignoring the advice of the State Treasurer Vyazemsky to raise taxes, Catherin preferred to print more money. Russia was in the throes of inflation, the assignat ruble fell to 108 kopeks while the value of the ruble declined on the foreign market. Catherine now proceeded to borrow abroad, and finally in 1794 she agreed to raise the poll-tax by thirty kopeks to one ruble, and introduced various other indirect taxes. To her belongs the credit of creating the Russian national debt. Yet though Russia was at war for so much of this time, and war evidently played a large part in the Russian financial crisis, expenditure on the armed forces as a percentage of total government expenditure declined throughout Catherine's reign, whereas expenditure on internal administration rose from 37.5 per cent of all expenditure in 1763 to 50.8 per cent in 1796.

Chapter 15

Catherine and the French Revolution

The impact of the French Revolution on Russian foreign policy has been discussed in Chapter 13. The Revolution also considerably influenced the domestic policy of Catherine in the last years of her life.

The news of the fall of the Bastille was, according to the French Ambassador in Russia, the Comte de Ségur, greeted with enthusiasm by the common people: 'Frenchmen, Russians, Danes, Germans, Englishmen, Dutch, all congratulated and embraced each other in the street, as though they had been delivered of a too heavy chain weighing on them.' The newspapers of the two capitals, the *St Petersburg* and the *Moscow Gazettes* (the latter no longer edited by Novikov) kept the public informed of events in France, if in somewhat dramatic tones. The circulation of both papers rose to record heights (2,000 and 4,000 respectively). The *Moscow Gazette*, even in the hands of its new editor, still reflected the freer intellectual climate of Moscow. On 7 August 1789 the *St Petersburg Gazette*, published by the Academy of Sciences, printed a description of the Fall of the Bastille: 'the hand trembles with horror in describing events in which people could show such lack of duty to the ruler, and to humanity'. The initiative in riots and disturbances was ascribed to the *meshchanstvo*, or the lower orders in the towns, composed of craftsmen, shopkeepers and petty traders. The Parisian National Guard was described as the *meshchanskoe voysko* (the common people's militia), thus stressing its lower-middle-class nature. The *Moscow Gazette* however attributed Parisian revolutionary activity to the *grazhdanstvo* or citizens.

If much of what occurred in France was described in terms intended to illustrate the seditious nature of events, yet readers were well informed about what was actually happening, and could form their own judgment. The summoning of the States General, its transformation into the Constitutional Assembly, speeches by Mirabeau, Barnave and others, the famous night of 4 August 1789, when feudal rights were voluntarily given up, the loss of noble privileges, 'reducing the nobility to a humiliating equality with those who today hold the legislative power', were events fully if critically described. The Declaration of the Rights of Man was printed in full in a Russian translation, in the *St Petersburg Gazette*, including the challenging article III: 'Supreme power derives from the people.' But reports of risings, the burning of châteaux, the killing of 'enemies of the people', that is to say nobles, were also published, to ensure that the reading public should be well aware of the implications of the revolution in the countryside, and remember what the Russian nobility had suffered during the Pugachev Revolt.

The Russian reading public could also draw on a large number of French revolutionary news-sheets, pamphlets and papers circulating freely, including *La révolution Parisienne*, which attacked the rich and 'unmasked' the treacherous doings of the Constituent Assembly, and Camille Desmoulins's *La Révolution de France et de Brabant*. Another favourite was the pamphlet of Jean Louis Carra, *L'Orateur des États Généraux*, in which the author called on the States General to draft a new constitution based on reason and natural law, and swore to die rather than be enslaved to royal absolutism. (Carra was guillotined in 1793.)

All classes among the literate were caught up to some degree in the excitement of the revolution. Young nobles wore French fashions and used French revolutionary jargon. Revolutionary songs such as 'Ça ira' were even sung in the presence of Catherine in the palace. In the Cadet Corps, the military academy which turned young nobles into officers and gentlemen, French revolutionary literature was openly displayed in the library. The debates over the drafting of the French constitution were followed with interest, and to a few of the more liberally inclined nobles the constitution adopted in September 1791 represented an approximation to the kind of constitutional monarchy they might themselves have hoped for. There were those among the magnates who preferred the English model, with its powerful and aristocratic House of Lords. Others found that a political structure which gave some degree of representation to a relatively small property-owning social class fitted in with their conceptions.

Catherine herself and most of the Russian nobles were much more sceptical and indeed were rapidly outraged by the excesses of the revolutionaries in France. At the beginning the Empress did not regard the news from France as likely to turn Russia upside down. The taking of the Bastille did not arouse her fears, though as she later wrote to her confidant, Baron Grimm, 'I don't like justice without justice, and these executions *à la lanterne.*' She was even prepared to discuss a treaty with France to strengthen her international position in 1789. Thus no steps were taken at first to impose censorship on news from France (just as information about the infant United States of America, which had just finished drafting its republican constitution, was freely published).

Perhaps because of her experience with the Legislative Commission, Catherine had no patience with legislative bodies, composed like the French Constituent Assembly, mainly of 'pettifogging lawyers' – the hydra with 1,200 heads as she contemptuously called it – which had abolished the French nobility, all that French families had earned by their labour and their service to the Crown. She blamed the weakness of the French nobles on the expulsion of the Jesuits and the decline in the quality of French education as a result of the closure of their schools. The flight of the French royal family from Paris and their recapture in Varennes in June 1791 showed clearly that they were no longer free agents, and led Catherine to refuse to receive the French Chargé d'Affaires at court. In September 1791 she was outraged by what appeared to her the supine way in which Louis XVI accepted and swore an oath of loyalty to the new French constitution of 1791. Even more important to her however was the proclamation of the new constitution in Poland on 3 May 1791 NS, which she viewed as the brainchild of a nest of 'Jacobins' on the very borders of Russia.

It is against this background that one must place the first really serious case of intellectual persecution of her reign, the prosecution and conviction of A.N. Radishchev in 1790. Radishchev is an extremely important figure in the history of Russian thought. In Soviet historiography he stands at the very beginning of the tradition of revolutionary ideas, though many western historians do not agree with the Soviet interpretation of his outlook. He came from a wealthy noble family, and had been chosen at the age of thirteen to join the Corps of Pages, which served Catherine at court. This gave him an inside view of the corruption of court society. Subsequently he was one of those sent to study abroad at government expense under Catherine's programme for subsidizing foreign study. He went to Leipzig in 1766, where he studied law and philosophy and was influenced not only by current German theories of natural law but also and particularly by the materialistic philosophy of the French thinker, Helvetius, in his work, *De l'esprit*.

Returning to Russia, Radishchev did not join the army, but entered civilian service in the first department of the Senate concerned with appeals and the revision of sentences throughout the country. Soon after he moved to the legal staff of the College of War, where his task was the gruelling one of supervising courts martial, at a time when Russian military law, in common with that of most countries including Britain, was marked by its extreme severity. He retired in 1775, but rejoined the service in 1777 in the College of Commerce, and eventually rose to be director of the St Petersburg Customs.

Radishchev had started writing and translating as a young man. He is supposed to have made various contributions to the periodicals published in the 1770s in St Petersburg, but his first known work is a translation of *Observations on the History of Greece* by the French *philosophe* Gabriel Bonnot de Mably. In this work Mably praised the 'democratic republics' of ancient Greece, particularly the egalitarian austerity and virtue of Sparta (based however on slavery) which had a particular attraction for eighteenth-century opponents of absolute monarchy, who contrasted it with the luxury and corruption of Periclean Athens (also based on slavery). Radishchev translated Mably's tirades against monarchy and despotism, and in a footnote of his own which he added to the text, he commented: 'Absolutism [*samoderzhaviye*] is the condition most repugnant to human nature. . . . Injustice on the part of the ruler gives to the nation as his judges a right over him which is just as great as, and yet greater than, that which the law gives the ruler over criminals. *The ruler is the first citizen of the national society*' (Radishchev's italics). It is an indication of the freedom of expression reigning in Russia at that time that the book was published in 1773 on the official press of the Academy of Sciences, and the translation was sponsored by a 'society for the publication of books', set up by Novikov and a colleague, for the marketing of books translated by the Society for the Translation of Foreign Books established and subsidized by Catherine II herself (see Chapter 8).

Radishchev published relatively little of what he wrote, but in 1789 he took advantage of the law allowing individuals to set up a private printing press to acquire one and in May 1790 he published *A Journey from St Petersburg to Moscow*. In form the book is a series of letters from a young man travelling between the two capitals, modelled on the *Sentimental Journey* of Lawrence Sterne. When Radishchev submitted it to the head of the Police Board of St Petersburg, the person charged with vetting forthcoming publications for offences against religion, decency and the government, the police official gave it the most cursory attention as a mere travelogue. But Radishchev could not have chosen a worse time to publish his book. Peace talks with the Turks had failed, and Catherine knew that the war would last for at least another campaigning season. At the beginning of June a great naval battle between the Russian and Swedish fleets took place in the Baltic, and the gunfire was clearly audible in St Petersburg.

The main themes of Radishchev's book, as expressed in letters from the various posting stations at which he stopped on the way, were indignation at the treatment of the serfs, and at serfdom itself as an insult to the equality and humanity of all men; the rejection of religious obscurantism; and a thoroughgoing attack on monarchical absolutism and all that flowed from it. This included the corruption and injustice of the law courts, the never ending wars and the cruelty of the recruit levy, the lack of accountability of officials, the prevalence of bribery and the arbitrariness of government. Radishchev expressed himself throughout in most impassioned tones, particularly when he denounced the monstrous treatment of serfs, and nowhere more so than in the allegory called 'The Dream'. Here, the traveller sees himself in a dream as a ruler enthroned, surrounded by evidence of the prosperity of his country, his victorious armies and the welfare of his people, and is then confronted by the figure of a woman, who removes the scales from his eyes and forces him to see the reality of injustice, poverty and death, of the commander-in-chief of the forces employed in war sunk in cowardly sloth while the soldiers are robbed and starved. In one of his chapters Radishchev uses the well-known device of finding some papers which prove to contain a plan for the emancipation of the serfs. He declaims against the inhuman habit of enslaving a fellow human being and the shame of maintaining the custom in the present enlightened days. Efforts by rulers to restrain this hundred-headed monster had failed because of the resistance of the hereditary nobility. Drawing on the theory of natural law Radishchev argues in favour of the equality of man, hence of the inadmissibility of slavery. Analysing the distorted relationship between master and serf, he begs the serfs to forgive the arrogance and oppressiveness of even the best of masters. The plan proposes making an immediate distinction between domestic serfs, slaves in all but name, and peasants. The former were to be freed at once. The peasants were to be guaranteed the ownership of the land they cultivated, the right to buy their freedom, the right to be judged by their peers, that is to say other serfs (a right which state peasants already enjoyed under the Statute of 1775), and no punishment without proper trial. Radishchev was also perceptive enough to see in the Table of Ranks instituted by Peter the Great the greatest obstacle to equality among Russians.

To ram his points home, Radishchev included an 'Ode to Liberty' written at the time of the American Revolution and which he had probably added after showing the book to the head of the Police Board. It describes how Liberty summons the Roman Brutus and the Swiss Wilhelm Tell from their sleep and strikes fear into the rulers' hearts; though it condemns Cromwell for having overthrown freedom, it praises him for having executed Charles I.

The *Journey* strongly reflects the influence of Radishchev's reading, notably Helvetius, Beccaria and the *Histoire des deux Indes*, of the abbé Raynal, one of the most vocal critics of slavery of all kinds, as well as of despotism, which had been published in several editions in the 1770s. But Radishchev transposes and applies Raynal's general strictures to Russian reality, and his book is the first and most powerful indictment of serfdom as a system and absolutism as a form of government published by a Russian in Russia. It is also the first attempt to publish an attack on the Russian ruler personally, on the Russian form of government, on the conduct of the war and on the social system. This is no doubt what aroused Catherine's anger. Attacks on classical or foreign tyrants and despots had nearly always been allowed. But Radishchev was closer to home.

Catherine immediately perceived the danger of his attack; she read the book very attentively; her marginal comments have survived and reflect her mounting indignation and the allegations that particularly outraged her. In Radishchev's comments on the ill-treatment of serfs Catherine who, in common with many Russians, believed the Russian peasants to be better off than most foreign peasants, saw the desire to arouse them against their masters – and called him a new Pugachev. (In fact Radishchev wrote disparagingly of Pugachev, and warned that *unless* serfdom became less cruel, the serfs would rise.) The Empress identified the source of many of Radishchev's tirades in Raynal's book, which she knew and despised for its anti-Russian tone. What seems most to have outraged her was the attack on her government in general and Potemkin in particular in 'The Dream': 'The author is filled and infected with the French mania, seeks out and seizes on every pretext to break down respect for authority . . . and to arouse the people against their superiors and the government . . . ', she commented.

Publication of a work which might destabilize Russian society while the country was fighting a war on two fronts, and which seemed to approve of the tenets being proclaimed by the revolutionaries in Paris, was bound to lead to trouble. Catherine, as soon as the author was identified, ordered his arrest and the confiscation of all the copies of the book. Radishchev seems to have been quite unaware of the danger he was incurring in publishing his *Journey*, but faced with arrest, a probable serious punishment and a long separation from his children, he decided that discretion was the better part of valour. He destroyed all the remaining copies of the book (only some twenty-five had been sold) and not only admitted his authorship but also said that his aim had been to make a name for himself as an author, and that he had had no intention of attacking the Empress. He did not retract his desire for the freedom of the peasants however, and begged the Empress for mercy.

Radishchev was charged with publishing a book 'filled with the most mischievous doctrines destructive of public order . . . tending to arouse among the people indignation against their rulers and government . . . and containing insulting outbursts against the imperial dignity and power', and with adding to his book after it had been passed by the censor. He was tried by the Central Criminal Court in St Petersburg and condemned to death on 24 July 1790. As usual in Russia, where the death penalty had fallen into disuse since 1754, the verdict was forwarded for confirmation to the Senate and then to the Empress, who as usual commuted the death penalty, in this case to ten years' exile (not, as is frequently stated, to hard labour) in the far-distant fort of Ilimsk in Siberia.

These were not the days of the Gulag Archipelago for political prisoners. Though Radishchev started out under guard and in chains on his journey to Siberia, the chains were promptly removed by imperial order, and Radishchev's patron, Count A.R. Vorontsov, the President of the College of Commerce, who thought the sentence excessive however much he deplored the book, supplied him with ample funds and clothes. He was allowed to linger in Moscow for a few weeks, and arrived in Tobol'sk at Christmas. Here he stayed until the spring, when he was joined by his sister-in-law (his wife had died) and two of his children, and he did not leave until July 1791. The party, which by now also included Radishchev's servants, did not reach Ilimsk until December 1791. Vorontsov continued to supply Radishchev with books and money, and the exile attempted to cultivate land, to teach his children and to physic the local people. Canon law forbade him to marry his deceased wife's sister, but he had three children by her in Siberia. He was allowed to return to live on his estates in 1797, after the death of Catherine and the accession of the Emperor Paul, and subsequently, under Alexander I, he worked in the legislative department of the Senate, but none of his later writings were published at the time. He committed suicide in 1802. The *Journey* was banned, and those copies which had not been destroyed by Radishchev himself were destroyed by the government. To this day only 15 of the 600 or so printed copies survive, though there are many manuscript copies. The book was published for the first time in Russian by the revolutionary Alexander Herzen, in London in 1859, but it did not appear in Russia until after the revolution of 1905. It was well known however among the members of the generation which grew up during the Napoleonic wars, providing young people with a programme and a political martyr.

The year of Radishchev's arrest, 1790, though a period of tension for Russia in the war, was however not the culminating point of French revolutionary ferment. Nevertheless, in mid-1791 the editing of the *St Petersburg Gazette* was handed over to a specially set-up translation department in the Academy of Sciences, which was ordered to shorten the accounts of events in France, and to accompany them with commentaries on their harmful nature to the French themselves. The increasing tension in France and above all Poland in 1791 was counterbalanced for Catherine by the signature of the peace of Jassy in December 1791, which left her more leisure. In March 1792 however she heard the news of the assassination of Gustavus III of Sweden. Though the attack on the King arose from motives which had nothing to do with the French Revolution, it was automatically assumed that Jacobin agents were behind it, and rumours circulated that attempts on Catherine's life were also being planned. Little by little Catherine closed down on France and French culture. The Governor-General of Moscow, General Prince A.A. Prozorovsky, warned Catherine that every kind of French revolutionary publication was clandestinely on sale in Moscow, and begged her to stop the importation of foreign books. She did not go so far, but she kept a close watch on what was being published, and in 1791 ordered all bookshops to register their catalogues of books for sale with the Academy of Sciences or the University of Moscow to ensure that no books should be sold which were opposed 'to religion, decency and ourselves'. Her attention was drawn in 1792 to the activities of the Moscow masons.

For most of her reign Catherine II had regarded freemasonry as a harmless but rather silly diversion in which her courtiers indulged. As a movement freemasonry provided an outlet for many of those who felt that traditional Orthodox Christianity as practised in Russia did not give them the spiritual comfort they required. But it was not, in the 1770s, regarded with hostility either by the Church or by the state. Many of Catherine's closest collaborators were freemasons, including her Foreign Minister, Count Nikita Panin. She herself did not at that time regard freemasonry as a dangerous political conspiracy but as so much absurd mumbojumbo. In 1779, the Italian charlatan Joseph Balsamo, who called himself Count Cagliostro and has been immortalized by Alexandre Dumas in the story of *The Queen's Necklace*, visited Russia, and Catherine seized the opportunity to caricature him under the name Kalifalkzherston in a play, *The Deceiver*, which she wrote in 1785 to discredit alchemy and freemasonry, and which was widely performed not only in Russia but in Germany, to her great satisfaction. But what had seemed at first merely comic began to take on a more sinister connotation in the more heated atmosphere of the late 1780s and early 1790s.

There was considerable confusion about the various masonic orders at this time. Broadly speaking there were two varieties, the so-called 'symbolist' masons, who were rationalists, drawing upon the scientific knowledge of the enlightenment; and the mystically inclined, who took their inspiration from the occult traditions of alchemy, the Jewish Kabala, Egyptian lore, and who also drew on the thought of the Swedish mystic, E. Swedenborg (1688–1772). In its early stages Russian freemasonry had gravitated more towards the former trend. Many of the most important Russian high officials and officers, like Count Nikita Panin and I.P. Elagin, were masons of this type. But by the 1780s the second trend began to dominate. The mystically inclined were frequently described as 'Martinists', after the followers of the converted Sephardi, Martines de Pasqually (1727–74) and his secretary and disciple Louis Claude de Saint Martin (1743–1803), and regarded as egalitarians and revolutionaries. This was quite unfair to Martines de Pasqually and to Saint Martin, whose doctrines were more concerned with enabling man to return to his state before the fall, by means of external rites and rituals for Martines de Pasqually, by means of internal communion with God for Saint Martin. Saint Martin published one of the key texts of mystical freemasonry in 1775, *Des erreurs et de la vérité*, under the pseudonym 'The Unknown Philosopher'. In the sense that he regarded the Christian Churches as having been superseded by the direct approach of the individual to God, Saint Martin was critical of the structures of Church and state in the Old Regime.

In general freemasonry was not anti-religious. It preached virtue, self-improvement, good works and above all fraternity and equality, though not to the extent of admitting the lower orders to membership. But there was one branch, not perhaps strictly masonic at all, namely the 'illuminists', founded by A. Weishaupt in 1776 in Bavaria, which was rationalist, anti-clerical, anti-monarchical and revolutionary, and was banned in 1784. The name 'illuminists' or 'illuminati' led many to confuse their followers with those of Saint Martin and other mystically inclined masonic movements such as the Rosicrucians, who advocated knowledge of God and self-improvement by means of spiritual illumination. The secrecy which surrounded freemasonry led to the belief, in those who knew little about masons, that they all formed part of a gigantic conspiracy to undermine the established order, and to 'allow the ex-Jesuits to climb back into the closets of kings on the backs of sorcerers and alchemists'.

Catherine began to discourage all masonic activity in the late 1780s because she had grown to suspect freemasons of links with the revolutionary movement. But there was nothing revolutionary about the Rosicrucianism of the Moscow group, of which N.I. Novikov was a prominent member. The Moscow masons, while officially members of the Strict Observance of which the Grandmaster was Duke Ferdinand of Brunswick, were in fact secretly committed to the Rosicrucian movement, of which the directors were two of the most important members of the court of King Frederick William II of Prussia in Berlin. The Moscow group had set up its two private printing presses, and a secret press, on which Russian translations of the classics of mysticism and alchemy were printed. They were closely supervised by their German superiors at the court of the King of Prussia, to whom they rendered an account of their publishing activities and to whom they sent the sums they raised. They also harboured a secret hope that the Grand Duke Paul might become a mason and the Grandmaster of the Rosicrucians in Russia.

Catherine's distrust of masons was now also being fed by one of her correspondents in Germany, Dr J.G. Zimmermann, who was particularly outspoken about the conspiratorial political and revolutionary activities of the illuminati of Bavaria and believed that freemasonry lay at the root of the French Revolution. As a result Catherine ordered a secret supervision of the activities of the Moscow masons in 1790, closed down the one independent masonic lodge in Russia, and, when Novikov's lease of Moscow University Press expired in 1789, she did not renew it.

The charge that Novikov had secretly published a book on the Old Believers replete with lies about the Orthodox Church led to his detention in April 1792. When searched, his house was found to be full of banned religious, occult and masonic literature. But what really told against him was the discovery of links with the Grand Duke Paul, and evidence that the Rosicrucians, of whom there were about sixty in Moscow and its surroundings, were being directed from abroad by a man, Johann Christoff von Wöllner, who had now become one of the ministers of the King of Prussia. This was the very time when Catherine had only just survived the pressure brought to bear upon her by the Triple Alliance, in which Prussia was a leading member, and when she regarded Prussia as a hostile power.

Novikov was never tried, but the accusations against him were listed in the sentence eventually pronounced. He was charged with holding secret meetings at which people swore submission to the Duke of Brunswick; he was accused of corresponding in cypher with the Prussian Minister, Wöllner, and with trying to lure 'a certain person', namely the Grand Duke, to become a mason. He was condemned to fifteen years' imprisonment in Schlüsselburg. But, again, this was not the Gulag Archipelago. He was allowed to take with him his private physician, also a mason, and his serf servant, and they were each allocated one ruble per day for their keep, in contrast with the three kopeks allocated to ordinary prisoners. He was released in 1796 but, though still only in his early fifties, his publishing career was over, and little is known about the rest of his life. He later sold the serf who was with him in Schlüsselburg.

Public opinion among intellectuals and in the University in Moscow was shocked by the severity of the sentence, for what to many seemed to be merely masonic activity. The attempt to recruit the Grand Duke and the subordination of the Rosicrucians to Prussian direction was known to but a few. Moreover three of Novikov's close masonic colleagues got off very lightly; two were exiled to their estates, and the third was even allowed to remain in Moscow. But a number of booksellers who had been distributing banned masonic works were detained, and eventually released, and large numbers of masonic books were burnt. The theological works were handed over to a monastery.

Catherine's treatment of Novikov has ever since remained controversial in the view of historians. Because it has been written about in isolation from her treatment of other printers and publishers, it has been assumed that the Empress was motivated by a particular animus against Novikov, deriving from the satirical attacks he published in his journals in the 1770s, and by dislike of his alleged independent social activity. He had engaged in large-scale charitable activities on borrowed money, to help landowners and serfs during a famine which afflicted the Moscow area in 1787, and Catherine's distrust was fed by the enormous sums of money of which he seemed to dispose. It is only in the last few years that additional evidence has been found by Soviet historians to fill in the background, which goes to show that Catherine continued to subsidize Novikov's journals in the 1770s, that she subsidized the schools founded by his masonic friends in St Petersburg, and that she did not single them out for persecution; and that her main objection to his activity as a publisher was the flood of masonic, hermetic and occult literature which issued from his presses.

The 1790s were however years of growing intellectual repression. The French Revolution was creating increasing revulsion and fear. The overthrow of the French monarchy on 10 August 1792, and the imprisonment of the royal family, followed by the lynching of prisoners in September in which around 1,200 people were massacred, most of them ordinary people of no political importance, horrified European public opinion. Moreover, this took place just when the French armies were starting to sweep victoriously through the Rhineland, annexing territory as they went. The execution of Louis XVI in January 1793 made Catherine physically ill, and she was deeply moved by the death of Marie Antoinette. In her attitude to the French Revolution she was certainly influenced by Edmund Burke, 'the Demosthenes of England' as she called him. To her France had become a country full of ravening beasts: 'they only know how to pillage and to kill', she wrote to Grimm on 6 December 1793. 'If the revolution spreads in Europe, one day a new Tamerlane will come to put a stop to it.' The appetite of the guillotine for victims of all ages, classes and sexes was something which Europe had never seen, and the execution of each wave of revolutionary leaders by the next was not to be seen again until Stalin set about removing all Lenin's friends and colleagues in the 1930s.

Publishers and printers were now more closely supervised. Even Princess Dashkova, at the head of the Academy of the Language, got into trouble in 1793 for printing a play by Ya. B. Knyazhnin (who had died two years earlier) called *Vadim of Novgorod*, in which the hero proclaims the virtues of republicanism. Catherine upbraided her in bitter terms and ordered her to call in and destroy all copies. Nevertheless, though over a hundred people were kept under surveillance (for reasons which are not always known) and some twenty passed through Catherine's Secret Chancery, the most assiduous search of the surviving records has not been able to produce many examples of really severe persecution. Censorship was more severe in revolutionary France, and there were far more people in prison for political reasons.

Many people, including Catherine herself, came to attribute the evils of the French Revolution to those authors such as Voltaire, Helvetius, Holbach and Diderot who had undermined respect for religion and authority over many years. 'Do you remember', the Empress wrote to Grimm on 11 February 1794, 'that the late King of Prussia [Frederick II] used to say that Helvetius had admitted to him that the aim of the "philosophes" was to overthrow all the European thrones, and that the *Encyclopaedia* had been created with the single aim of destroying all the kings and all the religions.' As a result she now turned her back on the intellectual friends of her younger days, and ordered the confiscation of a complete edition of the works of Voltaire in 1792; in 1794, two works, the one entitled *The Tragedy of the Death of Caesar*, the other called *Julius Caesar*, were both removed from the University library and the University bookshop in Moscow. Even Milton's *Paradise Lost* fell under the ban of the censor. Yet in many respects there was still considerable freedom of expression in Russia.

Finally, in September 1796, Catherine set up the first formal system of censorship of her reign. It is difficult to know why she delayed until then if her object was to seal Russia off from the infection of the French Revolution, and it is possible that she was more concerned with the repercussions of revolutionary outbursts in Poland where the final partition had just been put through. However, she now decreed the setting up of censorship posts in St Petersburg, Moscow, Riga and Odessa and on the Polish border, and the closure of all private printing presses; all books were to be submitted before publication to one of the censorship offices; all imported books were to be examined at the frontier.

The reign of Catherine II saw the birth of the Russian intelligentsia. Among the aristocracy, more people travelled, attended universities in Russia or abroad, spoke foreign languages, employed foreign tutors, subscribed to Russian and foreign journals, wrote plays, poetry and novels, or translated works from French, German and even English than ever before. There was a growing class of non-noble educated officials or members of the liberal professions, writers, poets, printers, artists of all kinds, doctors, surgeons, architects, surveyors, actors, who also participated in intellectual life of one sort or another. There were more institutions since the foundation of Moscow University, the Academy of Arts and the Academy of the Language. There was a number of people who now earned their living entirely by writing. But whereas at the beginning of her reign the Empress herself had been one of the leaders of intellectual development, with her Instruction, her periodical, her plays, the translations she sponsored, her general encouragement of writers and poets, by the end of her reign a new, young generation had grown up, seeking to establish its independence of state patronage and looking out on the exciting events taking place in France and elsewhere with a mixture of envy and fear.

Chapter 16

Catherine as Woman and Ruler

Catherine ruled Russia from 1762 to 1796. 'In an absolute monarchy, everything depends on the disposition and character of the Sovereign,' the British Envoy to Russia, Sir James Harris, observed in 1778. The ruler sets the tone in every field far more than in a limited monarchy, as Great Britain was at the time, or in a democracy, as the United Kingdom is today. Peace or war, prosperity or poverty, a free and easy intellectual and social life, or a society isolated from outside influences and dragooned into conformity, all this depended to a great extent on the character of the individual ruler.

The personality of Catherine thus merits some attention. Inevitably it changed a good deal over the thirty-four years of her reign. Yet some features of her character remained present throughout. She was to begin with a woman of an optimistic and cheerful temperament, looking on the bright side of things, not easily depressed or downhearted. This shows clearly in her letters to Potemkin, who, on the contrary, was subject to formidable bouts of despondency, for instance at the beginning of the second Turkish war in 1787, when after the loss of his precious fleet in a storm on the Black Sea he was prepared to throw up his command and evacuate the Crimea. Catherine wrote letters to him full of encouragement, urging him to believe that a bold spirit would overcome failures, advising him about his indigestion, which she was sure contributed to his depression. 'Goodbye, my friend,' she concluded one letter in 1788, 'neither time, nor distance, nor anyone on earth will change my thoughts of you and about you.'

It was this same positive temper which enabled her to steer her way through the shoals at the Russian court while she was still grand duchess and gave her the courage to embark on the *coup d'état* which brought her to the throne. Its success should not conceal from one how dangerous failure might have been. Imprisonment in a convent would have been the mildest penalty she might have had to suffer. Throughout her life Catherine showed very strong and steady nerves at moments of crisis: during the early plots against her; during the Pugachev Revolt, when she had to be dissuaded by her ministers from going herself to Moscow to restore morale after the sacking of Kazan' by Pugachev. But her health did not remain unaffected by these crises and she suffered from frequent headaches and digestive disorders.

By the standards of her time Catherine was a well-read woman of considerable breadth of interest and intellectual curiosity. She was interested in politics, history, education, literature, linguistics, architecture, painting. In her literary as in her legislative production she was pragmatic in her approach, pedantic in her execution, and eclectic as regards her sources. She seemed to feel that if the law described down to the last detail precisely how its provisions were to be implemented, better results would be achieved. In the Russian context, no doubt she was right to think that the careful drafting of laws would prevent misinterpretation. In her Instruction of 1767, she had quoted Montesquieu's dictum that you cannot change customs by means of laws but only by means of other customs; but her faith in the power of law to change conduct survived and shows through in her major legislative innovations.

A hard-working woman, Catherine rose early, lit her fire, made her black coffee and settled down at her desk to indulge in her 'scribbling'. A blank sheet of paper made her fingers itch to start writing. After a few hours devoted to her literary or political activities, she would see her secretaries and ministers, withdraw to perform her toilette in private and only appear in her dressing room for her hair to be dressed. She did not go in for the elaborate court ritual of the *lever* and the *coucher* (receptions on getting up and going to bed) still practised at the French court. In private Catherine dressed simply in a loose silk gown, but on state occasions she was richly dressed and wore splendid jewels. Dinner was usually at 2 p.m. and, since the Empress was not interested in food, it was notoriously bad. Catherine was also very abstemious, and did not drink even wine unless her Scottish physician, Dr Rogerson, prescribed it.

The afternoon was devoted to reading or working, or seeing specially invited guests, such as Diderot or Grimm. The Empress would then play for a while with her grandchildren, and adjourn to spend the evening at the theatre or at her private parties in the Hermitage. These were completely informal. It was forbidden to rise when the Empress stood up, and those who had the right to attend talked, gambled, played paper games or went in for theatricals until about 10 p.m. when the Empress, who never took any supper, withdrew attended by her current favourite, and the guests dispersed in search of a well-provided table and a better cook than Catherine's.

All those who ever attended the court bear witness to the grace and dignity with which Catherine conducted herself, to the ease and charm of her manners. Claude Carloman de Rulhière, who was attached to the French Embassy in St Petersburg at the time of Catherine's *coup d'état*, described her appearance in 1762:

> She has a noble and agreeable figure; her gait is majestic, her person and deportment is full of graces. Her air is that of a sovereign. All her features proclaim a superior character. . . . Her brow is broad and open, her nose almost aquiline. . . . Her hair is chestnut coloured and very beautiful, her eyebrows brown, her eyes brown [they were in fact blue] and very beautiful, acquiring a bluish tint in certain lights; her complexion is dazzling. Pride is the principal feature of her physiognomy. The pleasantness and kindness of her expression are, to the eye of a keen observer, rather the consequence of a great desire to please. . . .

George Macartney, British Envoy in 1766, was even more impressed:

> I never saw in my life a person whose port, manner and behavior answered so strongly to the idea I had formed to myself of her. Tho' in the thirty seventh year of her age, she may still be called beautiful. Those who knew her younger say they never remembered her so lovely as at present. . . . It is inconceivable with what address she mingles the ease of behavior with the dignity of her rank, with what facility she familiarizes herself with the meanest of her subjects, without losing a point of her authority, and with what astonishing magic she inspires at once both respect and affection. Her conversation is brilliant, perhaps too brilliant for she loves to shine in conversation. . . .

The desire to impress, not only by her physical presence but by her intellectual qualities, is noted by many observers of Catherine, beginning with the adventurer Count Casanova, and it explains the well-merited reputation she had for vanity. To Sir James Harris it appeared that:

> she has a masculine force of mind, obstinacy in adhering to a plan and intrepidity in the execution of it; but she wants the more manly virtues of deliberation, forbearance in prosperity and accuracy of judgment, while she possesses in a high degree the weaknesses vulgarly attributed to her sex – love of flattery and its inseparable companion, vanity; an inattention to unpleasant but salutary advice; and a propensity to voluptuousness, which leads her to excesses that would debase a female character in any sphere of life.

The Chevalier de Corberon, who was not admitted to Catherine's small court circle and was therefore somewhat jaundiced, regarded Catherine as a 'comédienne', always acting a part.

Whether she was acting a part or not, Catherine throughout her life showed her ability to get on with people in all ranks of life. Her servants adored her and remained with her for years; her secretaries were well treated, and the diary kept by A.V. Khrapovitsky, himself a poet and writer, who was her private secretary in the years 1782 to 1793 and also helped her with her literary works, illustrates her kindness, her consideration for his health and welfare. She was always well received by the common people on her various travels throughout Russia, and it was the aristocracy, not the people, who cold-shouldered her in Moscow. Of course personal access to the palace and to the presence of the Empress was much easier in those days than it is today to the presence of kings, presidents and ministers, for she did not have to be protected against terrorists, journalists or photographers. Catherine drove about the streets of St Petersburg in an open sledge at night, with just a few attendants, in perfect security. The public – decently dressed – was admitted to the imperial parks, and wherever she travelled Catherine gave receptions to which the local nobility and townspeople were invited. The French Ambassador, Ségur, describes how after one such lengthy reception the Empress emerged with her cheeks coloured bright pink with rouge from having kissed so many of the painted faces of the merchants' ladies.

Life was also made easier for her ministers by her commonsensical and unpretentious approach to work. Ministers did not have to stand in her presence like Disraeli or Gladstone before Queen Victoria. The letters and notes she wrote asking for advice, and the letters she received with advice, reflect a genuine partnership in the search for a solution to a particular legislative or administrative problem. Where her correspondence over a particular legislative project can be followed, as with Count Sievers over the Statute of Local Administration of 1775, it is clear that her advisers and ministers had no hesitation in countering her ideas and expressing their own. The minutes of the meetings of the Council of State frequently reflect the vigorous debate which took place. On the other hand Catherine could also write stinging rebukes to officials who failed her.

Within the mental climate of her time and of her position as ruler, Catherine also showed more originality than any previous ruler of Russia and than most rulers at the time in Europe, except perhaps the Grand Duke Leopold of Tuscany, in her thoughts about changing the nature and the structure of Russian central government by altering the relationship of the central power and the corporate forces in Russian society, forces to which she had herself given legal form. It is here that the influence of William Blackstone's *Commentaries on the Laws of England* (in a French translation) is so noteworthy. Catherine made over 700 pages of notes from Blackstone and wrote various drafts at different times of the changes in the constitutional structure she proposed to introduce.

In a manner typical of her industrious nature, she hoped to begin to draw up her final plans in the course of her journey to the Crimea in 1787, and ordered her secretary to collect all her notes on Blackstone to take with her, as well as a copy of her Instruction, which she wished to compare with her notes on Blackstone. Familiar with her plans and never at a loss for a compliment, Khrapovitsky exclaimed that one day Russians would treasure her work as the English treasured their Magna Carta. Throughout her journey Catherine continued to work on her plans for constitutional reform. From what one can tell of her intentions, she viewed her project as a means of consolidating absolute government in Russia by making it more responsive to the various estates and more efficient. The most novel feature she drew from her reading of Blackstone was her plan for a high court, which seemed to have some of the legislative features of the British Parliament and some of its judicial elements. The separate chambers into which the proposed High Court was to be divided would have appointed councillors, but also assessors, elected by the local nobles, townspeople and state peasants.

Though Catherine never completed even a draft law, these papers show that as late as 1787 she could still contemplate fundamental reform, which associated elected representatives of the free estates with the machinery of central government in a way which was not even to be thought of again until the reign of Alexander II (1856–81). It is not possible to tell what inspired her to think such institutions necessary or advisable in Russia. Did something remain of her lengthy conversations with Diderot in 1774, who had urged her to keep the Legislative Commission in being and who had warned her, 'All arbitrary government is bad, even the arbitrary government of a good, strong, just and wise master. . . . He deprives the nation of the right to deliberate, to wish, or not to wish to oppose, to oppose even that which is good. In a society of men, the right of opposition seems to me a natural right, inalienable and sacred.' The best of despots 'is a good shepherd who reduces his subjects to the condition of animals; he makes them lose the sense of liberty . . .'.

It is unfortunately also not possible to tell on the evidence available at present whether Catherine abandoned her projects because of the outbreak of war with Turkey in 1787, or because she was feeling old and discouraged, or because of her dismay at the use made of their power by elected 'representatives' of the people in the French Revolution. As Marc Raeff, the historian who has done most to illuminate Blackstone's influence on Catherine, points out, there is a direct line between her plans and those of M.M. Speransky in 1809 and those of the liberal reformers of the late 1870s. The secretariat of Catherine's Legislative Commission of 1767 continued in being, and worked on attempts at codification throughout her reign. There is no doubt that later reformers drew on the various projects and studies which were produced by this secretariat (most of which remain unpublished) and that later on the codification of Russian law undertaken in the reign of Nicholas I by Speransky also drew on its resources. Hence the continuity of ideas between the eighteenth and the nineteenth centuries.

It was Catherine's private life which really exercised the gossip-mongers of the time (and later). By twentieth-century standards there was nothing abnormal about it until her breach with Grigory Orlov in 1772 – he had been her lover for twelve years and was the father of her son, A. Bobrinskoy, never legitimized, but known to be hers, and recognized as his brother by Paul I. (The rumour that she had five daughters by Orlov is quite unsubstantiated.) During their liaison Orlov seems to have conducted himself in such a way as not to arouse violent hostility. He was brave, lazy, good-natured, neither very intelligent nor very cultured. He played a prominent part in court functions and festivities. But he was a liberal-minded man and he should be remembered for two initiatives: he invited the Genevese philosopher Rousseau, who quarrelled with everybody, to settle in Russia (presumably with Catherine's consent); and he sponsored a number of projects on his estates to find an alternative to serfdom for the establishment of peasants on the land, also with Catherine's knowledge and approval.

Catherine was induced to dismiss Orlov in 1772 because of his unfaithfulness, and she chose a new lover, whom she did not love and who was given no governmental post, simply because she could not live alone. Something of her emotional life at this time is known, for she described it in moving terms in a letter to Grigory Potemkin with whom the great love affair of her life began in December 1773. Potemkin was already a lieutenant-general in the army, and had distinguished himself in the war against the Turks. He was probably thirty-four years old – ten years younger than Catherine and a bold, enterprising, imaginative, moody, arrogant, witty and intelligent man. He ceased to be Catherine's lover in 1776, but he kept his official positions to the surprise of many at court, who expected him to be dismissed when Catherine took a new lover, P.V. Zavadovsky. But he remained the most powerful figure at court, and continued as Catherine's principal adviser and confidant. It is possible that he was her husband – there were rumours that a religious ceremony had taken place – at any rate she trusted him absolutely. His role at her side can be compared to that of Leicester beside Elizabeth I of England. A woman ruler, however able, needs someone very reliable indeed to command her armies, someone who will not turn against her (as Essex did against Elizabeth). Catherine found her helpmate in Potemkin, who continued to dominate the scene at her side until his death in 1791.

Potemkin was a favourite, since his power originated in his personal relationship with Catherine. But he was not only a favourite, he was also a statesman. Nevertheless, other senior ministers and officials were bound to resent his seemingly boundless power and authority, the fact that he, above anyone else, had the ear of the Empress, that he could overrule and dominate, that he could draw on the Treasury for his private and public needs. Courtiers might fear him, they might hate him, but they could not despise him. (He was also a man of considerable culture, who had the complete works of Rousseau in his library, and yet preserved close links with the Russian Church, and loved all exotic peoples and religions.) From her letters to Grigory Potemkin, and to Petr Zavadovsky, it is evident that Catherine was passionately in love with both of them (and they with her) but that for reasons which no one can really at this date fathom, the relationships did not last.

But the favourites who followed Zavadovsky (who was dismissed in 1778) did nothing to increase Catherine's reputation. She needed their companionship both as lovers and as partners in her intellectual and cultural activities, but only two of them, A.D. Lanskoy (1780–4) and A. Dmitriyev Mamonov (1786–9), seem to have been reasonably well educated and capable of providing Catherine the woman with the affection and friendship she craved for. But the first died in her arms, possibly of diphtheria, in 1784 leaving Catherine absolutely heartbroken. She poured out her grief to Baron Grimm:

> When I began this letter [on 7 June 1784] I was happy and gay . . . but things have changed [on 2 July]. . . . I am sunk in the deepest sorrow, my happiness is over. I thought I too would die at the irreparable loss of my best friend I suffered just eight days ago . . . my room has become an empty cave in which I drag myself around like a shadow. . . . I can neither eat nor sleep. . . .

The death of Lanskoy shows Catherine at her most human; she continued to work, but she could not bear to spend the rest of the summer in Tsarkoye Selo, or to resume normal court life. Finally, after some months, she found a new lover.

Later, A. Dmitriyev Mamonov betrayed Catherine's affection in a different way, by falling in love with one of her maids of honour. Deeply hurt, Catherine dismissed him and arranged his marriage. As the Empress grew older, her favourites became younger, and though they were not given prominent political positions, their closeness to Catherine meant that they were the channel by which private and even corrupt influence could be brought to bear. Catherine was now beginning to feel her age. She had grown very stout, though according to the French painter, Mme Vigée Lebrun, she remained very charming, with her white hair framing a noble face, and beautiful, very white hands. But she no longer had the energy, or perhaps the discrimination, to judge the harm Platon Zubov, her last lover, did to her reputation, though her impatience with his incompetence in the fulfilment of his public duties is duly noted by the somewhat biased diarist Khrapovitsky. The future Alexander I, who was often in the company of his grandmother, made quite clear his hatred and contempt for her favourite.

The great Russian historian N.M. Karamzin, though critical particularly of the corruption and neglect of the public interest in the last years of Catherine II, nevertheless wrote in a memorandum he drew up for Alexander I in 1811 that 'should we compare all the known epochs of Russian history, virtually all would agree that Catherine's epoch was the happiest for Russian citizens; virtually all would prefer to have lived then than at any other time.' This verdict is in striking contrast to the judgments of some late-nineteenth-century Russian historians which have influenced historians in the west. Soviet historians unanimously claim that peasants, and the serfs in particular, were more and more severely exploited in the reign of Catherine II to the extent that one wonders that any remained alive. And many contemporary western historians have echoed these judgments without examining the evidence on which they are based.

There was of course opposition both to Catherine's usurpation of the throne and to some of her policies. There were those who, like the Vorontsov brothers, Alexander, the President of the College of Commerce, and, even more so, Simon, the long-serving Ambassador to England, had supported Peter III in 1762, and had never forgiven Catherine for usurping the throne and dislodging their sister Elizabeth, who had been Peter III's mistress. There were others who had hoped that Catherine would merely be regent for her eight-year-old son Paul. This was the case above all with Count Nikita Panin, who had hoped to benefit from his position as governor of the young Grand Duke to achieve a position of considerable power in a regency council.

It is essential to realize how little opposition there was to the form of government, absolutism, in Russia. The bulk of the population accepted the legitimacy of the regime however much some people might disagree with some policies. Government operated largely as a partnership between the nobility, the townspeople and the Crown, and the political class in a largely illiterate and materially still very primitive country was minute. Individuals might criticize specific policies, but the Russian political system provided no channels for groups to form with common programmes. There were only small patronage and clientele circles around specific magnates. This explains the importance of the favourites and of high-ranking ministers like Prince A.A. Vyazemsky or Alexander Vorontsov. They all became rich (or richer) and Catherine's favourites were given high rank. Nobles anxious for promotion gravitated towards one or other of the magnates as long as their favour lasted.

The most important clientele group, as long as he lived, formed around Potemkin. Another very influential group, deeply opposed to Potemkin, formed around Count Nikita Panin, Foreign Secretary and governor of the Grand Duke until his dismissal in 1781 (he died in 1783). It continued to some extent around the Grand Duke after Panin's dismissal. At one time some members of this group of courtiers and high officials, notably the playwright Denis Fonvizin, even drafted plans for constitutional changes in Russia, to be implemented by the Grand Duke on becoming emperor, changes which would turn Russia into a proper monarchy, as distinct from a despotism, namely a state in which the ruler abided by principles laid down in 'fundamental laws' which he would himself be unable to alter. In the event, Paul proved to be one of the most despotic rulers Russia has ever known, and these plans only came to light much later, in Alexander I's reign. This kind of clandestine constitutional criticism of Catherine's rule tended rather to be expressed either in odes to the Grand Duke, or in fables such as that of *Callisthenes* published by Fonvizin in 1786, in which Alexander the Great is made to choose between the virtuous advice of a moral philosopher and the capricious and arbitrary whims of a favourite and ends up by choosing the latter and condemning the philosopher to a cruel death. At this stage Catherine seems to have been indifferent to such indirect criticism of her rule but it cannot have helped Fonvizin when he attempted to launch a periodical in 1788.

The two most serious plots, aimed against Catherine as a usurper and at placing the ex-Emperor Ivan VI on the throne have already been mentioned (see Chapter 1). In the following years there were several noble conspiracies, mainly among officers in the Guards Regiments. Some originated among officers who had expected Paul to be proclaimed emperor with Catherine as regent; some represented a reaction to the rumour that she intended to marry Grigory Orlov. Several more alleged plots were investigated by the Secret Chancery between 1762 and 1772, some of them originating among common soldiers wanting to proclaim Paul emperor – many of them merely incoherent ranting by very young men who had drunk too much. Nevertheless Catherine took such plots very seriously, and most of those involved ended up in Siberia condemned to hard labour or settlement.

What was particularly disturbing for Catherine was that anyone plotting against her had a pretender to hand in the person of her son. These fears all came together in the early 1770s. Some loose talk among the Guards who complained about rumours that freedom was to be given to the serfs ('and then how shall we live?') and that an officer had been arrested for beating a sergeant ('previously officers were not arrested without a personal order from the tsar') and several other incidents of a similar nature seemed to indicate a seditious temper among the minor nobility serving in the Guards. The plotters had not failed to remark in their confused speeches that Paul was now of age (he was eighteen years old in 1772), and Catherine could well be expected to step down from the throne and let him reign. The use of Paul's name by Pugachev in 1773–4 was also alarming, though since Pugachev was rebelling on behalf of the restoration of 'Peter III' Paul was not a real threat in that context.

Catherine dealt with the situation in several ways. In the first place she acknowledged Paul's maturity by arranging his marriage, which took place in September 1773. The bride was a princess of Hesse Darmstadt; she did not learn Russian; she flirted, she intrigued and she got into debt. Two years after the wedding she died in childbirth and a second wife was soon found for the Grand Duke. But with Paul's marriage Catherine was able to sever the ties which linked him to Count Nikita Panin, who had continued to be governor and Master of the Court of the Grand Duke. Panin now ceased to live in the palace and see his charge daily. He was no longer able systematically to disparage Catherine's policies nor to direct Paul's political judgment, though he had already sown the seeds of an unbounded admiration for Frederick II of Prussia in his young pupil.

At the same time Catherine, in 1773, this time together with Panin, was able to complete the transfer of the Duchy of Holstein Gottorp, which Paul had inherited from his father, to the King of Denmark. Denmark had always had claims on the duchy, and Catherine had been glad to negotiate a treaty by which her son lost the duchy which might provide him with a territorial base outside Russia in which he might seek refuge and from which he could mount an attack in the event of a breach with his mother. The treaty had been negotiated in 1767, but its ratification had to wait for Paul's majority. Holstein Gottorp was now exchanged for the duchies of Oldenburg and Elmenhorst, which went to a minor branch of the Holstein family. At this very moment, however, Catherine was faced with a plot to urge Paul to demand his rights, this time led by the man who was negotiating the Holstein exchange on her behalf,

Count Saldern. The details of the plot have never been made clear, and though Saldern was undoubtedly largely bribed by the Danes, he seems to have been acting on his own behalf. He left Russia never to return. In fairness to Paul, it must be added that though he was often very critical orally of his mother's policies, and sometimes countered her plans in foreign policy, he never actually encouraged any attempt to dethrone her.

Looking back, the historian may well be tempted to think that the years 1771–4 were the most difficult and dangerous of Catherine's whole reign. Had the plague continued to ravage Moscow in 1771; had Pugachev succeeded in setting the centre of Russia ablaze; above all had the Russian army been defeated by the Turks, she might well have been overthrown in favour of Paul. But her luck held, and in the middle of this tremendous crisis she found the man – Potemkin – who inspired her with self-confidence as a woman and as a ruler. From the peace of Kutschuk Kainardzhi in July 1774 Catherine's authority as empress was unchallenged.

There were probably more critics of Catherine's policies than we have any means of knowing. The absence of a free press, indeed of any kind of press other than the government gazettes, makes it very difficult to assess the nature of public opinion, and one must rely on memoirs, letters and diplomatic dispatches written by foreigners who were often prejudiced or ill-informed. In general, opposition to Catherine's policy, apart from that arising among disgruntled courtiers passed over in the race for what they considered well-deserved promotion, seems to have centred on foreign policy, particularly war, which many opposed, and on the role of Catherine's favourites in government, more particularly that of Grigory Potemkin, accountable only to the Empress in all that they did.

Bezborodko and some of Catherine's other ministers fully supported the annexation of the Crimea. In the 1780s and 1790s there was certainly a war party, which supported the acquisition of the steppes in the south and of territory in Poland. Many nobles saw in these Russian acquisitions opportunities to acquire estates or land for themselves. But quite apart from considerations of whether Russia needed to grow larger, or whether expansion for the sake of expansion fitted in with the moral precepts of a just war, as some nobles thought they should, many nobles resented the loss of manpower consequent on the conscription of serfs in wartime, and the policy of Potemkin of offering a refuge to fugitive serfs in order to people the empty lands of the south. One cannot, of course, tell to what extent the opposition to Catherine's expansionist policies was really a disguised form of opposition to the personality and power of her favourite, and to the reforms which he was inaugurating in the army. There is some evidence that this was the case because the person around whom this opposition crystallized was again the Grand Duke Paul. He hated Potemkin, and he disapproved of the former's policy as President of the College of War, of increasing the number of lightly armed cavalry regiments, and of simplifying the soldier's uniforms to make them more comfortable. It has been argued by one historian that Radishchev's *Journey from St Petersburg to Moscow* for which he was sentenced to ten years' exile in Siberia (see pp. 191–6) should be regarded much more as an attack on the incompetent and corrupt conduct of the war of 1787–91 by Potemkin than as an attack on serfdom. Radishchev, it is argued, was tried in fact for sedition in time of war rather than for his revolutionary opinions on serfdom.

One can fairly assume the existence of other critics of the role of favourites and of Catherine's policies. But they did not make their criticism public. Prince M.M. Shcherbatov wrote *On the Corruption of Morals in Russia* in 1787, but it was published for the first time by Alexander Herzen in 1859 in London. Shcherbatov was a disgruntled aristocrat who felt that he had not achieved the rank which should have been his, though Catherine was very generous to him. In his book he attacked the materialism, corruption and immorality of the Russian court from the time of Peter I and compared it unfavourably with the simplicity of seventeenth-century Russia. He accused the Empress of arbitrary and despotic conduct, and 'although she is in her declining years, although grey hair covers her head and time has marked her brow with the indelible signs of age, yet her licentiousness does not decline'. It certainly would not have been possible to publish Shcherbatov's, extremely frank criticism of the public and private lives of eighteenth-century Russian rulers during the reign of one of them. Indeed even today such an attack on a living person would undoubtedly fall foul of the laws of libel.

On the other hand the rising of the assigned peasants in the Urals in 1763–4 and the rising led by Pugachev in 1773–4 are clear indications of popular dissatisfaction with specific government policies among Cossacks, state peasants, industrial serfs and privately owned serfs. But the discontented did not normally coalesce into one single, massive opposition; they usually formed single-issue groups among the peasantry, anxious to escape from the tyranny of a particular landowner. Moreover the dissatisfaction felt by the peasants was part of a widespread, formless hatred of and revolt against the modern state, which taxed them, called them up to serve in the army (or, worse, the navy), instead of leaving them in peaceful occupation of all the land, without any officials, officers or landowners intervening between them and a benevolent tsar.

There is one aspect of the opposition to Catherine which has so far been much less well documented. The example which the Empress so glaringly provided of total disregard for the rules of domestic morality – acceptable at that time in a man, totally unforgivable in a woman – turned many of the Church hierarchy, such as Metropolitan Platon of Moscow, and of the more straitlaced nobles, of which there were many, and the Moscow freemasons against her. Catherine's private life was contrasted with the apparent domestic happiness of Paul (he was more discreet). She was accused of corrupting young people and family life by her example, and the Russian court, particularly in its later years, rivalled French society, or the grand Whig society of England, in its dissoluteness, though high standards of decorum were always maintained in public.

Lower down the social scale, there was considerable opposition to Catherine's secularization of Church lands, to the widespread closure of monasteries and convents, and the concentration of monks and nuns in a smaller number of larger establishments. Local minor nobles and townspeople appealed to be allowed to keep open at their own expense small convents which they had often endowed in the past and which acted as refuges for their wives and sisters – requests which were sometimes granted. Unofficially, women's groups in provincial towns set up self-supporting 'women's communities', in which women could live a disciplined and religious life, and undertake good works without being officially rated as nuns. What one might call the conservative opposition to Catherine's 'enlightenment policies' needs further study.

It is still too early today to make a considered judgment on the impact of Catherine's reign in Russia, and to interpret her policies with any certainty. Research on her reign has been so neglected in the USSR for so many years that there are many aspects of the government of Russia which remain totally unstudied. To mention but a few, almost nothing is known about the operations of the law courts set up in 1775; about the operation of the noble provincial assemblies and the town assemblies; about the activities of the treasury chambers; about the activities of the land commissars (*zemskiy ispravnik*), and the social class they were actually drawn from; about the exploitation of small agricultural estates belonging to nobles and about the state peasant villages. Some of these topics have been touched on in more general works, but there has been no systematic study of how particular institutions actually worked. There are very few biographies of the statesmen and ministers who worked with Catherine, and none of them reach the standard expected in the west for biographies of let us say William Pitt or Charles James Fox, or Choiseul. There are no studies of merchant dynasties which might illustrate the development of trade and industry.

The traditional view for a long time has been that Catherine was so badly in need of noble support to keep the throne that she deliberately increased the power of the nobles over their serfs, and governed in such a way as to consolidate noble domination and exploitation of the human and material resources of the country. This theory is still found in some modern histories of her policies, but it no longer commands general agreement. In the light of the work that has been done mainly by British and American historians it is now more possible to see both what the Empress tried to achieve and what obstacles faced her. By temperament, as well as because she was aware that she had no legitimate claim to the throne, Catherine wished to prove herself a reformer, in the spirit of German cameralism as modified by the enlightenment. Her policies were presented to the Russian (and to the European) public clothed in the language of the enlightenment. But there was a considerable discrepancy between her aims and her achievements. It is this discrepancy between the rhetoric in which she expressed her aims and hopes and the actual performance of the institutions she created which has left her open to the charge of hypocrisy. But she was no hypocrite. She believed in her reforms, but she had to use the human tools to hand, and there is no doubt that, while she found many great administrators, most of the officials on whom she had to rely did not live up to her expectations. Was she informed of these inadequacies? Did she turn a blind eye? We cannot tell at this stage. What remains true however is that Catherine was the first ruler of Russia to conceive of drawing up legislation setting out the corporate rights of the nobles and the townspeople, and the civil rights of the free population of the country. The nobility, the townspeople and the free peasants were given a legal framework within which these rights could be pressed. She was also the first ruler ever to establish special courts to which the state peasants had access and in which they could and did sue merchants and nobles. During her reign the individual – other than the serf or the soldier – was allowed more space, more responsibility, more security, more dignity. For a while an increasingly diversified Russian society escaped from the overwhelming pressure of the militarization imposed on it by Peter I and restored by Paul I.

Catherine did not increase the power of the nobles over the serfs, nor did she turn large numbers of Russian state peasants into private serfs. She did not, as we know, free the serfs, or even attempt to regulate relations between serfs and landowners by law. Her hold on the throne was not strong enough to enable her to put through a policy which would have been opposed by the whole of the Russian political elite, both the nobility and the townspeople. She did not have the power of coercion necessary to enforce a policy which would have to be put through by the very people who benefited from the *status quo*. But that should not be the sole criterion by which she is judged.

Catherine was not a revolutionary like Peter I, who forced his policies on a reluctant society without counting the human cost. She paid attention to public opinion; as she said to Diderot, 'what I despair of overthrowing I undermine'. Her absolute authority rested, as she well knew, on her sensitivity to the possible.

After the death of Potemkin in 1791 and the disappearance of many of Catherine's long-serving ministers in the late 1780s and early 1790s, the Empress was surrounded by lesser men. There were still many remarkable governors active in the provinces, but the new men who took up posts in the centre were inexperienced and lacking in character. Catherine herself was suffering by now from the shrinking of horizons which comes with age, just when the storms of the French Revolution were being unleashed all over Europe. She was tired and she could no longer control events and people. In September 1796 the young King of Sweden, Gustav IV Adolf broke off the negotiations for his marriage with Catherine's granddaughter over her conversion to Lutheranism. The insult was public and the Empress suffered a slight stroke. It was followed by a more serious stroke which surprised her in her closet on 16 November. She died on 17 November without recovering consciousness. In the words of a contemporary American historian, J.P. LeDonne, she 'remains the finest gift of the German lands to her adopted country'.

Bibliographical Note

This book has no footnotes. This is quite deliberate, since it is intended to be an introductory survey rather than an academic history. It is nevertheless, I hope, scholarly, and no statement has been put forward which is not based on the evidence of documents or on the work of other scholars. The evidence comes from many sources: collections published in Russia and the Soviet Union: monographs by pre-revolutionary Russian historians and by Soviet historians; and the extensive monographic literature published in the last twenty-five years or so in Europe and America. I must, therefore, place on record here the great debt I owe to a number of scholars whose work I have drawn on and whom I am glad also to call my friends: Professor J.T. Alexander, Dr R. Bartlett, Professor A.G. Cross, Professor P. Dukes, Professor David Griffiths, Dr J.M. Hartley, Dr Gareth Jones, Professor R.E. Jones, Professor J.H.L. Keep, Professor G. Marker, Professor Brenda Meehan Waters, Professor George Munro, Dr Jennifer Newman, Professor K. Papmehl, Dr Pia Pera, Professor M. Raeff, Professor D. Ransel and Dr W.F. Ryan. I have also used the work of other scholars with whom I am not acquainted; they will be mentioned in the following bibliography.

For a general survey of Catherine's reign the most up-to-date work is my own *Russia in the Age of Catherine the Great*, Weidenfeld & Nicolson, London, 1981, which has a wide-ranging bibliography of works published in pre-revolutionary Russia, the USSR and abroad. A useful additional bibliographical survey is P. Clendenning and R. Bartlett, *Eighteenth-Century Russia: A Select Bibliography of Works Published since 1955*, Oriental Research Partners, Newtonville, Mass., 1981.

I do not propose to repeat here the full bibliography I published earlier. Since 1981 when the two books mentioned above were published many more contributions to Catherinian scholarship have appeared, mainly in the United Kingdom and in the United States. I propose to list here all those books and articles which I have actually used or quoted from, a selection of works published since 1981, and some works which readers who wish to pursue a question further could usefully consult.

A brief list of further reading in English follows: For the young Catherine, see J.T. Alexander, *Catherine the Great – Life and Legend*, Oxford University Press, 1989 (Macartney's description of Catherine on p. 205 is quoted from him); M. Raeff, 'The Domestic Policies of Peter III and His Overthrow', *American Historical Review*, LXV, No. 5, June 1970, 1289–310; Princess E.R. Dashkova, *Memoirs*, ed. K. Fitzlyon, John Calder, London, 1958.

For Russian society, see M. Raeff, *The Origins of the Russian Intelligentsia: The Eighteenth Century Nobility*, Harcourt Brace and World, New York, 1966; J.M. Hittle, *The Service City: State and Townsmen in Russia, 1600–1800*, Harvard University Press, Cambridge, Mass., 1979; see also J.T. Alexander, *Bubonic Plague in Early Modern Russia: Public Health and Urban Disaster*, Johns Hopkins University Press, Baltimore and London, 1980, which ranges far more widely than the plague; for the peasantry see J. Blum, *Lord and Peasant in Russia from the Ninth to the Nineteenth Century*, Princeton University Press, 1961, and my own 'Catherine II and the Serfs: A Reconsideration of Some Problems' in the *Slavonic and East European Review*, 52, No. 126, January 1974, 34–62. Peter Kolchin in *Unfree Labor: American Slavery and Russian Serfdom*, Harvard University Press, Cambridge, Mass., 1987, draws some interesting conclusions from a comparison between serfdom and slavery. 'The Administration of the Borderlands', Part V of J.P. LeDonne's *Ruling Russia – Politics and Administration in the Age of Absolutism, 1762–1796*, Princeton University Press, 1984, deals with the eastern and southern borderlands of Russia.

The official contemporary English translation of Catherine's Great Instruction or *nakaz* has been republished in *Documents of Catherine the Great. The Correspondence with Voltaire and the Instruction of 1767 in the English text of 1768*, ed. W.F. Reddaway, Cambridge University Press, 1931, reprinted in 1971; a second English version, also dating from the eighteenth century, and with a useful introductory article discussing sources and pre- and post-revolutionary interpretations of the Instruction has been published by P. Dukes, *Russia under Catherine the Great*, vol. II, *Catherine the Great's Instruction (NAKAZ) to the Legislative Commission, 1767*, Oriental Research Partners, Newtonville, Mass., 1977. On the Legislative Commission see also by the same author, *Catherine the Great and the Russian Nobility: A Study Based on the Materials of the Legislative Commission of 1767*, Cambridge University Press, 1967. On the attempt to limit Catherine's power in 1762, see M. Raeff, *Plans for Political Reform in Imperial Russia, 1730–1905*, Prentice Hall, Englewood Cliffs, NJ, 1966. Some problems of the translation of political terms into Russian are discussed in my 'Autocracy and Sovereignty', *Canadian American Slavic Studies*, 16, Nos 3–4, Fall–Winter, 1982, 369–87.

Very little new has been published recently on the first and second Turkish wars or the Armed Neutrality or the annexation of the Crimea or the partitions of Poland. On Russian relations with Sweden, see M. Roberts, *British Diplomacy and Swedish Politics 1758–1773*, University of Minneapolis Press, 1980.

The crisis of the 1770s can be studied in J.T. Alexander, *Emperor of the Cossacks*, Coronado Press, Lawrence, Kansas, and his *Autocratic Politics in a National Crisis: The Imperial Government and Pugachev's Revolt*, Indiana University Press, 1969, and also in his *Bubonic Plague in Early Modern Russia: Public Health and Urban Disaster* (see previous page). An excellent literary portrayal of the revolt is given by the poet Alexander Pushkin in his tale *The Captain's Daughter*.

The unpublished doctoral dissertation by Dr Janet M. Hartley, 'The Implementation of the Laws Relating to Local Administration with Special Reference to the Guberniya of St Petersburg', University of London, 1980, casts much new light on the reforms of 1775 and 1785. The reform of local administration has been treated by R.E. Jones, *Provincial Development in Russia: Catherine II and Jacob Sievers*, Rutgers University Press, New Brunswick, NJ, 1984; and in a somewhat idiosyncratic way by J.P. LeDonne in *Ruling Russia: Politics and Administration in the Age of Absolutism, 1762–1796*, which can be contrasted with the approach of M. Raeff in *The Well-Ordered Police State: Social and Institutional Change through Law in the Germanies and Russia, 1600–1800*, Yale University Press, 1983. See also the article by J.M. Hartley: 'Catherine's Conscience Court – An English Equity Court?' in *Russia and the West in the Eighteenth Century*, ed. A.G. Cross, Oriental Research Partners, Newtonville., Mass., 1983, and her 'Philanthropy in the Reign of Catherine II: The Theory and the Practice' in *Russia in the Age of the Enlightenment – Essays for Isabel de Madariaga*, ed. Janet M. Hartley and Roger Bartlett, Macmillan, London, 1990. On Catherine and Blackstone, M. Raeff, 'The Empress and the Vinerian Professor', *Oxford Slavonic Papers*, VII, 1974,

18–40, is essential. See also on the abolition of torture my own 'Penal Policy in the Age of Catherine II' in *La 'Leopoldina', Criminalità e Giustizia Criminale nelle Reforme del Settecento Europeo*, Università degli Studi di Siena.

New light has been thrown on Russian eighteenth-century intellectual life by G. Marker in *Publishing, Printing and the Origins of Intellectual Life in Russia*, Princeton University Press, 1984; see also W. Gareth Jones, *Nikolay Novikov: Enlightener of Russia*, Cambridge University Press, 1984, and Charles A. Moser, *Denis Fonvizin*, Twayne Publishers, Boston, Mass., 1979. On Catherine's relations with the French *philosophes* see my 'Catherine and the *Philosophes*' in *Russia and the West in the Eighteenth Century*, ed. A.G. Cross (see previous page), and 'Catherine II and Montesquieu between Prince M.M. Shcherbatov and Denis Diderot' in *L'età dei lumi – settecento europeo – saggi in onore di Franco Venturi*, vol. II, Jovene editore, Naples, 1985, 611–50. On censorship see K. Papmehl, *Freedom of Expression in Eighteenth Century Russia*, Martinus Nijhoff, The Hague, 1971. There is a useful anthology of Russian literature in Harold B. Segel, *The Literature of Eighteenth Century Russia*, 2 vols, E.P. Dutton, New York, 1967. *The Eighteenth Century in Russia*, ed. J.G. Garrard, Clarendon Press, Oxford, 1973, is also a useful survey of Russian intellectual life.

The implementation of the charters of 1785 is dealt with by R.E. Jones in *The Emancipation of the Russian Nobility*, Princeton University Press, 1973, and Janet M. Hartley, 'Town Government in St Petersburg Guberniya after the Charter to the Towns of 1785', *Slavonic and East European Review*, 62, 1984, 66–84. On schools see Janet M. Hartley, 'The Boards of Social Welfare and the Financing of Catherine II's State Schools', *Slavonic and East European Review*, 67 No. 2, April 1989, 211–27. Policy towards Little Russia has been illuminated in Zenon E. Kohut, *Russian Centralism and Ukrainian Autonomy – Imperial Absorption of the Hetmanate, 1760s–1830s*, Harvard University Press, Cambridge, Mass., 1988. J.D. Klier, *Russia Gathers her Jews – the Origins of the 'Jewish Question' in Russia 1772–1825*, Northern Illinois University Press, 1986, includes an up-to-date study of Catherine's policy towards the Jews. The relevant chapters of *Soldiers of the Tsar*, by J.L.H. Keep, Clarendon Press, Oxford, 1985, are most informative on army life.

The Russian Journals of Martha and Catherine Wilmot, ed. the Marchioness of Londonderry and H.M. Hyde, Macmillan, London, 1934, are a most delightful account of Russia at the beginning of the nineteenth century. Other very readable memoirs are *An English Lady at the Court of Catherine the Great: the Journal of Baroness Dimsdale*, 1781, ed. A.G. Cross, Crest Publications, Cambridge, 1989, and John Parkinson, *A Tour of Russia, Siberia and the Crimea, 1792–1794*, ed. William Collier, Frank Cass, London, 1974. *Years of Childhood*, *A Russian Gentleman* and *A Russian Schoolboy* by S.T. Aksakov, trans. J.D. Duff, World Classics, Oxford University Press, 1982, 1983, 1984, provide a beautifully written chronicle of Russian life seen by a boy and a youth. On the problems of the nobility see A. Kahan, 'The Costs of Westernization in Russia: the Gentry and the Economy in XVIIIth Century Russia', *Slavic Review*, XXV, 1965, 61–85.

On Russian economic history see A. Kahan, *The Plow, the Hammer and the Knout: An Economic History of Eighteenth Century Russia*, University of Chicago Press, 1985. James Duran, 'Catherine the Great and the Origin of the Russian State Debt'; George Munro, 'The Role of the *Veksel*' in Russian Capital Formation: A Preliminary Inquiry'; and R.E. Jones, 'Ukrainian Grain and the St Petersburg Market' are three useful articles published in *Russia and the World of the Eighteenth Century*, ed. R.P. Bartlett, A.G. Cross and Karen Rasmussen, Slavica Publishers, Columbus, Ohio, 1988; see also R.E. Jones, 'The Dnieper Trade Route in the Late Eighteenth and Early Nineteenth Centuries, A Note' in *International History Review*, XI, No. 2, May 1989, 303–12; Jennifer Newman, 'The Russian Grain Trade 1700–1779' in *The Baltic Grain Trade: Five Essays*, ed. W. Minchinton, Exeter, 1985, and 'The English Contribution to the Economic Revolution in Russia in the Eighteenth Century' in *Britain and the Northern Seas*, ed. W. Minchinton, Pontefract, 1988. Ian Blanchard, *Russia's 'Age of Silver'*, Routledge, London, 1989, studies the role of Russian gold, silver and copper production in Russian and European eighteenth-century economic history; figures for the standard of living of the peasants in Chapter 12 are quoted from the section 'Russian Economic Growth' of his book; see however the review by B. Mironov, which casts doubt on Blanchard's conclusions, *Slavonic and East European Review*, 69, No. 2, 1991, 361–3. For financial history see James A. Duran, 'The Reform of Financial Administration in Russia during the Reign of Catherine II' in *Canadian Slavic Studies*, 4, No. 3, Fall 1970, 485–96, and relevant section of John P. LeDonne, *Ruling Russia* (see p. 221).

On the 'conservative' opposition to Catherine see Brenda Meehan Waters, 'Russian Convents and the Secularization of Monastic Property' in *Russia and the World of the Eighteenth Century* (see above); *On the Corruption of Morals* by Prince M.M. Shcherbatov has been published with an English translation by A. Lentin, Cambridge University Press, 1969; R.E. Jones, 'Opposition to War and Expansion in Late Eighteenth Century Russia', *Jahrbücher für Geschichte Osteuropas*, 32, 1984, 34–51. D. Rausel, *The Politics of Catherinian Russia: The Panin Party*, Yale University Press, 1975. The constitutional ideas of Nikita Panin as expressed by Denis Fonvizin have been published in *Russian Intellectual History: An Anthology*, ed. Marc Raeff, Harcourt Brace and World, New York, 1966.

N.M. Karamzin's *Memoir on Ancient and Modern Russia* has been published in translation and with an introduction by R. Pipes, Harvard University Press, Cambridge, Mass., 1959. The quotation on the last page is from J.P. LeDonne, op. cit.

Useful articles can also be found in two anthologies, *Catherine the Great – A Profile*, ed. Marc Raeff, Hill & Wang, New York, 1972; *Canadian American Slavic Studies*, 4, No. 3, Fall 1970, a special issue, devoted to the reign of Catherine II; and in the proceedings of the two international conferences organized by the Study Group on Eighteenth Century Russia, *Russia and the West in the Eighteenth Century*, ed. A.G. Cross (see p. 222), and *Russia and the World of the Eighteenth Century*, ed. R.P. Bartlett, A.G. Cross and Karen Rasmussen (see previous page).

GLOSSARY

Boyar high-ranking noble and official in Pre-Petrine Russia; not a hereditary title.

Dvoryanin, dvoryane noble, nobles.

Guberniya province.

Provintsiya sub-province.

Uezd district.

Kupets, kupechestvo merchant, merchantry.

Magistrat, Glavnyy Magistrat town administrative and judicial council; Main Council.

Ukaz decree, order issued by the ruler or the Senate.

Zemskiy ispravnik land commissar.

WEIGHTS AND MEASURES

Desyatina (land measurement) 2.7 acres.

Verst 0.663 miles.

Pud Forty Russian pounds, thirty-six pounds avdp.

Vedro (liquids), pail 2.7 gallons.

One ruble One hundred kopeks

GENEALOGICAL TABLE

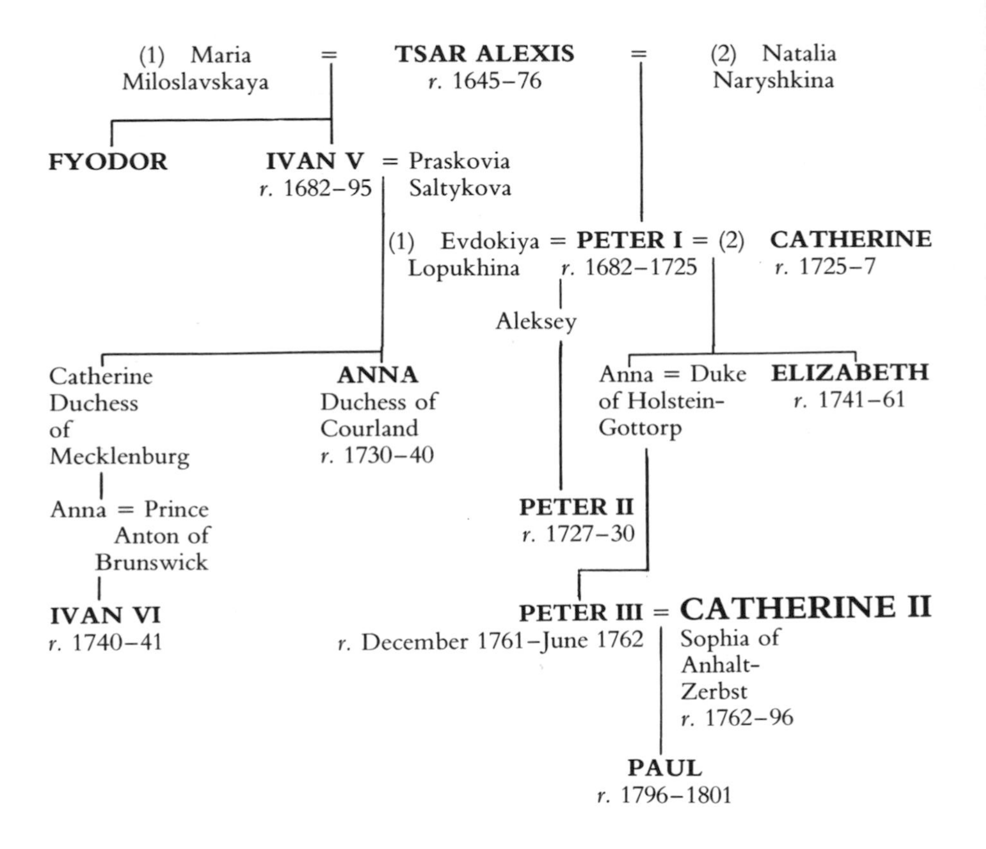

CENTRAL GOVERNMENT 1764–96

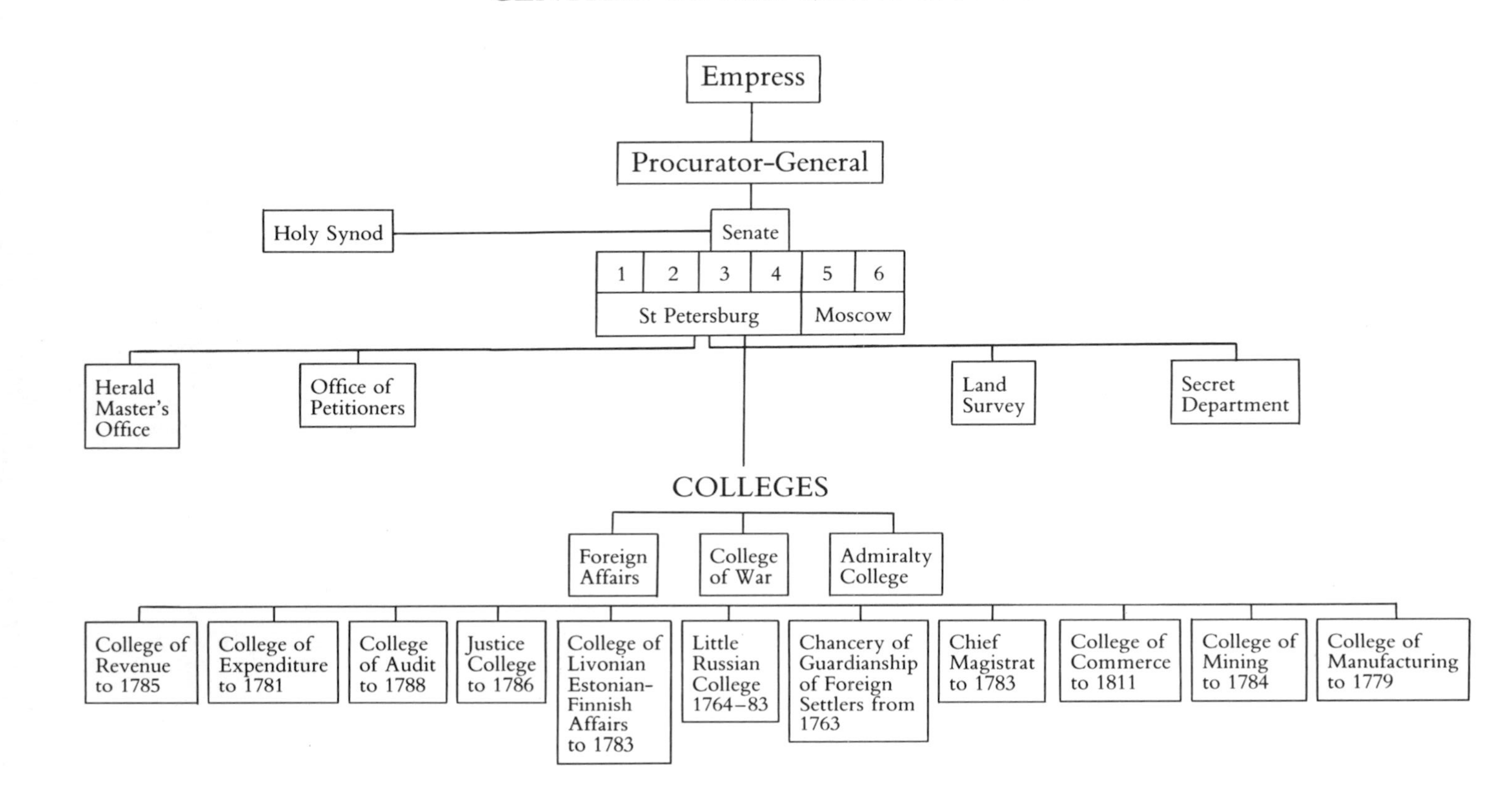

LOCAL GOVERNMENT 1775 ONWARDS

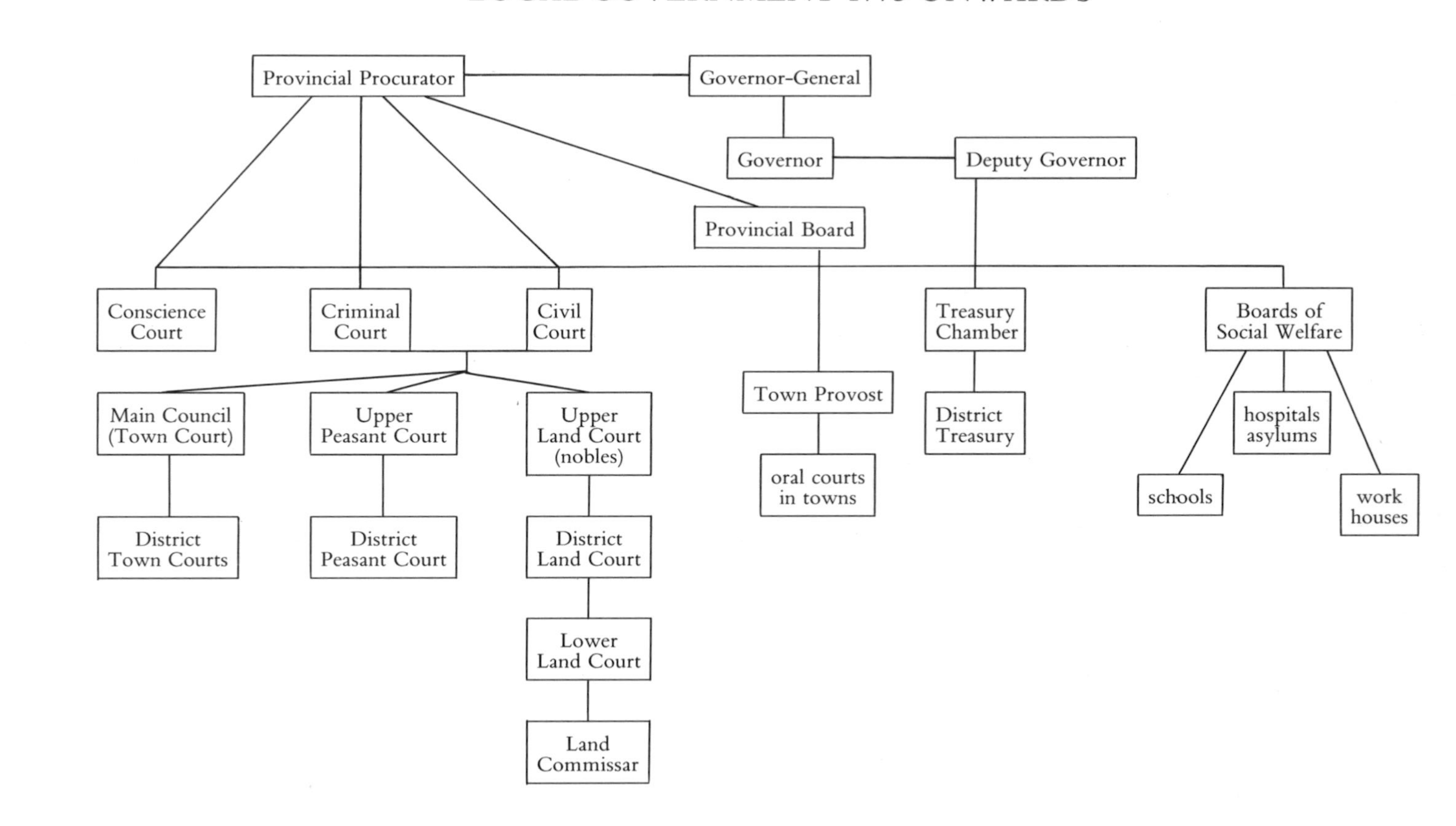

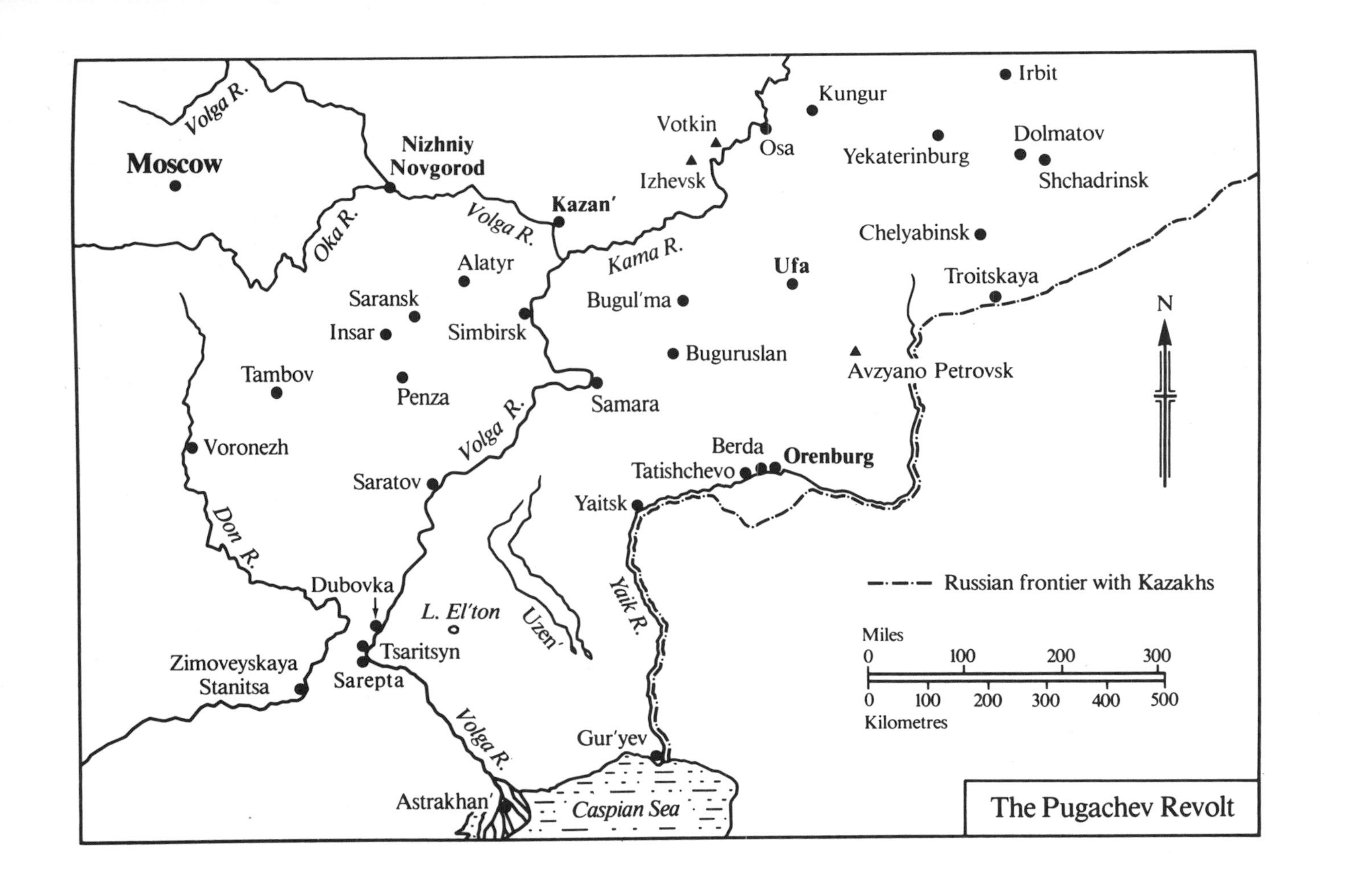

The Pugachev Revolt

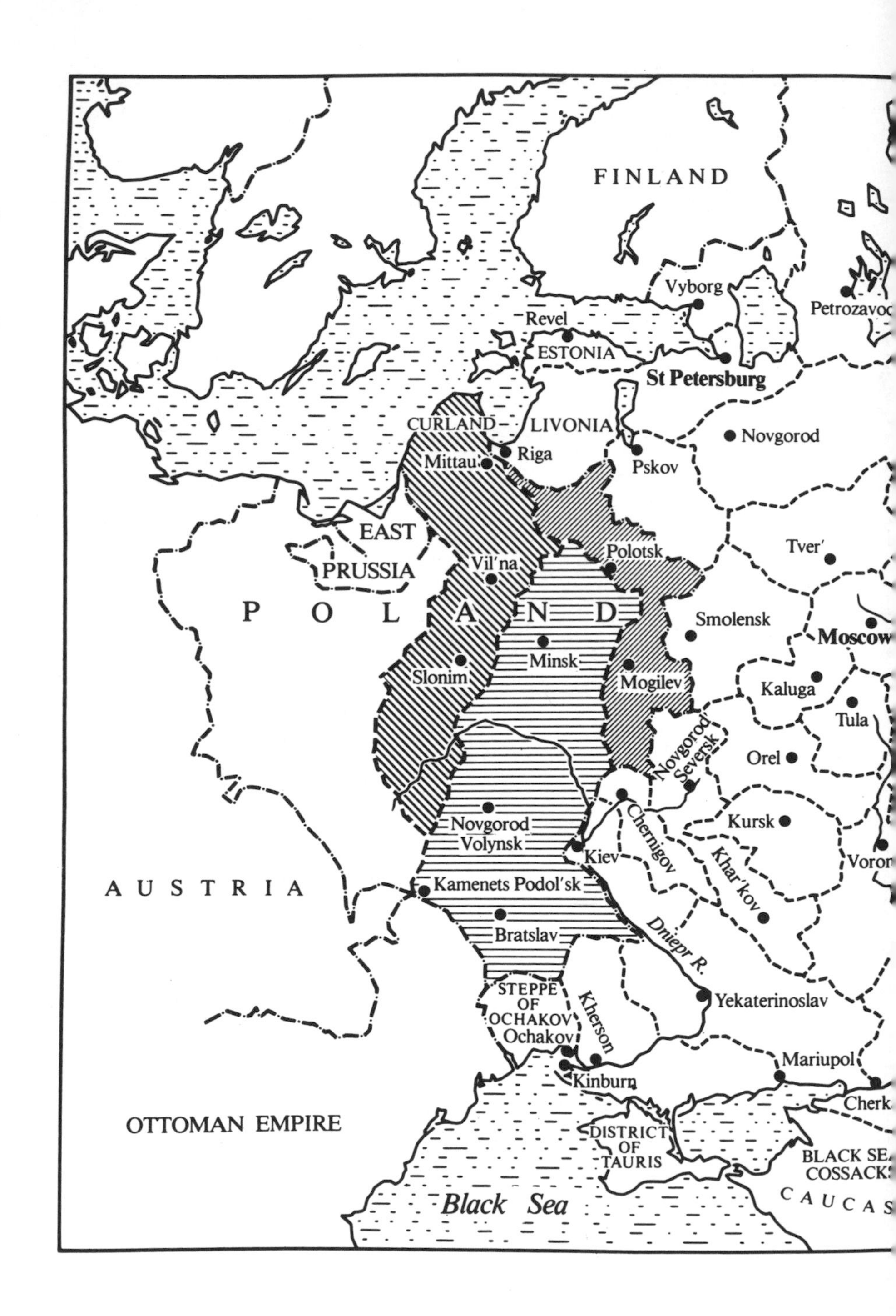
FINLAND
Vyborg
Petrozavo
Revel
ESTONIA
St Petersburg
CURLAND
LIVONIA
Riga
Mittau
Pskov
Novgorod
EAST
PRUSSIA
Vil'na
Polotsk
Tver'
P O L A N D
Smolensk
Moscow
Minsk
Slonim
Mogilev
Kaluga
Tula
Novgorod Seversk
Orel
Chernigov
Kursk
Novgorod Volynsk
Kiev
Khar'kov
Voron
AUSTRIA
Kamenets Podol'sk
Bratslav
Dniepr R.
STEPPE OF OCHAKOV
Ochakov
Kherson
Yekaterinoslav
Mariupol
Kinburn
Cherk
OTTOMAN EMPIRE
DISTRICT OF TAURIS
BLACK SE
COSSACK
CAUCAS
Black Sea

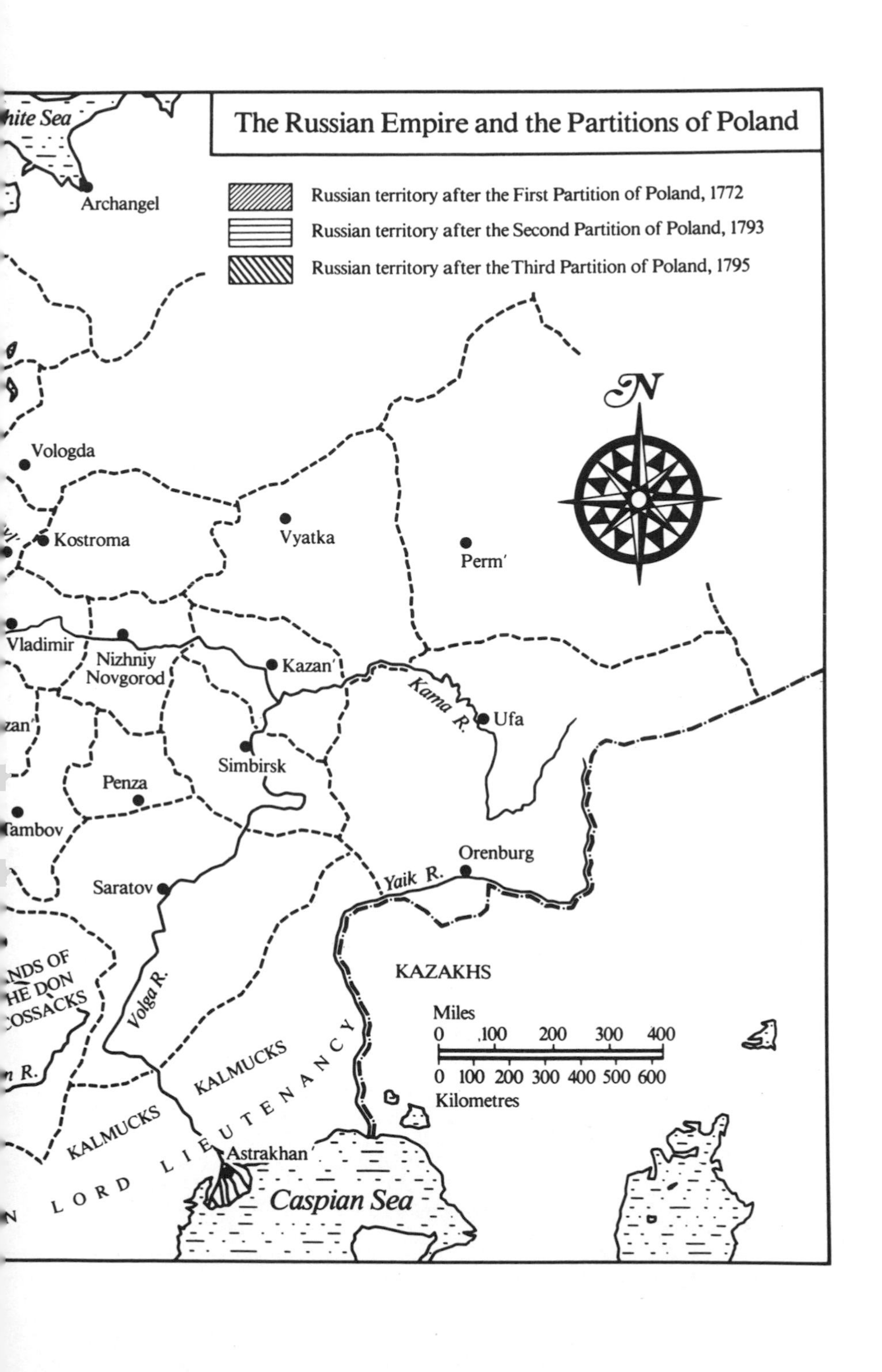

The Russian Empire and the Partitions of Poland
Russian territory after the First Partition of Poland, 1772
Russian territory after the Second Partition of Poland, 1793
Russian territory after the Third Partition of Poland, 1795
hite Sea
Archangel
Vologda
Kostroma
Vyatka
Perm′
Vladimir
Nizhniy Novgorod
Kazan′
Kama R.
Ufa
zan′
Simbirsk
Penza
Tambov
Orenburg
Yaik R.
Saratov
KAZAKHS
NDS OF HE DON COSSACKS
Volga R.
Miles
0 100 200 300 400
0 100 200 300 400 500 600
Kilometres
KALMUCKS
KALMUCKS
n R.
N LORD LIEUTENANCY
Astrakhan′
Caspian Sea

Index